THE GREEN-TOOTHED WITCH & THE YELLOW CANARY

IAN CHESTER

1st Edition: v.5 (6th June 2021)

ISBN: 9798639039744

www.chesfoxbooks.com

DEDICATION

To Colleen, my wife, for allowing me to realise a dream, sharing in my experiences, both good and bad, and assisting with many of the illustrations.

ACKNOWLEDGEMENTS

To James Chester and Sophie Mayer for their technical assistance in Microsoft Word and Adobe photoshop.

To Ian Hudson, my press ganged proof reader, who is now lying in a hospital bed somewhere 'comma-tosed'.

To John Shipley for his encouragement and guidance on vocabulary and style.

To Tom Isitt (Author: Riding in the Zone Rouge) for his guidance and assistance with the maps of 1919.

To David Guenel (Author: Petit-Breton: Gentleman cycliste) for his assistance in dating photos and his general advice on French cycling terms.

To Rob Kennedy for a giving me a laugh.

To the country of France for providing the wonderful weather (H.A.A.R.P. ?), great food and wine.

Les Ètapes

Chapter 1 : The Prologue

Henri Desgrange was a complete and utter sadistic bâtard!

There are no other words to describe Henri Desgrange. I've searched the French-English dictionary from back to front and none of them come close to describing a man, so driven, so single minded in his endeavour to create the ultimate test of human physical endurance, that nothing got in the way of HIS vision of the Tour de France!

Ok, so he didn't actually create the Tour. That honour fell to Géo Lefèvre, a young journalist Desgrange had employed on his failing sports newspaper L'Auto. Desperate to boost ratings, Henri had called a crisis-meeting at their headquarters on the Rue de Faubourg in Paris. Unsure as to what to say, but knowing the reporting of 'Les Grands Tours' such as Paris – Bordeaux and The Tour of Flanders, had boosted newspaper circulation in the past, the twenty-six-year-old Géo blurted out,

"Let's organise a race that lasts several days longer than anything else. Like the six-days on the track, but this time on the road. All the big towns of France will welcome the riders."

Henri Desgrange, knew this had only ever been done once before, by car, in what was known as the 'Tour de France Automobile' and he exclaimed,

"What you are suggesting, my little Géo, is a Tour de France."

Henri was sceptical to begin with, but when he put the idea to the paper's finance manager, Victor Goddet, he was so excited by the idea, he gave Desgrange the keys to the company safe,

"Take whatever you need."

This was approval indeed, from the man with his hand on the company coffers, and on the 19th January 1903, Henri Desgrange made this announcement on the front page of L'Auto,

"We intend to run the greatest cycling trial in the entire world. A race more than a month long; from Paris to Lyon, then to Marseille, Toulouse, Bordeaux, Nantes and back to Paris."

And so; the Tour de France was born.

Henri Desgrange and Géo Lefèvre look happy with their 1919 route and agree the 5,560km course should kill off all sixty-seven riders!

However, the great man distanced himself from the Tour. He made the announcement under the name of Henri Desgrenier rather than Desgrange, and uncertain of its success he stayed in Paris, and left the reporting to little Geo, who was to follow the Tour by bike and train, writing his column inches from key locations along each stage.

My own interest in cycling started at an early age, with a vintage Triang Noddy trike complete with Harley Davidson handlebars, wobbly stabilisers and a bread-bin basket, large enough to squeeze in a folded-up Action Man and three copies of the Beano. Christmases came and went, and as the bike size grew, so did the freedom to venture out into the Northamptonshire countryside. A visit to the iron ore pits of the local British steelworks was a must.

The great pools and lakes left by the excavation of the ore were better than any Disney theme park, and with the addition of the local limestone caves, there was a prehistoric feel to the landscape. So much so, it was chosen as one of the film locations for the 1970s film based on Edgar Rice Burroughs' novel, The Land That Time Forgot, starring American actor Doug McClure, famous for his role in the 1960s TV Western, 'The Virginian'. What the film crew thought about their marauding gangs of giant dinosaurs and prehistoric cavemen being interrupted by an occasional spotty teenager on a Raleigh Chopper bike, heaven knows, but the film was a success. I've cycled all my life, enjoying the freedom of the open road, the chance to clear your mind and get life back into perspective.

My earliest memories of the Tour de France were similar to many of my era. 'Eddy Merckx, Eddy Merckx, Eddy Merckx.' The Belgian 'Cannibal' was ever-present on the back pages of sports newspapers in the seventies. Eddy is widely viewed as the most successful rider in the history of competitive cycling. His victories include an unequalled 11 Grand Tours, consisting of five Tours of France, five Tours of Italy, and a Tour of Spain. The later dominance of Bernard Hinault, the 'Breton Badger' in the late seventies and early eighties passed me by, as the attraction of the punk music scene and college life dominated my attention. Even Plastic Bertrand's 'Ca Plane Pour Moi' couldn't divert my attentions to cycling events on the other side of the Channel. Still I had a love of cycling, and a love of France and the French language, and in my early business career, I was offered the opportunity to live and work in the forests of Fontainebleau, one-hour south of Paris. It was not a difficult decision to make, as I looked out of my rain splattered office window, with its view of the nearby Halal slaughterhouse, and the grey Birmingham skyline. The chance to live and work abroad doesn't come your way that often and so I jumped at the opportunity. I swapped the city of Tommy Shelby's Peaky Blinders for the town where King Louis XIII built his weekend retreat, the 'Chateau de Fontainebleau', where he would regularly retire with Paris' finest to hunt wild boar in the forest.

My early days at work were interesting as I tried to master the French business language from the three ladies who worked in the accounts department. None of them could speak a word of English, so I would point at things and they would kindly write down the equivalent French word or phrase for me. My knowledge of sporting words came from Philippe 'Flies Undone' (guess why?) who came in each day with L'Èquipe, the major French sports newspaper and the modern-day successor to Desgrange's L'Auto. He pointed out words such as 'but' (goal), 'arbitre' (referee) and 'velo' (bicycle). Mind you, as his only words of English were Bobby Charlton and Cadbury's chocolate fingers, I was not sure how well my French was going to progress! Then there was Gerard, the company salesman and lovable rogue, who came into my office and taught me all the words you can't find in the French dictionary! So, after weeks of making schoolboy errors and trying to book my boss a room in the Hôtel de Ville (Town Hall), inviting people to the pub, maison-publique (brothel) and announcing at the company annual conference that the company's profits were down 'baisser' but inadvertently using the wrong pronunciation 'baiser'. I soon found out I'd told the gathering throng the company was 'fucked' and, to my great surprise, I got a standing ovation and suddenly I felt part of the team.

As my French improved, and I got into conversation with my fellow co-workers, talk often turned to what our plans were for the weekend. I said in England, weekends tended to revolve around watching a football match on a Saturday, and maybe playing golf or football on Sunday. For my French colleagues the instant reply was that Saturdays were for playing tennis, and on Sundays it was out for a long ride with their local cycle club. So, what is the lesson to be learned here? For fifty years England haven't won any major competition in International Football and meanwhile the French have won two World Cups and the European Championships. On the other hand, its over thirty years since a Frenchman Bernard Hinault last won the Tour de France in 1985, and recently the 'La Grande Boucle' (The Big Ring) has been dominated by British riders and Team Sky.

Still, as I was now living and working in 'La Belle France', the Tour was beginning to work its way into my psyche. In my first summer there, in 1991, it was announced the Tour would pass close to the village of Vulaines-sur-Seine, where I was living, with the final stage into Paris, departing from the nearby town of Melun, before heading off to the Champs Èlysées. I thought it might be difficult to drive and park in the centre of Melun, so I took the logical decision to cycle there. It was a beautiful 20km ride along the banks of the river Seine, the only problem being a few hundred Frenchmen had come to the same decision. Arriving at the 'Quai de Marechal Joffre' it was impossible to get up the steps from the river into the main town to see the start of the race. Instead I had to content myself with the sight of the silhouettes of the riders as they filed across the bridge above me. Then I had to guess which rider might be the Spaniard, Miguel Indurain, who was wearing the yellow jersey on his way to his first ever Tour de France victory in Paris. This was to be the first of his five consecutive Tour wins, equalling the record held by Jacques Anquetil, Eddy Merckx and Bernard Hinault, as the softly spoken Spaniard dominated the race in the 1990s.

The following year in 1992, my in-laws visited from the UK, and I planned a road trip for them through the Dordogne and Auvergne regions of France. I'd completely forgotten Stages 16 and 17 of the Tour were forming a two-hundred-and-fifty-mile barrier across our route. In a sunflower field, somewhere in the middle of nowhere, we were brought to a standstill behind a long row of Peugeots, Renaults and Citroen 2 CVs. A fully kitted out gendarme waved his arms and shouted ***'Arrête, c'est Le Tour qui arrive,'*** and so we sat and waïted patiently for the race to pass. One consolation was, Stephen Roche, the Irish rider, actually won Stage 16, the last of his three career stage wins, following his Tour de France victory in 1987. By now, the Tour, and its interwoven connection to French culture and the French way of life was permanently imprinted on my brain, and my interest in following 'La Grande Boucle' only increased from thereon.

Back in 1903, Henri Desgrange had reduced the race from five weeks to three, due to a lack of initial interest. This was confirmed when only fifteen riders signed up, due to the long-time commitment involved. His masterstroke was moving the race to the middle of July, which coincided with the French two-week national holiday, and so began a long-term love affair between the French people and his 'free to view' race. The Tour became an annual tradition and the French citizens would plan their holidays to follow the three to five-thousand-kilometre race around their country. It was whilst following the 1993 Tour, and studying the map of the route, I noticed half of the race took place completely in the north of the country, and the other half completely in the south, with absolutely no cycling in between. The two separate routes were connected by two 500km flights from Nancy in the north-east to Grenoble in the south-east and then from Bordeaux in the south-west back up north to Paris. Hang on. This isn't a Tour de France. It's a 'demi-tour' at most. So, the following summer, whilst lying on a beach, I got out my Michelin road atlas of France and started plotting a cycle journey which would hug every coastal road, every border crossing and every mountain range lying on the hexagonal shape which is France. I worked out it would take me somewhere between two and half to three months to complete the 6,000 or so kilometres required. The plan was in place, but like all plans, real life came along, and for want of a better phrase, 'put a spoke in the wheel!'

It was time to move back to England after two enjoyable years working in France. The subsequent exciting arrival of a new baby boy and the four F's (Football, Family, Friends and Frothy beer) meant any cycling dreams had rightly to be shelved as work and raising a family must always take priority. The dream didn't go away though. The ambition was still there, sitting on a dusty shelf, it just needed the time and the place to get it back on the road. Years later, studying the history of the routes of the Tour de France, I soon discovered that whilst the original Géo Lefèvre Tour formats in 1903 and 1904 were limited to a lap of 2,428km, it didn't take Henri long to sort out the most punishing route ever. Yes, the Bâtard Desgrange soon got his claws stuck into what would soon become known as HIS Tour de France. By 1906 Henri extended the Tour to a complete circuit of the French nation, resulting in a staggering 4,637km of racing over 13 stages. Almost double the size of the original Tour.

His quotes on HIS Tour … "***The ideal Tour is one in which one rider finishes.***"

HIS ideal … "***Suffering on a bike is noble as it equates to the ultimate expression of willpower.***"

On the potential introduction of gears, brakes and light weight bikes…. "***I still feel that variable gears are only for people over forty-five. Isn't it better to triumph by the strength of your***

muscles than by the artificial aid of a 'derailleur'? We are getting soft.... As for me, give me a fixed gear!"

As to the race itself, his rules reflected his arcane vision of extending the limits of human achievement. There would be no 'domestiques', he banned pace making and the use of tactics. If you broke down you had to mend your own bike. You were not allowed any outside help at all. His motto was 'SUFFER AND SWEAT!'

And you wondered why I called him a complete and utter sadistic bâtard! His 'piece de resistance' had to be the Tour de France of 1919, coming as it did, straight after the end of the First World War. Most of the well-known 'kings of the road' had long been consigned to the cemeteries of northern France. All in all, three previous winners had been killed.

Lucien Petit Breton, the first rider to win the race in consecutive years 1907 and 1908, died in a car crash colliding with a horse and cart behind the front line at Troyes, south of Paris. The driver of the cart was tragically thought to have been blind drunk.

François Faber, from Luxembourg, was the first foreigner to win the Tour in 1909. He was also the first person to win five consecutive stages, a record which still stands today. François met his end fighting in the French Foreign Legion near Arras. It is thought he was struck by a German bullet whilst trying to rescue a colleague from No-Mans-Land.

Octave Lapize who, despite winning the Tour in 1910, shouted at race officials (Henri Desgrange maybe?) on the climb up the Col Du Tourmalet. ***"Vous êtes des assassins! Oui, des assassins!"*** *('You are murderers! Yes, murderers!')*. Octave joined the French air force as a fighter pilot and was eventually shot down somewhere in the Meurthe-et-Moselle region in eastern France. He died later in hospital from his injuries.

On the eleventh hour of the eleventh day of the eleventh month of 1918, the Armistice was signed in a railway carriage in Compiegne, bringing to an end 'The Great War'. By the twelfth hour Henri had got his pen out and was writing these words for the following week's edition of the L'Auto.

'The next Tour de France, the thirteenth in name, will take place next year in June and July, with a stage to Strasbourg'

Never mind the fact that the roads and towns in the north of France had been completely decimated during the First World War. Never mind the fact that any riders signing up for the race would be completely lacking in training, some of them having been held as prisoners of war and therefore had not sat on a bike for four years. Henri Desgrange chose to ignore all of this, and on the 22nd November 1918 (just 11 days after the Armistice was signed), he published the rules for his new Tour de France 1919. He followed this by revealing his most punishing route yet measuring a staggering 5,560km over 15 stages. (Average stage length 370km). This is still the second longest Tour ever in its history, with only the 1926 Tour beating it at 5,745 km. The race would contain six punishing stages, crossing the entire mountain ranges of the Pyrénées, the Alps, the Jura and the Vosges. All this was to be done on fixed-wheel bikes, which effectively had two gears. A high gear for riding along the flat terrain, and then, when faced with a mountain climb, the cyclist had to dismount, flip his rear wheel over, and select the sprocket on the other side, which gave a lower gear to tackle the ascent. On top of this, some of the mountain roads were not even on the national route map. They were nothing more than goat tracks, or tracks which local farmers used to drag felled-wood down from the mountains.

In comparison to the 1919 route, the current 2019 Tour de France measures 3,460km in length and will be held over 21 stages. It will have an average stage length of less than half that of 1919, 165km. The 1919 Tour also contained the longest single stage distance ever. Stage 5 between Sables D'Olonne and Bayonne was noted to be an incredible 482km in length! 2019's longest stage will be Stage 7, which runs from Belfort to Chalon-sur-Saone, and measures 280km.

Still Henri wasn't completely unreasonable. He agreed that as rationing was still in place, and with food hard to come by, he would allow feed stops twice a day. This was the first time this had ever happened in the Tour and each rider would get a bag of food and a fresh bidon (bottle) of water. What a great guy!!

And so that was it. My route was decided. The chance to follow in the footsteps of the 1919 riders. The chance to witness what these war-torn heroes of the road had gone through, exactly one hundred years to the day. It was also an opportunity for me to discover the personal story of my grandfather, Emmanuel Tarver, who had fought at Ypres, on the Somme and at Passchendaele during the Great War. As it happened Stages 1 and 14 of the 1919 Tour would pass through the battlefields where he had witnessed all the horrors that mankind could throw at a young man of his generation. Henri Desgrange's 1919 Tour de France would be the route for me.

Oh, and by the way did I mention the famous yellow jersey was also born on this Tour – Le Maillot Jaune – One hundred years old - Bonne Anniversaire!

Chapter 2 : The 3 R's - Runners, Riders and Rules.

Henri Desgrange hated the commercialism of the pre-First World War fashion of grouping cyclists into teams sponsored by the major bike manufacturers. He preferred the purity of a race ridden by individuals with no outside support. Therefore, in 1919 he reverted to the system of having two different classes of rider as there had been in the original Tours. The total field of 69 riders registered for the race would be split between Licence 'A' – the professional riders, of which there were 44, and Licence 'B' - the amateur riders, which were made up by the remaining 25. Henri wasn't entirely successful in his quest as the bike manufacturers clubbed together and under the name 'La Sportive' sponsored nearly half of the riders anyway.

On the eve of the race, the newspaper L'Auto stated who they thought the favourites might be amongst the runners and riders. Henri Desgrange gave his own forecast of the outcome for his specially selected top ten riders. A list which I'm sure will have gone down well with the rest of the 59 hopeful riders who were about to set off on his 5,560km course. So here are his predictions.

Henri Pélissier: NON, he will still be exhausted by his efforts in the Paris-Bordeaux race in May.

Francis Pélissier (younger brother of Henri): NON, too young.

Philippe Thys: NON, he looked over-trained in the Paris-Brest race and it will be too much to think he can win three Tours in a row.

Eugéne Christophe: NON, too old!

Jean Alavoine: NON, too old! He's spent too much time on the heavy fruit juice.

Louis Heusghem: NON, He's way too heavy. (flattering indeed)

Alexis Michiels: NON, too young and he may be feeling the effects of riding Paris-Brussels, two weeks earlier.

Honoré Barthélémy: NON, too young. I like him but he's not a great tactician.

Hector Tiberghien: PERHAPS, but he may be feeling the results of Paris-Tours, three weeks ago.

Emile Masson: YES, with no Paris-Bordeaux on his conscience, and having done a fantastic Tour of Belgium, this is the man who can become one of our cycling greats, and win the Tour de France.

So, there we have Henri Desgrange's choice. It's now time for you to choose from the main runners and riders.

Number 55: 'FACING HIS WATERLOO' ODDS: 50/1

Joseph Vandaele, the professional Belgian cyclist, will be hoping for an improvement on his previous two GC placings, where he finished 9th in both. Born in Waterloo he will be hoping that unlike Napoleon, he doesn't surrender over fifteen stages and will be looking for a podium finish at least. His ability to go the distance is without doubt.

Age: 29
Weight: 72 kilos,
Development: 5.50
Previous Tour placings:
1912 DNF, 1913 9th, 1914 9th

Number 42: 'Mr. JOHN' (GARS JEAN) ODDS: 5/1

Age: 31
Weight: 74 kilos,
Development: 5.25
Previous Tour placings:
1909 3rd , 1914 3rd.

Ridden by Jean Alavoine who emanates from the royal city of Versailles. As the Peace Treaty was signed there only yesterday **'Gars Jean'** will be keen to give a good showing in this year's race. A thoroughbred with over ten years' experience in cycle racing, Jean is carrying a bit of weight at 74 kilos, as can be seen from the ripples in his lower quarter, but despite carrying a bit of timber, he is still expected to show well. He finished third in the pre-war 1914 Tour de France winning Stage 7.

Number 15: 'THE BASSET HOUND' ODDS: 5/2

Age: 29
Weight: 69 kilos,
Development: 5.10
Previous Tour placings:
1913 1st, 1914 1st.

Ridden by Phillipe Thys from the city of Anderlecht in Belgium. Philippe is known as the **Basset Hound (Le Basset)** or 'Fat Dog' because of his low cycling position. A strong favourite with two previous Tour wins under his belt already. As both of these victories came just before the Great War, the Belgian should be well placed for three Tour wins in a row. Also, a recent good showing of second place in this year's Paris-Roubaix shows that the Basset Hound has lost none of his touch and is well worth sticking a few of your French Francs on.

Number 57: 'THE LOCOMOTIVE' ODDS: 40/1

Age: 30
Weight: 81 kilos,
Development: 5.50
Previous Tour placings:
1913 DNF, 1914 14th.

Léon Scieur comes from the cycling hotbed of Florennes in Belgium. Taught to ride by his good friend and local rival in this year's race, Firmin Lambot, **the Locomotive** weighs in at 81 kilos, Léon, the son of a farmer, is not the heaviest in the race (that honour goes to Hector Heusghem at 86 kilos) but all the same 'Léon the Locomotive' will need to get a full head of steam to pull his fulsome frame up the 'Col du Galibier'

Number 46: 'THE OLD GAUL' ODDS: 6/1

Age: 34
Weight: 67 kilos,
Development: 5.50
Previous Tour placings:
1906 9th, 1907 DNF
1909 9th, 1911 DNF
1912 2nd, 1913 7th,
1914 11th

Not known as 'Le Vieux Gaulois' **(The Old Gaul)** for nothing. Eugéne Christophe comes into this race with a wealth of knowledge and experience. Known for being as organised as one of the toolboxes in his workshops, Eugéne always carries a 10 and 20FF note, a chain link and a spoke key in his cycling bib. Famous for his misfortune on the 'Col du Tourmalet' in 1913, where he had to repair his broken front forks himself, Eugéne will be hoping that his bike doesn't let him down this time and he can win his first Tour de France.

Number 45: 'THE SADDLER' ODDS: 3/1

Age: 33
Weight: 66 kilos,
Development: 5.50
Previous Tour placings:
1911 11th, 1912 18th, 1913 4th, 1914 8th.

We have already spoken of the Sellier **(Saddler)** of Florennes. At the age of 17, Firmin Lambot used to cycle 50km to work every day and despite the fact he trained on the lowlands of Belgium, he is considered to be one of the best climbers around. He is said to be prudent like the Sioux Indian, calm, reflective and perfectly organised. He is known to drink tea, suck mint pastilles (against thirst) and to carry 600FF around in his pocket in case he needs to buy a new bike. With his progression in the Tour to date you wouldn't bet against him achieving a 'podium' finish.

Number 37: 'THE GREYHOUND' ODDS: 3/1

Age: 30,
Weight: 67 kilos,
Development: 5.50
Previous Tour placings:
1912 DNF, 1913 DNF, 1914 2nd.

The French cycling equivalent of football's 'Neymar' this stubborn and difficult man was once described by Henri Desgrange as a 'pig headed and arrogant champion'. Thrown off the family farm at the age of 16, Henri Pélissier thought he was far better than a labourer who had to deliver milk from a horse drawn cart. Henri saw his future was in cycling and with wins in this year's Paris-Roubaix (April) and Bordeaux-Paris (May) plus a second place in the Tour last time out, who is to argue with him?

Number 40: 'THE UNKNOWN' ODDS: 40/1

Age: 30
Weight: 77.5 kilos,
Development: 5.00
Previous Tour placings:
1913 DNF

A good outside bet, and Henri Desgrange's tip to win the 1919 Tour, is Emile Masson. He achieved a 2nd place in the Tour of Belgium in 1913 and was the winner of the terrible stage Erquelines-Namur. Travelling in the terrible conditions of western Flanders, he beat that day Défraye, Gauthy and Buysse, who are in a nutshell, all of the best Belgian riders around. He is little known to the general public but Henri believes he has what it takes to win his great race. Do you believe him?

Number 48: 'THE MAN OF IRON' ODDS: 50/1

Age: 29,
Weight: 71.5 kilos,
Development: 5.60
Previous Tour placings:
1912 DNF, 1913 DNF, 1914 DNF

If Henri Pélissier is the French equivalent of football's 'Neymar' then surely Louis Mottiat is Belgium's version of Christiano Ronaldo. Called the Man of Iron because of his endurance, not only physical but cosmetic, Louis can still look like a film star, dressed in a flat cap and goggles, after sixteen hours riding in the saddle. One for the ladies to put their money on and let the 'Iron Man cometh'

Number 49: 'GLASS EYE' ODDS: 5/1

Age: 28
Weight: 69 kilos,
Development: 5.50
Previous Tour placings: 0

The Parisian Honoré Barthélémy looks more like Tweedle–Dum or Tweedle-Dee, with his striped shirt and cap sat atop his round face. I've taken his name of 'glass eye' from the 1920 Tour de France when he crashed on the Stage near Aix-en-Provence. He thought he had concussion and didn't realise that it was actually blindness as he had got a bit of flint stuck in his eye. He somehow managed to finish the stage riding with his handle bars in the upright position and with a broken shoulder and dislocated wrist. Not only did he finish the stage but he also completed the Tour finishing 8th. In subsequent tours he used to take his, by then, 'glass eye' out and replace it with a cotton wool plug if it got too dusty. He often complained that he spent more on replacing lost glass eyes than he got from winning races. Still this shows the tenacity of the man. He is also known as the 'Red Squirrel' due to his bright red hair. Third in this year's Paris-Roubaix, fourth in Paris-Tours and sixth in Paris-Brussels shows that Honoré is coming into this Tour in fine form and surely can never be written off.

Number 19: 'THE ITALIAN JOB' ODDS: 70/1

Age: 25
Weight: 67.8 kilos,
Development: 5.40
Previous Tour placings: 0

There are only three Italians gracing this year's Tour and one of those is Luigi Lucotti from Voghera in the Lombardy region of northern Italy. Riding in the colours of the Bianchi team, it's his first Tour de France. Luigi will be looking to improve on his good showing of third place in the 1914 pre-war Giro D'Italia. With his slicked back dark hair, and the steely grin and look of Chris Froome, Luigi will be determined to put his country back on the map. The only previous podium finish for the Land of 'La Dolce Vita' was a third place showing by Cesar Garin in the infamous 1904 Tour de France. However, the race was rocked by rumours of scandal and cheating (riders were thought to have caught trains between stages) and Henri Desgrange vowed that this, the second Tour de France, would be the last. After a thorough investigation, by the wonderfully named Union Vélocipédique Française (UVF), the top four finishers were disqualified and the disgraced Cesar Garin eliminated.

Number 44: 'THE APPLE' ODDS: 15/1

Age: 35
Weight: 68 kilos,
Development: 6.10
Previous Tour placings:
1908 11th, 1909 4th, 1911 2nd, 1914 31st.

Paul Duboc is an experienced rider from Rouen in Normandy. He comes with a wealth of experience in the Tour, not all of it good. In 1911 he was close to winning when he was poisoned, after drinking from a bottle given to him by some opposition fans, supporting the eventual winner Gustave Garrigou. It was never proven, but poor old Paul ended up finishing 2nd, which is still his best placing. 'Le Pomme' will be hoping that all he drinks is apple juice in this year's race as he looks to right those wrongs. For the occasion Paul has grown a massive moustache to match the handlebars on his bike.

Number 51: 'THE YOUNG MAGICIAN' ODDS: 50/1

Age: 24,
Weight: 78 kilos,
Development: 5.80
Previous Tour placings: 0

Francis Pélissier, younger brother of Henri, comes from the same strong farming stock. Known as the 'Le Sorcier **(Magician)** de Bordeaux - Paris' Francis' pedigree is assured. He is also fondly known as 'Le Grand' or the 'Big One' and weighing in at 78 kilos at the tender age of 24 you can see why. His 6th placing in this year's Paris-Roubaix shows he will not rest in the shadow of his older brother and he may well have a few magic tricks of his own to show us in the days to come.

Number 50: 'THE UNWANTED' ODDS: 20/1

Age: 30
Weight: 72 kilos,
Development: 5.55
Previous Tour placings:
1909 DNF, 1912 1st, 1913 DNF, 1914 DNF.

A strong favourite for this year's Tour has to be the 1912 winner, Odile Defraye, the first Belgian to win the Tour de France. **Unwanted** originally by the Alcyon team, Odile, the winner of the recent Tour of Belgium, was taken on to help Gustave Garrigou repeat his 1911 Tour victory. It was soon realised that Odile was actually the stronger rider and he was made the team leader. This decision turned out to be fully justified as he won the Tour on the points system beating Eugéne Christophe. If the race had been decided on pure time alone then Christophe would have held the yellow jersey all the way to the final stage in Paris.

Number 151: 'THE UPSTART' ODDS: 500/1

Age: 29
Weight: 61 kilos,
Development: 5.50
Previous Tour placings: 1911 DNF, 1914 27th

It's good to have an outsider to back in the race and Jules ('Julot') Nempon from Calais fits that category perfectly. One of the promising Licence 'B' riders Jules will be riding under his own team name 'Nempon Cycles' His first Tour outing was in 1911 when he did not finish but he got all the way to Stage 13 out of 15. He followed that up in 1914 with a promising 27th place riding for the J.B. Louvet-Continental team. Jules is definitely a dark horse and, in his photos, he looks like one.

Number 115: 'THE SOLE SPANIARD' ODDS: 500/1

Age: 23
Weight: 58.5 kilos,
Development: 5.10
Previous Tour placings: 0

You may want to put your money on the **sole Spaniard** in the race, Jose Orduna. A young rider from Madrid, Jose becomes only the second Spanish rider to enter the Tour in the history of the race. His predecessor was Vincente Blanco who rode for the marvellously named 'Casanovas' team. Unfortunately, Vincente only managed to complete the first stage so let's hope that Jose can better the Casanovas performance. He can certainly beat their outfits.

Number 63: 'THE SMOKER' ODDS: 50/1

Age: 29
Weight: 65 kilos,
Development: 5.50
Previous Tour placings: 1912 17th, 1913 DNF, 1914 19th.

Jacques Coomans was christened the Smoker by Henri Desgrange. He repeatedly reported in L'Auto, that this great Belgian rider would never reach his full potential, due to his penchant for smoking, either pipes or large cigars. Jacques is quoted as saying that he may struggle on Stage 12 of this year's Tour from Geneva to Strasbourg as he would have to stop regularly to sample the tobacco leaves grown on the plains of Alsace.

Number 41: 'ETERNAL SECOND' ODDS: 20/1

Age: 29
Weight: 66 kilos,
Development: 5.40
Previous Tour placings:
1913 DNF, 1914 4th.

This will be Jean Rossius's third Tour de France. After having to abandon on Stage 7 of the 1913 Tour, he finished in a creditable 4th position in 1914, behind Phillipe Thys, Henri Pélissier and Jean Alavoine. He is one to watch out for with his two stage wins in 1914 on Stage 2 Le Havre to Cherbourg and Stage 9 Marseille to Nice. He was also race leader for four days. The nearest he has come to winning a Grand Tour is 2nd in the Tour of Belgium in 1914. Could it be a case of third time lucky for the Eternal Second?

Number 56: 'THE KID (LE GOSSE) ' ODDS: 50/1

Age: 26
Weight: 65 kilos,
Development: 5.40
Previous Tour placings: 0

Alfred Steux, is known as Le Gosse, The Kid, due to his boyish looks. His face is said to look like a bright shiny button. Well, the Belgian had shone well in the recent Paris–Roubaix race in April 1919, finishing tenth behind Eugéne Christophe. No mean feat. This is his first Tour de France and it will be interesting to see if Alfred can endure the fifteen gruelling stages and grow up to be a man.

Some other riders that are worth a flutter if only because of their names or professions are:

Number 59 - Félix GOETHALS – 'THE SOCK SELLER' named after his pre-war profession. Ever the salesman René has brought a small stock of his foot garments along with him to sell to the riders en-route.

Number 61 - René CHASSOT – 'CHEEKY MONKEY'. You always need one joker in the pack and René is not backward when it comes to pulling a stunt or two.

Number 143 - Paul THONDOUX – 'MR. SOFT TUNA' who at 20 years old is the youngest rider in the race.

Number 106 – Etienne NAIN – 'THE DWARF' who ironically at 1.95m is one of the tallest riders in the race.

Number 125 - Henri MOREILLON who at the grand old age of 43 earns the title of **'THE DEAN'.**

There are two non-runners **Georges DEVILLY** and **Marcel MISSEREY** (enough said) as both missed signing 'La Feuille' at the allotted time. So, this leaves us with a final field of 67 riders that will leave the Parc des Princes at 3 a.m.

And so, the choice is yours. You've seen the field, now pick your favourites and see if you can predict the top three riders of this 'Tour to end all Tours'

Number ____ Rider ______________________________ Odds______
Number ____ Rider ______________________________ Odds______
Number ____ Rider ______________________________ Odds______

The Rules of the Tour de France 1919

1. The rider must complete the race on the same bike;
2. Any rider of the Tour de France is placed in an 'out-on-the-road situation' and will do his training alone. He mustn't prepare anything for the road trip, such as refreshments. It follows that:

a) he cannot help his friends or competitors in any way and they, in turn, cannot accept any help from him;

b) on the route the rider must take any refreshments himself, without having ordered anything in advance. He also cannot receive any help from anyone. For example, he must only draw water for himself from springs or fountains that he may come across on the route.

3. The rider, at the outset, may take away anything he wants with him;

4. The rider, at the stage finishes, can do anything he wants, provided he has, before the start of each stage, approved this with L'Auto;

5. The race is undertaken without coaches and /or masseurs, except at the stage finishes and a rider must compete on a punched bike. *(one stamped with the rider's race number – to ensure the same bike is used throughout the race)*

6. Any rider not looking after his own fate, or who is seen to be sacrificing himself for the opportunity of a friend, will be excluded from the race.

An essential bit of advice to all the riders, whoever they are, is that they must legibly sign the 'control' sheets, both in the mobile control points, as well as in the fixed control points, and they must affix their seal in the special box assigned to them in front of their names and on the printed sheets. Failure by them to sign will incur the penalties set out in the rules.

The Machines

L'Auto noted with great regret the fact that only 67 riders would take part in this year's tour. After all, 140 had entered the 1914 Tour prior to the war. They put the lower number down to the scarcity of materials to build cycles, in particular the lack of rubber available for making tyres. This mainly affected the number of registered riders in the Licence 'B' category who had to find their own bikes, as they were not sponsored by a manufacturer.

In 1919 the bikes were typically of the fixed wheel variety. The rear wheel had a sprocket on either side of the hub. To change gears, the rider had to stop, dismount and remove the wheel, flipping it around and remounting it. Derailleurs were in their infancy, being developed in France between 1900 and 1916. In fact,

Stephanois Panel had experimented with the system in the 1912 race and was immediately banned. As we have already seen Henri Desgrange was totally against any sort of assistance from a 'derailleur' and believed that the cyclist should propel the bike with his own strength, not through the mechanical assistance of gear ratios.

'La souffrance à bicyclette est noble car elle correspond au plein épanouissement de la volonté.'

'Suffering on a bike is noble because it represents the full blossoming of your willpower'

Whether you believe in Henri's ideal or not 'derailleurs' were not allowed in HIS Tour de France until 1937! L'Auto did have one essential recommendation for the bikes though:

We recommend that riders equip their machines with extremely solid brakes for the crossing of the Vosges, Jura, the Alps and the Pyrénées. We warn them that the Pyrenean descents are excessively dangerous. Extreme caution should be observed, not only from time to time, but always. Sound advice indeed!

It was now up to the bike manufacturers to come up with a machine that they could be confident would complete the 5,560km journey over the roughest of terrains. They did battle with each other on the advertising pages of L'Auto. It is interesting to compare their approaches to convince the reader to purchase their products.

PEUGEOT, the world-famous manufacturer of cars and bikes, publish a simple understated advert of their strengths. 10 Specialised Factories, 12 branches and 3,000 agents across France and the entire world.

AUTOMOTO take the same approach 'Automoto' cycles are manufactured with all their parts, (very handy), in their six factories around Saint Etienne.

J.B. LOUVET from Puteaux in Paris take a different approach and announced confidently

'5,560 kilometres on a single punched bicycle A. DEJONGHE, B. MATHIS, U. ANSEÊUW, C. MENAGER, J. NEMPON, J. VERDICKT, A. HURET, F. DHERS have all entrusted their chances to the excellent green bicycle with the red band, plus the addition of PIRELLI tyres. SPORTSMEN, AGENTS, when you see a green bicycle with a red band passing you on the road, remember it is stamped: J.B. LOUVET'

It will be interesting to see how many of their eight quoted riders make it to the finish at the Parc des Princes.

ALYCON, is another well-known manufacturer from the Courbevoie region of Paris. Residing just two kilometres down the road from the J.B. Louvet factory, they decide to sing their own praises across the tree tops of 'the Bois de Boulogne'

'For four consecutive years ALYCON has won the Tour de France. 1909-Faber, 1910-Lapize, 1911-Garrigou, 1912-Defraye.'

There's no mention of what happened in the last two tours of 1913 and 1914!

Chapter 3 : 'Squeezing Germany so hard the pips squeak'

So, where should I stage my own personal 'Grand Départ' in recognition of the 1919 Tour de France? I needed to be located somewhere near the official start at the Parc des Princes in south-west Paris. I toyed with the idea of staying at the café 'Au Reveil Matin' (the early morning wake-up call) in the town of Montgeron, to the south of the City. This was the actual café from which Maurice Garin and 59 other riders had set off on the 1st July 1903, embarking on the first ever Tour de France. But after further study, it soon became obvious that there was only one candidate for the place I could start this 1919 post-war Tour de France. I needed to be to the west of the Parc des Princes on the 28th June 2019, the day before the start of the 1919 race. Wasn't it exactly one hundred years ago, on this day, that the famous Treaty of Versailles was signed at Louis XIV's home just down the road, bringing an end to the First World War? A quick check on Google maps revealed that the Palace of Versailles was only 12km away from the Parc de Princes, and that I could cycle to the starting point of the 1919 Tour in under an hour. Magnifique!

I was concerned as to whether I would be able to access the Palace and grounds on the 100th anniversary of the treaty being signed, as there would probably be official private celebrations scheduled to commemorate this historic event. It seemed not. In fact, there didn't seem to be any indication that the Palace of Versailles was going to acknowledge the 100th anniversary of the most significant event in its history in any way at all. Mind you, they were celebrating the 300th anniversary of the death of Louis XIV's secret wife, Françoise d'Aubigne, who later became the Marquise de Maintenon. Born in a prison, Françoise rose to fame by marrying Louis XIV, the self-proclaimed Sun King. The marriage, between two social unequals could not be recognised officially and therefore Françoise never became Queen. She was, however, an influential advisor to the court and the King and obviously in French eyes, she was more important than the signing of the Treaty of Versailles. After all, this had only brought about world peace. And so, I found myself in front of the Palace gates, at 2 p.m. on the 28th of June 2019 on the 100th anniversary of the arrival of the delegations of the 32 nations that would sign the Peace Treaty.

*

The crowd was enormous. There were soldiers and sailors still in uniform, mixing with civilians both young and old, lining the Avenue de Paris, which leads from the city of Versailles down to the Palace gates. There were gentlemen dressed in plus-fours and smart jackets with waist-coats, smoking their pipes and chatting about the great event that was about to take place. Ladies and young children sat around the edges of the Chateau's great fountains waiting for the day's events to unfold. Some had brought their own fold-up chairs, to rest their weary legs, as they waited and watched the children playing in the midday sun. A vendor was wandering around outside the gates selling national flags to the crowd from his wicker baskets. The flags were predominantly French tricolours and the stars and stripes of the USA. The crowd were now armed and ready to wave their chosen flag at the appropriate moment. A vendor pushed his cart into the middle of the throng, and proceeded to sell drinks and cakes to the thirsty and, by now, hungry masses. As the excitement rose and the official cars arrived, soldiers stood on top of their parked motor bikes, holding on to each other for balance and hoping to get a better view over the heads of the thickening crowd. Some brave souls climbed up one of the nearby telegraph poles, straining to see the action.

The Big Four arrived. David Lloyd George, the 'Welsh Wizard' and Prime Minister of Great Britain. Georges Clemenceau, the 'Tiger' and Prime Minister of France. Woodrow Wilson, President of the United States of America 'the sign of Hope' and creator of the League of Nations and Vittorio Orlando, Prime Minister of Italy.

Upon entering the Palace, I checked again with the Information Desk to see if there were any special celebrations lined up for today.

"Non, Monsieur. Our Management is bad, yes?"

I replied that I was stunned that the Palace had let this major event pass without any recognition at all. The guide on the Information Desk agreed. He thought something may have been arranged in the War Rooms later on that evening but he wasn't sure. I joined the queues and started to make my way towards the Hall of Mirrors, where the Treaty was signed, aiming to be there for the historic hour of 3 p.m. As I passed through each room, dawdling to look at some of the great treasures and paintings that the Palace contains, I found the crowd getting thicker and thicker. Time was marching on! Was everybody planning the same timed visit as me and secretly everybody knew of the momentous event. It was now 2.50 p.m. and I was almost there. A guided Tour stopped in front of me and they thronged around their leader blocking my way through to the Hall of Mirrors. I saw a gap and went for it. Suddenly, from nowhere, an old Japanese man appeared on crutches. What was he doing here hobbling around in these hordes of tourists? I waited for him to pass slowly through the doorway and then politely body-swerved a mother with three children and I was there. Just in time! I waited for the allotted time to appear on my iPhone. 14.58, 14.59, 15.00. I looked around to see if anyone else recognised the significance of the moment.

Nope, nobody had a clue! Somebody took a photo of the magnificent ceiling and the glass chandeliers glistening with the reflections of the hundreds of candle-lights placed above each one. A young boy was break-dancing in front of one of the 17 arches of mirrors, each containing 21 individual pieces of mirrored glass. Maybe he was dancing in joy at the thought that the war was finally over. An American couple stopped and took the obligatory selfie.

"Hang on! Do you think you can move out of the way? We're expecting some very important people to enter this room to bring peace to the world after four years of the bloodiest war in history."

*

So, at 3 p.m. on the 28th June 1919 the signing of the Treaty commenced. The Germans had sent a delegation of two to do their dirty work and sign the Treaty. Hermann Muller, Minister of Colonial Affairs and Doctor Johannes Bell, Minister of Foreign Affairs. They arrived sheepishly, dressed in black suits, their shiny black top hats glistening in the sun. They were ushered into the Hall of Mirrors as if they were convicts. They were trembling, their ashen white faces contrasting dramatically with their dark formal suits. There were tears in their eyes, genuine tears that could not have been simulated.

Hall of Mirrors – Palace of Versailles – 3 p.m. 28th June 2019

This whole scene had been carefully stage managed by the French Prime Minister, Georges Clemenceau. He had chosen the venue of the Palace of Versailles on purpose, as this was the exact place where the Germans had proclaimed their New Empire, after their victory in the Franco-Prussian War of 1871. Germany had taken back the provinces Alsace and Lorraine, much to the disgust of the French.

Henri Desgrange was so shocked by his countries capitulation in the 1871 war, he felt his nation was 'tired, without muscle, without character and without willpower'. It was partly this sense of disgrace in the overall fitness of his compatriots that drove him to create the punishing routes and long stages in the Tour de France, to create a lean fit nation which was ready for anything.

Georges Clemenceau added to the Germans' discomfort by placing a special writing desk and ink stand, belonging to Louis

XIV, in front of the two signatories. In the front row, directly facing them, he had also deliberately placed some horrendously mutilated French war veterans, so the Germans would not forget their crimes. They would sign, underneath the ceilings of the 30 legendary paintings of the artist Charles Lebrun, depicting the famous French victories of the 'Sun King'.

Hall of Mirrors – Palace of Versailles – 3 p.m. 28th June 1919

At the allotted 3 p.m. the Hall was crowded with delegates, reporters and journalists from all the Allied nations across the world and not, as in 2019, groups of Japanese and American tourists! Box cameras stood on fixed tripods, poised to capture the historic moment. The crowd outside pressed their faces against the windows, straining for any view of this historic event. It was exactly five years to the day that the assassination of Archduke Franz Ferdinand had taken place. The catalyst that started the Great War. Germany signed, accepting as they did Article 231, which became known as the War Guilt Clause.

"The Allied and Associated Governments affirm, and Germany accepts the responsibility of Germany and her allies, for causing all the loss and damage to which the Allied and Associated Governments and their nationals have been

subjected, as a consequence of the war imposed upon them by the aggression of Germany and her allies."

The terms of the Treaty were many. The bill that the Germans were faced with was 296 billion golden marks, which is probably about £570 billion in today's money. Significantly though Germany had to return the lands of Alsace and Lorraine back to France (more to come later on this subject in Stage 12 of the Tour - Geneva to Strasbourg). The Germans also had to give France the exclusive use of their coal and iron minefields in the rich and plentiful Saar Valley for 15 years. This would enable France to replenish her mineral resources. The mines, railways, bridges and factories in the north of France had been deliberately flooded or blown up by the Germans during their evacuation of the front line in November 1918.

Georges Clemenceau had achieved his aim, although some still thought the treaty to be too lenient. Woodrow Wilson had realised his objective of creating a League of Nations, which would work together with the exclusion of Germany, to achieve global stability and world peace. Britain, themselves, had a policy of 'Squeezing Germany until the pips squeak'. This certainly had been achieved, although privately Lloyd George, did not want a treaty of revenge, but he preferred a more conciliatory stance that would not cripple Germany and her economy.

At 3.45 p.m. the Treaty had been completely signed by all of the 32 nations. The Germans rose from their chairs and were the first to leave the Palace followed by all the other delegates. The scenes outside were ecstatic as the crowd burst into celebration.

It must be remembered that, although the Armistice had been signed on the 11th November 1918 in a railway carriage in Compeigne, war was not officially over. In fact, even at the beginning of the month of June 1919, the Germans had stated that they would sign the Treaty subject to the removal of certain clauses. The Allies responded in anger and stated that if the Treaty was not signed, as it stood, within 24 hours, the Allies would take up arms and invade Germany, crossing the River Rhine.

The diplomatic cars drove out through the Palace gates and onto the streets of Versailles. Bowler hats and boaters were thrown into the air in celebration that the Great War was over. People sang and danced in the streets.

TREATY SIGNED; WAR OVER

The Evening World.

FINAL EDITION

WILSON LEAVES PARIS; SAILS SUNDAY

GERMANS PLEDGED TO ACT IN GOOD FAITH

CITY'S BELLS RING TIDINGS AS PEACE TREATY IS SIGNED; FLEET JOINS IN CELEBRATION

TREATY SEVERE ON GERMANY, SAYS WILSON, BUT IMPOSES NOTHING SHE CANNOT DO

President in an Address to the American Public Says It Furnishes a Charter for a New Order and Ends Rule of Selfish Groups

GUNS BOOM, PLANES FILL AIR; FRENCH CROWDS CHEER PEACE

GERMANS PLEDGED TO ENFORCE TREATY; NO RESERVATION

WILSON, STARTING FOR HOME, BIDS FRANCE GOODSPEED

Soldiers Break Ranks and Join in the Demonstrations of Joy—Chinese Refuse to Attend Ceremony and Gen. Smuts Signs Under Protest.

In the Fench capital the celebrations were in full swing. Giant fireworks were being let off into the night sky to celebrate the moment that peace had finally arrived. Mind you, this momentous event was given scant coverage in the following days edition of Henri Desgrange's L'Auto newspaper. A tiny paragraph could be found, half way down page two, that stated,

AU DESSUS DU PALAIS DE VERSAILLES
(above the Palace of Versailles)

Yesterday, at the very moment of the signing of peace treaty, at 3H.12 many planes flew over the Palace of Versailles in a cannonade of joy that shook the air. The English airmen have made a name for themselves with the audacity of their twists and turns and on board the French planes, many ladies took their seats and admired the magnificent spectacle of the 'Panorama of Versailles' and below them swarmed a huge and enthusiastic crowd.

To be fair the L'Auto team had other things on their mind. After all this was the morning of the 'GRAND DÉPART' of their 13th Tour de France, and Henri and his fellow organisers were creeping out of their offices on the Rue de Faubourg in Montmatre, in the still of the night, and heading across the city to the Parc des Princes. They drove in the 'Brasier Dictoriale', (the official car in which they would follow this year's Tour). A full chapter was written in L'Auto, describing the features of this magnificent new motor, using more words than had been used to describe the celebrations of world peace.

Henri and his team were in a hurry, as they needed to get to the Parc in the Bois de Boulogne by 1 a.m., for the weighing and signing in of this year's group of riders. As they drove down the dark streets, they could hear the singing of the 'Marseillaise' in the far distance. They thought because of the magnitude of the peace celebrations, the usual race crowds may desert them and the Tour would head off unnoticed.

This was a big mistake on their part!

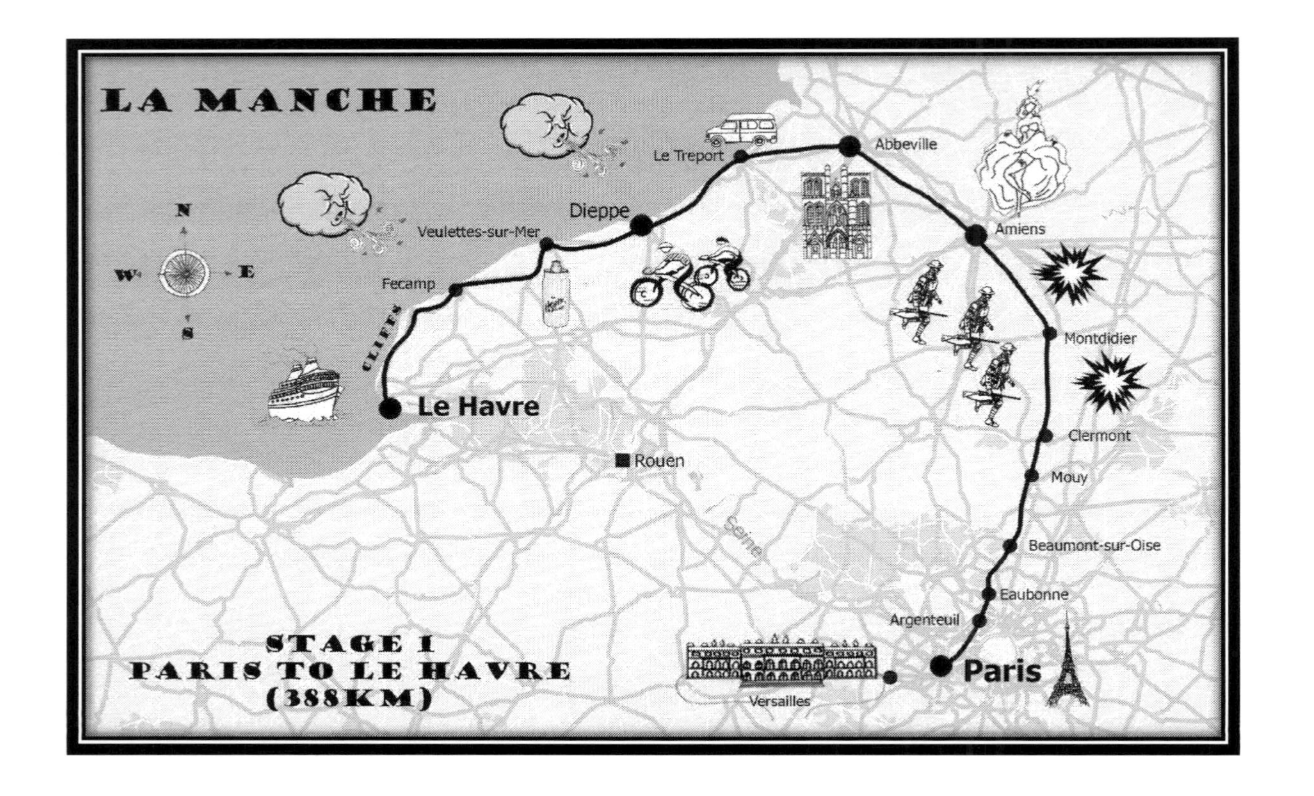

LA MANCHE
N
W
E
S
CLIFFS
Le Havre
Fecamp
Veulettes-sur-Mer
Dieppe
Le Treport
Abbeville
Amiens
Montdidier
Clermont
Mouy
Beaumont-sur-Oise
Eaubonne
Argenteuil
Paris
Versailles
Rouen
Seine
STAGE I
PARIS TO LE HAVRE
(388KM)

Chapter 4: Grand Départ – 'Allons Y'

Stage 1 - Sunday 29th June 1919 (Paris – Le Havre)
Friday 28th June 2019 (Versailles – Paris)

"Désolé' (Sorry) Monsieur Desgrange, but there is no way I am going to be at the control point at the Parc des Princes, ready to sign in, at one o'clock in the morning."

Apart from the unearthly hour, it is probably not the best time for a lone Englishman, to be hanging around the backstreets of Paris, crossing the notorious alleyways which are home to the ladies of the Bois-de-Boulogne. I had already worked out that the best way for me to sign in, was to get there first, the night before, the closest I would get to 1 a.m. and at least get a head start in the race.

This meant a few additional kilometres cycling into the centre of Paris from the Palace of Versailles, but at least my intended route would be of significant interest to Tour de France aficionados, as I would pass through the Ville d'Avray, the site of the official finish of the inaugural Tour de France of 1903. It was in this very town that Maurice Garin was crowned the first ever Tour champion and 'Le petit ramoneur' (the little chimney-sweep) took his place in Tour history, despite his proven misdemeanours the following year, when he and three others were disqualified for blatant cheating. No one officially knows what he was supposed to have done. The Tour records went missing, whilst being transported to the south of France in 1940, in an attempt to stop them falling into the hands of the invading Germans. However, years later, a cemetery attendant heard the elderly Garin bragging about his great Tour victories and about hitching a ride on a train in the Tour of 1904.

And so, I set off on my own Grand Départ, in the blistering heat of the late afternoon sun, following my visit to the Hall of Mirrors in Versailles. I had arrived in France in one of the most intense heatwaves that the country had known for decades.

One advantage of 'la canicule" (heatwave) was that the French government had recently banned vehicles of a certain size accessing a predefined area, circling Paris, to try and prevent high levels of street pollution. The upside to this was that Versailles was an excluded zone and my cycle route into the centre of Paris would at least, given that it was a Friday night, be subject to lower levels of manic traffic.

And so, I set off along the tree-lined boulevards and cycle paths of the royal home of the Kings of France. I passed elderly ladies, heavily manicured, parading their petit chihuahuas and dachshunds in the dappled afternoon sunlight. Obviously, these delicate treasures didn't know how to distinguish between a path and a cycle route, and on a couple of occasions, I only just managed to avoid sending the little darlings into the awaiting guillotine of my spinning front wheel.

Soon I was heading out of town, up a fairly steep rise, when suddenly a row of police cars greeted me, their flashing lights signalling that traffic could go no further. Bolloques, I thought in my best French, surely my Grand Départ wasn't going to be thrown off course after a measly three kilometres. I made my mind up. I was going to stick to my route and see what happened. I cycled up to the barricade, said 'Bonjour' to a female gendarme and kept on pedalling. No one stopped me so on I went. I wondered what might lie ahead, a mangled car crash, a violent robbery? Maybe a speeding cyclist had lopped the head off a wandering toy poodle. Heaven forbid!

In another kilometre, it soon became apparent why the road had been cordoned off. On either side stood two large stone monuments, each carrying a statue of a mounted officer, facing one another. On my side of the road there was a mixed group of what appeared to be young French and American students. On the other side of the road French and American soldiers were starting to line up together in preparation for the main event.

I soon worked out what was happening. A few metres in front of me stood an unmanned microphone stand waiting for the dignitaries to commence proceedings. I needed to act quickly or I would be stuck there for an hour or more. I got myself into a Chris Boardman time trial position and WOOSH off I went, hurtling through the middle of proceedings and escaping into the woods beyond. I subsequently found out that I had passed the Pershing-Lafayette memorial built to celebrate Franco-American friendship and the decisive role played by the Americans in the victory of 1918!

Ah, so that's where everybody's been today, and here's me thinking nobody cared about celebrating the end of the Great War.

As soon as I arrived in the historic cycling town of Ville d'Avray, I searched for number 147, Rue de Versailles (now an Italian restaurant), which was the address of the Hôtel-Restaurant Pére Auto, the control point deciding the first winner of the 1903 tour. The Tour had to finish here due to a Parisian bylaw forbidding road races to end on cycling tracks such as the Parc des Princes. Consequently, Maurice Garin and the 23 other riders who had completed the Tour, celebrated their achievement by downing their complimentary bottles of champagne and then they continued on a ceremonial ride into the city and the Parc where they were welcomed by a bugler and 20,000 paying spectators.

I continued on my own ceremonial ride, happy in the knowledge that I was following in their esteemed wheel-tracks. Soon the leafy wooded areas surrounding Versailles changed into the sprawling towns of suburban Paris. I passed through the town of Sèvres and immediately the traffic began to increase. The protection from traffic, thus afforded me by the police barricade outside Versailles, was now over. It being early Friday evening, the Parisians were heading home from their air-conditioned offices in some haste to enjoy the evening sun and get ready for a weekend in the predicted heatwave. I soldiered on, heading for the Pont de Sèvres. I managed to cycle across the bridge, following the other cycling commuters, and avoided the many pedestrians heading for the Metro. As I got onto the Avenue du General Leclerc both the traffic and footfall were starting to increase. The pavement cafés and bars spilled out onto the streets as thirsty Parisian workers met friends and colleagues for a swift aperitif or two before heading home with the masses. I must admit it was tempting to join them but I had a control point to report to. I decided that for my safety, and that of the general public, I should push my bike for the last kilometre or so as it seemed that the area was now becoming unusually busy. Cars, small vans and people carriers pulled over and disgorged their passengers onto the streets. I noticed a few of them were wearing football shirts and scarves bearing the name of their favourite French players, Kante, Griezmann etc. As I reached a mishmash of subways disappearing under the busy autoroute of the Périphérique, I thought it was time to check my directions.

"Excusez moi monsieur, could you tell me the best way to get to the Parc des Princes, s'il vous plait?"

"Sure, I'm going there myself. Suivez -moi."

I soon noticed that he was also wearing a red, white and blue FRANCE football scarf. I asked if there was indeed a match on tonight.

Fervent supporters of the French Women's football team – Parc des Princes

"Bien sur," he replied looking at me quizzically, "It's only the quarter-final of the Women's World Cup. Tonight, it's France versus the favourites, the USA! I thought you Engleesh loved football?"

Well I do, we do, and I had been aware that Phil Neville's England team had beaten the Norwegians ladies' team last night 3-0 in Le Havre. In fact, I had driven by the impressive L'Ocean stadium when heading down to Versailles that morning.

And so, I arrived at the Parc de Princes stadium to be greeted by 40,000 or more paying spectators. Although unlike Maurice Garin and his 1903 buddies, I don't think they had come to see me do two celebratory laps of the stadium and festoon myself and my bike with bouquets and garlands of flowers. In fact, nearing the stadium I was swamped by a large group of happy French girls singing 'ALLEZ LES BLEUS'

I wondered what the 1903 riders would have made of this sight. The Stade Velodrome du Parc de Princes had only been built a few years earlier in 1897 to host the nation's favourite sport of cycling. Built on the old hunting grounds of the French royal family (hence the name) the stadium originally hosted 3,200 spectators and a 666-metre cycle track. As football increased in popularity there were a few matches between local Parisian sides played in the Parc, and it also hosted the finals of the inaugural French league. It was actually in the year of 1903 that the first international football match took place in the Parc des Princes. Mind you, the 11-0 defeat of a team of largely Parisian players to an all-England team would hardly have contributed to the popularity of the round ball game.

*

This minor sport wouldn't have entered into the mind of the Parc's director, one Henri Desgrange, as he and his editorial team wound their way across Paris in the still of the night. Henri was more concerned about how many spectators would come out to see the rebirth of his Tour de France, given the minor distraction caused that night by the celebration of world peace. He needn't have worried. There were huge crowds circling the crossroads that led to the Parc. Despite the early hour, and despite the fact that the stadium wasn't open yet, masses of people swarmed along the entrance road, ready to cheer on their heroes. Henri and his team drove past the waving throng, showing off the new official car 'La Braserie Directorale'. The team managers of La Sportive, the commissaires of the Parc and of the Tour de France and of course the inimitable Monsieur André Bazin, the 'Official timekeeper', were already there waiting for the gates to open.

The first rider who arrived to sign the book was the License 'B' rider Maurice Borel, followed wheel to wheel by his compatriot Jean Deyries, both from Clermont-Ferrand in the Auvergne region of

France. They were weighed in, their height taken and race numbers were affixed (punched) under the crossbar of their bikes.

All of a sudden, there was a shout rising from the streets outside the velodrome announcing the arrival of a few of the ACES of the Tour, Edgard Roy of the Charente, Albert Heux and Léon Leclerc from Paris and Alfred Brailly from Chateaurault.

By now it was 2 a.m. and time was ticking on.

Next in the line was Emile Masson (The Unknown), Henri Desgrange's favourite, who arrived along with the youngster Alexis Michiels who, with a broad grin on his face, approached the rope of the control and affixed his seal on the sheet. Then it was the turn of the Heusghem brothers, Louis and Hector. After the weigh-in, it was decreed that Hector had the right to weigh a kilo more than his brother Louis, as he was two centimetres taller. Next, we saw the arrival of another pair of famous brothers, Henri Pélissier (The Greyhound) and Francis (The Young Magician), who both looked as serious as each other and who obviously meant business. More cycling greats arrived. Hector Tiberghien from Waterloo was calm and smiling. Jean Rossius (Eternal Second) was apologetic. Apparently, he had left the rubber number that needed to be punched onto his bike in his suitcase back in the hotel.

Henri Desgrange wasn't always flattering in his descriptions of the 'Kings of the Road' as they arrived at the control; Jean Alavoine (Gars Jean) apparently had great hands; Louis Engel, was fresh and looking well, but Paul Duboc, (Le Pomme -The Apple) and a cycling legend, apparently had a more pointed nose than before, and the Belgian Alphonse Spiesens' proboscis was positively scary. Joseph Vandaele (Facing his Waterloo) looked serious, but so would I at two o'clock in the morning. Alfred Steux (The Kid) was laughing like a little babe. The Belgian Albert Dejonghe was followed by his immense compatriot Urbain Anseeuw, and he was in turn followed sneakily by the tiny French microbe, Napoleon Paoli.

Roll on the libel suits!

It is now 2.45 a.m. and most of the riders had signed in. Some lay down and relaxed in the corner of the control area, whilst others were busier, stretching their limbs in preparation for the great ordeal ahead.

"It's time to go – ALLONS Y"

All the official cars were ready to go and they led the riders out into the dark night, along the Rue de la Tourelle, that runs parallel to the stadium. The state of the roads in Paris was still pretty bad with most of them having been neglected during the war years, and so to avoid any accidents through speeding, it was decided that the race would be neutralised for the first few kilometres up to Argenteuil.

"Now, no more than two minutes", exclaimed the timekeeper André Bazin.

"Now, no more than one minute!"

"No more than thirty seconds."

"Everybody into the SADDLE."

"Only ten seconds."

Then, with a great roar from the crowd, the peloton headed off on the thirteenth Tour de France. They followed the headlights of the leading car into the darkness along the Rue de Tourelle.

"ALLONS-Y!" (Let's GO!)

It was exactly 3 a.m.

67 riders had signed in but apparently there were another two riders still hurrying to the start. They were permitted to join the peloton and a decision regarding their fate would be made in Le Havre.

*

I set off as well. The Rue de la Tourelle was quiet, given the hour, and the fact that the women's football match was about to kick off in an hour's time. The real reason for this was that there was another police blockade, at the far end of the street, across the main entrance to the stadium, where the UEFA dignitaries and official cars were being allowed in. There seemed to be a nice symmetry with my start, and that of the riders in 1919, and maybe the French gendarmes had heard of my epic journey and were putting up road blocks to assist me on my way. I turned right out of the Rue de la Tourelle and onto the busy Route de la Reine. The pavements and bars were now full of spectators chatting about football, and downing a final beer, before heading off to the match. Those not lucky enough to have a ticket were getting into pole position, in front of the TV screens ready to watch. I followed the road up to the Pont de Saint Cloud, turned right and followed the 1919 route along the banks of the Seine. It was somewhere here, that in 1919 disaster suddenly struck the peloton. Only a few kilometres out from the Parc de Princes and there had already been a crash. Surely, The Green-Toothed Witch hadn't struck already?

'Voir la Sorcière aux dentes verts' (Seeing the Green-Toothed Witch) was a phrase used by the peloton to describe any bad luck suffered in a race. It could be a puncture, a chain breaking or worse still, permanent damage to the bike. The witch could strike without warning, leaving the rider at the side of the road, with a sick feeling in his stomach, knowing his race could be over. Why the Witch? Well according to the legend, and cyclists love legends, at the fatal moment, when a cyclist can be at their lowest, deprived of strength, a vision of a witch with green teeth will appear. She towers over the unfortunate rider, giving him the evil eye, and pointing her craggy finger towards the object of his misfortune. The character of the Green-Toothed Witch was immortalised and given a face by the French cartoonist, René Allos, in the comic book adventures of Les Pieds Nickelés, in the 1950s.

So, what had happened? Who had been struck down ?

It turned out that it was none other than the younger of the Pélissier brothers Francis (The Young Magician) whose bike had suffered a breakage. There was always the possibility of this happening to a bike, given the scarcity and quality of materials that were used in their manufacture after the war. Poor old Francis was left, distraught, leaning over his bike, cursing the Green-Toothed

Witch, on the banks of the river Seine. Thankfully no other incidents occurred up to Argenteuil. In Suresnes, there were several hundred spectators lining the route, cheering the peloton on in the darkness.

*

Luckily for me, it was still light and in the bright evening sunshine I made my way along the banks of the river Seine, past boat-houses, restaurants and cafés and surprisingly, I saw my first poster for 'FREXIT'. I hadn't realised there was a French version.

I followed the riders' route to Puteaux, which was home to the famous J.B. Louvet cycle factory, on 8-12, Rue Eugéne Eichenberger. I wondered whether Francis Pélissier would be giving them a call to see if they could fix his bike. Interestingly, both he and his brother Henri raced in the famous red and green of the J.B. Louvet team shortly after the 1919 Tour. Anyway, upon arriving at the Puteaux factory I discovered it was now a row of plain shuttered four-storey houses, the factory having moved around the corner to 23 Rue Parmentier in 1924. Soon I entered the suburb of Neuilly-sur-Seine, sitting alongside the renowned island, Île de La Grande Jatte, whose beauty has been captured in many impressionist paintings by famous artists such as Georges Seurat, Claude Monet, Alfred Sisley and even Vincent Van Gogh.

*

The 1919 riders turned and started to head out from the centre of Paris, north towards Colombes. The crowds cheered them on despite the slow pace. The peloton was headed by René Gerwig, all full of ardour, Louis Engel, Paul Duboc and Constant Menager, all following Mr. Ravaud, driving the official car.

In Colombes, the riders were reminded to pay their respects to the great Luxembourg rider François Faber, who had been killed in the First World War. François was born in France to Luxembourgeois parents and was known in cycling circles as the Giant of Colombes.

Louis Engel shouted out to the official driver in front.

"You slow yourself, Ravaud,"

"Remember ten years ago, our good evenings with François and my poor brother?"

"Oh yes!" replied Ravaud, all saddened, "I remember!"

Louis Engel and his younger brother Emile were also from Colombes and had been great friends with François. Emile was also a prominent cyclist who had even won stage 3 of the Tour de France in 1914. Like François he had signed up in the French army only to be killed immediately in September 1914 in the Battle of the Marne, a matter of weeks after his cycling victory. Ravaud respected the solemn silence as the riders passed by and put his headlights on full-beam to honour the two brave men. It was still dark, as the riders cycled carefully towards the bridge of Argenteuil, the official start of the race.

*

The air was getting cooler and it was time for me to head back to Versailles before nightfall. I got to the campsite bar and restaurant just in time to catch a cold beer and a hot burger and watch the last minutes of the French Women's World Cup match, France 1 – USA 2. Ah well, at least there would be no wild French celebrations until the early hours tonight. It had been a long day for me, since arriving on the overnight ferry from Portsmouth to Le Havre at 6.45 a.m., and I needed to get some sleep!

Chapter 5: Not so quiet on the Western Front

Stage 1 - Sunday 29th June 1919 (Paris – Le Havre)
Saturday 29th June 2019 (Paris – Mesnil-Val-Plage)

BOUCHON A 3 KILOMETRES!

My heart sank. The overhead sign on the Boulevard Périphérique (Paris' outer ring road) told me what I already knew, everyman and his 'chien' (dog) was heading out of the city to escape the intense heatwave, due over the weekend, and by the looks of it we were all headed in the same direction. On top of this, 90 km/hour speed restrictions had been out in place around the city, to reduce the effects of pollution from the combination of exhaust fumes and heat from the sun. Not the best start to a Saturday morning.

My plan was to pick up the 1919 race at Eaubonne (good water) in the north of Paris. This was the next town noted on the route after Argenteuil and, with the neutralisation of the first part of the race in Paris, the start of the Tour proper. Eaubonne was originally a Roman settlement on account of the excellent waters discovered here. The highly sulphated water was good for the kidneys, and with the advent of the railways in the early 1850's, it soon became a popular health destination for Parisians.

*

The 1919 riders wouldn't have been able to see much of this spa-town as 66 of the official 67 starters jostled for position as they left the outskirts of the city. (There were only 66 riders as poor old Francis Pélissier was still trying to repair his broken bike on the banks of the river Seine.) By now, it was approaching 3.45 a.m. and there were still another two hours to go before dawn broke. They rode up the Rue de General Leclerc, following the gas-lit street-lamps, which threw some flickering light on the quaint houses and tiny shops of the village. The peloton was still together at this point, with some of the stronger riders taking the lead, as they headed off over the fairly flat terrain, maintaining a good pace through the villages of Moiselles and Presles and onto their second river crossing at Beaumont-sur-Oise.

*

I arrived in Eaubonne at around 10 a.m., so already over six hours behind the peloton. The once tiny rural town is now completely engulfed by the suburbs of Paris and any signs of its former glory as a health retreat have all but disappeared. The quaint railway station, welcoming would be patients, was now a humming three-line commuter connection. Today, Eaubonne consists of a mixture of the original garden-walled houses, three-storey apartment blocks and shops of a new build design, which shout out functionality, rather than spa elegance. The only connection I could see with the original spa-town, was the line of twenty fountains, spouting out of the elongated oblong-shaped roundabout, in front of the modern SNCF station. Mind you I was tempted to go for a dip, as despite the hour, the temperature was already in the low thirties and rising. Still, I had some catching up to do and I headed out of town following the route. Within three kilometres I was into open countryside, as the route passed through the 'Forêt Domaniale de Montmorency', an ancient sweet chestnut wood and historic royal hunting ground. The forest is now an ideal rural escape for Parisians looking to spend the weekend walking, mountain bike riding or horse riding.

I suddenly thought this must have been quite an eery moment for Henri Desgrange's 'Giants of the Road' heading through the thick damp woodlands in the dark of night, but to be honest, most of his 'valiant riders' would have been used to cycling in these night-time conditions, with only each other for company, and following the lights of the official cars. After all most of them had taken part in pre-war Tours or the recent Paris-Roubaix, Paris–Brussels, Tour of Flanders, Le Circuit des Champs de Bataille etc.

*

As to who was in the lead, it was not clear at this point. All we know is that Géo Lefèvre, L'Auto's roving correspondent, posted his first report from Mouy, 30km on from here. At this point we knew a group of 40 leading riders had broken away from the other riders. Travelling on the route up to the town of Mouy, it soon became clear to me where the breakaway may have taken place. Once the cyclists left the forest near Moiselles, there is a gradual descent down through Presles, into the Val d'Oise (valley of the river Oise) and the town of Beaumont-sur-Oise. The 1919 cyclists would have headed into the town, past the imposing Eglise-Saint-Laurent, with its dominant renaissance bell tower, appearing as an apparition in the lightening grey skies above them. Crossing the old town bridge, they would suddenly have hit a sharp incline taking them up and out of the valley to Neuilly-en-Thelle, a pretty little village at the summit. At 150m above sea level, this would be the highest point of Stage 1 to Le Havre, and a perfect place for a breakaway.

*

It was 5.40 a.m. when the group of 40 riders arrived in Mouy and, as it was now light, Géo Lefèvre could identify each rider that passed in front of the large crowd. The applause for the leader, Louis Engel, was great and Géo noted that the leading group contained Marcel Buysse, Philippe Thys (The Bassett Hound), Albert De Jonghe, Urbain Anseeuw, and Henri Desgrange's personal favourite Emile Masson (The Unknown). Apparently, Robert Jacquinot had an accident when coming into the Oise region, but had managed to fix his bike and carry on. The good news was at 7.30 a.m. the desolate young magician Francis Pélissier arrived only two hours behind. He had fixed his bike and was back in the Tour. The same group was reported passing through the town of Clermont, but this time led by Odile Defraye (The Unwanted) and Henri Pélissier (The Greyhound) who were now making a showing at the front of the pack.

*

I arrived in Clermont and parked in the Place de l'Hôtel de Ville. I had done my research and was interested to have a look around this ancient town. The Hôtel de Ville (Town Hall) was built by none other than the French King Charles IV, who was born in the town in 1294. The town itself is built on a hill and became an important military post in the middle ages. It had passed hands many times during the Hundred Years' War, between the English and French, as they fought for the right to rule the country. The 40 riders in the peloton would not have been thinking about the Hundred Years' War, but rather the four years of war that had ended only six months previously. They were now only a few kilometres from the Western Front and each of the riders had been touched by the war in some way.

The Pélissier brothers had lost their younger brother, Jean, killed in action, in the battle of Champagne in March 1915. Francis Pélissier had been shot twice, but still managed to survive, as he had done again this morning. Jean Alavoine lost his younger brother Henri following an airplane crash near Pau in July 1916. Whilst he survived the crash, he died later from his wounds in hospital. As we know, Louis Engel had lost his younger brother, Emile and his close friend François Faber. It was probably with some sense of dread that they again approached the battlefields of the Great War, although some had already confronted their darkest fears, by taking part in the earlier 1919 Tour of Flanders, the Circuit des Champs de Bataille and Paris–Roubaix, all of which had passed through the killing fields of the Western Front.

Leaving Clermont, I too headed north towards the Western Front. The enfolding scene was one of rural peace, with wide rolling fields of wheat dominating the landscape. I came across the tiny village of Crevecoeur-le-petit, (the little heartbreak), which I thought was quite an appropriate name, given the horrors that had occurred here, one hundred years ago. The 1919 Tour was only 100km from its start-point in the Parc des Princes, and the riders were already preparing themselves for the war torn, bomb shelled roads ahead.

Soon I arrived in the town of Montdidier, which had been the site of some fierce fighting at the end of the war, as the Germans had one last roll of the dice, in their attempt to break through the Allied Forces and capture Paris in 1918. The town was repeatedly bombed, lost to the Germans and recaptured, leading to the obliteration of the town itself. The battle of Montdidier marked the end of the stalemate of trench warfare on the Western Front, with the Allies' effective use of a combination of infantry, air support and tanks. It was the first of several long battles fought between August and November 1918, which later became known as the Hundred Days Offensive. It was a black day for the German Army. It was also a black day for the town of Montdidier, as it was now effectively a pile of bricks and rubble.

And so, a ghost town greeted the peloton of 40 riders as they cycled up the Rue d'Amiens. Not one building had escaped untouched from the bombardment during the intense fighting. Large swathes of bricks and blasted mortar spewed from the windows and doors of once proud town houses and shops. The ruins stood like sentinels pointing towards the grey sky, the skeletal fingers of the remaining chimney breasts and bared inner walls, revealing the secrets of the families that had once lived within. Both the imposing churches of Saint Sépulcre and Saint Pierre had been shelled and razed to the ground. It was still early, around 7 a.m., and there were a few civilians and military servicemen greeting the riders, before continuing their hazardous task of trying to rebuild their lives, businesses and homes. Many civilians were still being killed and wounded from the unexploded shells, bullets and grenades in the area. This crop of unexploded ordnance became known as the 'iron harvest'. In his notes in L'Auto Henri Desgrange was a subtle as a sledgehammer as usual, and called the Rue d'Amiens, the road blown up by the Krauts!

Rue d'Amiens (Brick Lane) Montdidier – circa 1919

I followed the route northwards, following the exact line of the Western Front, that had changed hands so many times between 1914 and 1918, with little or no progress being made by either side. It was difficult to imagine the bloody muddy mess and carnage this small section of road would have seen. The road passed through the tiny rural villages of Pierrepont-sur-Avre and Thennes, with their closed-shuttered-windows, keeping the heat of the midday sun out of the single-storey farm houses. The wide-open expanses of the surrounding fields changed colour, as I drove through this patchwork quilt of green, yellow, blue and red. Fleets of tractors dominated the skyline, as the local farmers brought in their harvest. Was it any coincidence that the red poppies of Flanders started to appear in abundance, on this 18km stretch of road, intermingled with the crops of wheat and barley?

*

For the 1919 riders, this must have been tough going both physically and mentally. The original roads can't have been more than farm tracks, and now after four years of fighting, they were barely passable. There is no mention in L'Auto as to what took place on this section of the route, but what we do know is, that by the time the race reached Amiens, the leading group was reduced in number from 40 to 25. One can only imagine the toll this section of the route took on the less experienced riders, who were coming across these conditions for the first time.

*

It was now 8.44 in the morning, and the leading group of 25 riders had been on the road for nearly six hours, having cycled a total of 150km. Amiens was the first official feeding point of the stage, and by now the riders would have consumed all they had stored in the pockets of their racing jerseys and satchels, and they would have emptied their 'bidons' of whatever liquid they had contained. This would be a welcome chance to replenish their supplies and refuel for the gruelling 238km ahead. Typically, a 'ravitaillement' (feeding station) would provide items such as cooked chicken, pork cutlets, bread, cheese, pieces of chocolate, bananas and fruit tartlets from the region. The riders would be served from large trestle tables by the cycling dignitaries of the region. There may be wine from Burgundy or Bordeaux to drink. It was not unknown for an occasional glass of champagne to be slipped into the bidon of one of the top riders. There would also be milk, water and coffee for those otherwise inclined. It was also an opportunity to make some quick repairs to their bike and maybe change a tyre or pick up some new inner tubes. The race itself was neutralised for five to ten minutes, and the professional cyclists were well drilled in passing through the feeding station, without losing any time to the clock.

The crowds greeting the Kings of the Road in Amiens were enormous. People, young and old, lined the streets, two or three-deep, hanging out of the upstairs windows of houses, shops and restaurants and straining to get a view of their heroes. The smell of coffee and cigar smoke was strong in the air. Géo Lefèvre reported that in the group taking refreshments, he observed Félix Goethals (Sock Seller), Alfred Steux (the Kid), Henri Pélissier (The Greyhound), Emile Masson (The Unknown), Eugéne Christophe (The Old Gaul), Jules Masselis, Honoré Barthélémy (Glass Eye), Alexis Michiels, Jean Alavoine (Gars Jean), René Vandenhove, Jacques Coomans (The Smoker) Louis Engel, Louis Mottiat (The Man of Iron), Lucien Buysse, Firmin Lambot (The Saddler), Albert Dejonghe, Alphonse Spiessens, Hector Heusghem, Philippe Thys (Bassett Hound), Paul Duboc (The Apple), Basil Matthys and Robert Jacquinot. Apparently, the riders were complaining about the many punctures they were suffering on the poor roads, particularly around Montdidier. Now, they were complaining about a lack of nourishment as the feeding station in Amiens struggled to cope with 25 riders all arriving at the same time.

Feeding station -Oloron Sainte Marie (ravitaillement) Tour de France

I followed the 1919 riders into Amiens, through the tiny village of Boves, with its ancient 12th century chateau, laying in ruins. The road ran parallel to the train tracks which took me into the railway town of Longueau, which had lain behind the enemy lines of the Western Front, on a junction between the river Ancre and the river Somme. The large railway sheds which had been built on this junction soon developed into a strategic location for the Allies. It had become a loading station for troops and stores from 1915 onwards, and was also a returning station for the many casualties requiring more treatment than could be offered at the clearing hospitals on the front line. It was here, I came across the footsteps of my grandfather, Emmanuel Tarver, for the first time. He had arrived in France in May 1915, aged 21, and after nine months of fighting on the fields of Flanders, his regiment, the Oxfordshire and Buckinghamshire Light Infantry, had received orders to proceed to a station in Esquelbec near Dunkirk. The battalion thought they were being transferred to Egypt, and were happy to be leaving the bloody fields of Flanders, and saluted the Menin Gate as they passed through Ypres. They got on the train, which passed through Arras, only to pull into Longueau station. They had been transferred to fight on the Somme!

Train station- Longueau – south of Amiens

I stopped in Amiens, and took a short walk up to the magnificent cathedral, the tallest complete cathedral in France. Constant Ménager, the French cyclist, who finished seventh in the 1909 Tour, would have looked upon it with pride. This was his home town and after the Tour in 1919, he lived happily here until his death in 1970 at the ripe old age of 81. The riders would have seen some damage to the Cathedral de Notre Dame, as it received nine direct hits during the Battle of Amiens, but luckily the main structure was intact.

I was interested to discover the other, less righteous aspects of Amiens, and wondered if the 1919 riders knew all of its secrets. Lying as it did, a few kilometres from the Western Front, and being in Allied hands for most of the war, Amiens became a place of relaxation (?) and respite for the soldiers from the death and horror close by. I walked to The Carlton Belfort Hôtel (now simply 'Le Carlton') opposite the station, which had played host to many of the famous war correspondents and artists of the time, such as the poet Siegfried Sassoon and the poet and novelist Robert Graves. Just around the corner from here was the Comedie de Picardie theatre, which in 1919 was the renowned 'Godbert's Restaurant'

'The food was excellent and we all had money to burn' wrote Dennis Wheatley, the subsequent well-known author of many thrillers and occult novels. It was not only the good dining that attracted the officers of the British Army, but also the waitresses such as 'little Marguerite', who made eyes at all the boys, desperate for a kiss after the lousy trenches. The commission that Second Lieutenant Dennis Wheatley received when he was just 17, entitled him to patronise one of the most luxurious brothels in Amiens reserved for officers. Upon arrival, 'the Madame took me to an eight-sided room, the walls and ceilings of which were entirely covered with mirrors. The only furniture in it was a low divan, on which a pretty little blonde was displaying her charms. She welcomed me most pleasantly and later we breakfasted off an omelette, melon and champagne.'

Captain T.P. Cameron Wilson of the Sherwood Foresters captured the atmosphere of the city, at the time, brilliantly in his **Song of Amiens**

Lord! How we laughed in Amiens!
For here were lights and good French drink,
And Marie smiled at everyone,
And Madeleine's new blouse was pink,
And Petite Jeanne (who always runs)
Served us so charmingly, I think
That we forgot the unsleeping guns.

Ah! How we laughed in Amiens!
For there were useless things to buy,

Simply because Irène, who served,
Had happy laughter in her eye;
And Yvonne, bringing sticky buns,
Cared nothing that the eastern sky
Was lit with flashes from the guns.

The subject of sex during the Great War was a difficult one for the authorities to handle. Lord Kitchener himself was against any such activity and issued a pamphlet to every Tommy on the frontline warning them to 'keep constantly on your guard against any excesses. In this new experience you may find temptations both in wine and women. You must entirely resist both.'

Of course, most of the soldiers arriving at the Front ignored this advice. They soon realised that their life expectancy on the Western Front could be as little as six weeks. Most of them were young recruits and the last thing they wanted was to die a virgin. And so, for the price of one franc paid to the madame of the house and another payment of one franc or more to the girl herself, the pride of British youth could experience the pleasures of the flesh for the first time.

However, it was not only the single men of Britain that took advantage of this ancient trade. It was widely believed, during this period, that regular sex was necessary for men's physical health. For married men, the need was considered to be even more imperative. They had become so accustomed to regular sexual fulfilment that the routine needed to be continued, even while away from the marital bed. And so, the many brothels of the major towns, cities and seaports became **'maisons tolérées'** (tolerated houses).

A young French prostitute shows off her sticky buns and a British officer plays the piano in a brothel in Amiens. WW1

While married men were considered to have greater carnal needs than single men, sexual opportunity also varied according to rank. Officers and rankers were serviced in different brothels, known as Blue Lamps and Red Lamps respectively.

'The officers are better off. Comparative luxury, knowledge and armour (condoms) stands them in good stead. It is one thing sleeping the night in Lina's arms, after a not too good dinner and minding one's p's and q's: it is another making the best of it in a thorny ditch.'

Another touchy aspect of 'Sex on the Somme' was the subject of venereal disease or syphilis. It was thought that over 150,000 British soldiers contracted the disease during the war, not always unintentionally. Catching V.D. or another sexual disease was seen as an easy way out of the fighting, and it was not unknown for certain prostitutes, who had contracted the disease, to earn more money than their clean and healthy counterparts. One such establishment was Madame Prudhomme's brothel in Amiens and one hopes the owner was no distant relation to Christian Prudhomme, current Director General of this year's Tour de France.

*

It was hard to imagine Amiens, as a hotbed of sin, on this balmy Saturday morning, as the shoppers went quietly about their business. Still, it was now time for me to leave the pleasures of Amiens behind and continue on the route by bike. I had earmarked the next section of the race 'The Somme Cycle Path' as my route for the day. Like the 1919 riders, I too required some 'ravitaillement', so I headed to the nearest boulangerie and picked up a ham and cheese croissant and a 'Chausson Pomme' (an apple turnover without the cream) Delicious!!

Blooming Heck, it's HOT!!

As I climbed out of my camper-van, the heat of the sun hit me full square on the back of my neck. The temperature must now be in the thirties, and it was still only 11 o'clock in the morning. Before leaving Amiens, I was happy to see the website for the town hall offered me a document called the 'Plan Canicule' – a plan for dealing with the heatwave.

- **Boire regulairement de l'eau (drink water regularly)**
  Yep, two full bottles of water on the bike. (TICK)
- **Mouiller son corps et se ventiler (Wet your body and take fresh air)**
  Well I'd got some wet wipes and I'd had the van windows open whilst driving. (TICK)
- **Maintenir sa maison au frais : fermer les volets le jour (Keep your home cool, close your shutters)**
  Yep, I'd put down all the shutters on the camper-van windows (TICK)
- **Donner et prendre des nouvelles de ses proches (Give and receive advice)**
  I'd said hello to some passing hikers (TICK)
- **Manger en quantite suffisante (Eat in sufficient quantities)**
  Yep, croissant and chausson pomme. (TICK)
- **Ne pas boire d'alcool (Don't drink alcohol)**
  I'd only had one pint of beer last night in Versailles (TICK)
- **Eviter les efforts physique (Avoid physical exercise)**
  Oops !

The original 1919 route between Amiens and Abbeville passed along the D1001, which clings to the top of the Somme valley some distance from the river itself. My research had shown me that the Somme cycle-path ran parallel to this main road, and took me along the tree-lined banks of this famous river, through pretty villages, offering some shade from the blistering heat. So, I chose this route and followed the canal section of the Somme, to the outskirts of Amiens, with the cathedral at my back. I was soon heading through leafy suburbs and passed allotments growing all types of vegetables. I couldn't help but notice most of the plots contained at least one crop of marigolds, growing close to the fruit bearing trees and vegetable patches. A quick search on Google advised me that the strong odour given off by marigolds wards off all sorts of pests, protecting the hard-grown produce, and at the same time attracting the pollenating bees. So, there we go. Gardeners Question Time answered here as well.

Further out from the city, the Somme alternates between straight sections of canal and a winding river bed. I'm not entirely sure why, but can only imagine that this was to make the river navigable to boats, as certain sections of the river expand out into marshland. Soon I was passing lock keeper's cottages with well-kept lawns, sweeping down river banks, where local fisherman sat in the shade, casting their rods hopefully into the water, trying to hook a well sized carp or barbel. As it was the weekend, I soon came across numerous families, out for a day trip on the river, paddling brightly-coloured canoes. Shouts of glee rose up from the river as the younger members of the family took great delight in soaking their weary parents. Mind you, given the extreme midday heat, I'm sure the parents didn't mind.

Lock gate plus missing cyclist near Ailly-sur-Somme, north of Amiens

After a wave and a friendly 'bonjour', it was time for me to witness some more serious weekend water pursuits. On one tributary of the river, a gang of supervised teenagers, in life-jackets, were jumping from the nearby sluice gates into the fast-flowing river. Upon surfacing, they worked their way back to some large waiting dinghies, holding onto a trip wire. Once aboard, they rowed back downstream, in groups of ten, punching the air with glee. It seemed hard for me to imagine the contrast with my own grandfather who, just over one hundred years ago, had himself jumped into the nearby River l'Authie. He had been on a route march back to Amiens, after a raid on some German trenches at

Beaurains, south of Arras. Whilst the raid had been successful, the battalion had made the mistake of stopping for a well sized lunch, whilst returning to camp. In the afternoon, the unbearable heat caused 60 to 70 members of the troop to fall out, as they marched across the flat open terrain of the Somme valley. The river in the village of Mezerolles was just what the men needed to cool off and escape the agony of marching in trench-coats and hobnailed boots, carrying their firearms and heavy back packs.

My journey, along the cycle path on the banks of the Somme, took me past boats of all sizes, from tiny schooners, medium sized house boats, up to the large 'peniches' (barges) which were originally working boats carrying their cargo to and from the large French industrial cities. These boats are twice the size of the traditional British working narrow boats, and as the canal system is much wider than in the UK, they could carry significantly greater loads. These boats could often be seen carrying the owner's family car, a Renault 5 or small Citroen, on the rear deck. I remember when I worked in France, the receptionist Annie, was brought up on one of these boats. When I told her, I used to spend some of my holidays on the canals in the UK, she was astounded. 'Tu es fou, (You're mad) I've worked hard all of my life to get enough money to buy a house and get off living on the water!'

*

I'd reached the end of my cycle journey on this stretch of the Somme and I caught up with the Tour de France 1919 riders in Abbeville. It was still only 10.50 in the morning for them, and they were exactly half way, having cycled 194 of the 388km to Le Havre. They were welcomed by an enormous crowd of around 5,000 spectators, and the town was in summer mode, despite the inclement weather. At each corner of the street, there were masts with banners indicating the route to follow for the competitors of the 'Grande Boucle'.

Louis Heusghem of Belgium arrived first, winning the first prize of 25FF. assigned to the best rider cycling into Abbeville. Behind him followed another Belgian, the giant Hector Tiberghien who won the second prize of 15FF. and in third place (the 'Greyhound') Henri Pélissier, who won the last prize of 10FF. Quite quickly behind these three riders came a group of 16 containing Philippe Thys (the Bassett Hound), Léon Scieur (the Locomotive), René Vandenhove, Jean Rossius (Eternal Second), Jules Masselis, Eugéne

Christophe (the Old Gaul), Emile Masson (the Unknown), Alfons Spiessens, Félix Goethals (Sock Seller), Louis Mottiat (The Man of Iron), Paul Duboc (the Apple), Alfred Stèux (the Kid), Joseph Vandaele (Facing his Waterloo), Jacques Coomans (The Smoker) and the first of the Buysse brothers Lucien.

Spread out, after the first group came:

At +2 minutes, Firmin Lambot; (The Saddler)
At +3 minutes, Jean Alavoine (Gars Jean)
At +5 minutes, Louis Engel;
At +10 minutes Robert Jacquinot;
At +12 minutes, Marcel, the second of the Buysse brothers and Albert DeJonge;
At +20 minutes, Jules Nempon (The Upstart) the first of the licence B riders to arrive, Charles Juseret, René Gerwig and René Chassot;
At +27 minutes, André Huret, Constant Ménager, Joseph Verdickt;
At +50 minutes, Gaston Van Waesberghe and Alfred Brailly;
At +52 minutes, Odile Defraye (The Unwanted) and Alois Verstraeten;
At +58 minutes. Henry Allard;
At +1 hour 5 minutes, Luigi Lucotti (the Italian Job), Maurice Bissière, Paul Zlenck, Edgard Roy and Napoleon Paoli;
At +1 hour 30 minutes, Jose Orduna (the sole Spaniard) and Jean Deyries.

This accounted for 44 of the 67 riders who had set out from the Parc des Princes. Surprisingly there was no news of Honoré Barthélémy (Glass Eye) or of the unfortunate Francis Pélissier (the Young Magician). Still I don't think the roving reporter, Géo Lefèvre, could hang around for the straggling riders, as he needed to get to the next 'control' point and feeding station in Dieppe, and there was no train link to get him there.

The town of Abbeville had been bombed repeatedly during the First World War, and although it was partially destroyed, it was never occupied by the German Army. There were still many familiar ghostly ruins to be seen by the riders as they passed through the last major town of the Western Front. The riders had to make sure they followed the banners, showing them the correct route, as there were still plenty of unexploded bombs (ordnance) to be found in the ground.

Well, there were nowhere near 5,000 spectators to welcome me into Abbeville, but with it being a Saturday, I followed the canal, avoiding the town centre. I could see the imposing 'Collegiate church of Saint Vulfran' in the distance, but having recovered my camper-van, I now headed off and followed the riders towards the coast. Whilst it was midday for the riders, it was now early evening for me and I needed to aim for my first campsite. I followed the riders along the D925 from Abbeville to the small fishing port of Le Treport. The countryside was at its best and the rolling hillsides were covered in fields of poppies, cornflowers and a great variety of other wildflowers. Towards Le Treport, the countryside is hilly and the cultivated slopes are a beautiful sight, with acre upon acre of crops of varying shades of green, and wild flowers adding their splashes of colour. Le Treport nestles at the foot of the surrounding white chalk cliffs. The riders would have seen the recently opened (1908) grand funicular railway cutting through the chalk and taking passengers up to the clifftops. During the Great War, Le Treport was an important location, with five established military hospitals, containing around ten thousand beds, showing the scale of the injuries being incurred just down the road on the Somme. During the latter stages of the war it was also used as a tank training site and there was no doubt our riders would have seen a number of these huge beasts waiting to be decommissioned. A diary of the Australian nurse Sister Elsie Tranter who at the time was working at the No. 3 Australian General Hospital in Abbeville, describes a trip to Le Treport in her extensive diary:

13.5.1919 We have had a beautiful trip today. Nineteen of us went by charabanc to Le Treport. The woods were such a picture, with the dear copper beeches and the blooms on the chestnut trees, and in the undergrowth, millions of bluebells. We spent quite a long time on the beach. Some young girls were hard at work there. They carried big square wicker baskets with a light wooden frame. The baskets they filled with shingle and then placed them onto stands, lifting them from there onto their shoulders. They carried such heavy loads. What the shingle was to be used for we did not find out. On the cliffs there was a tank 'park'— hundreds of tanks and armoured cars there from the battlefields. There are hundreds of flowers about – the lilacs and tulips are at their best just now.

The 1919 riders were welcomed at the control point in Le Treport, by a top-quality French sportsman, Tirmont from Abbeville, a current tenor of the comic opera. They must have felt they themselves were playing a part in a comic opera, as the wind picked up and, with the steep ascents from the coast to the cliff top, many of the riders started to struggle.

*

For myself it was the exact opposite, there was no wind and the glare of the sinking sun started to dazzle me as I drove along the clifftops of the Côte d'Albatre (the alabaster coast). My campsite at Mesnil-Va- Plage was a delight as I parked up on one of the clifftops overlooking the beach. As I ate my hastily cooked 'Spaghetti Bolognese', a stone chat sang from the top of a conifer tree, as the sun slowly sank into the English Channel (La Manche). I took the time to reflect on what had been a glorious day and realised, that at 240km in, I had only completed half of Stage 1. The 1919 riders were now way ahead of me as they continued the 'roller-coaster' clifftop route down to the port of Le Havre. The schedule was set for them to get there in time for Henri Desgrange's 6 p.m. publishing deadline, which would allow enough time for the headlines of the day to be written. I could only sit and wonder in awe at the physical feat they were undertaking.

Still, one day in and only 5,340 more kilometres to go!!

Stage 1 - Monday 30th June 1919 (Rest Day)
Sunday 30th June 2019 (Mesnil-Val-Plage – Le Havre)

Today was a rest day for the brave riders of 1919 Tour. The chance to have a long hot bath and recover after the exertions of the previous day. It was also a chance to study a copy of L'Auto and read up on the race leaders and the overall standings and try and get their brain 'into gear' to think about Stage 2. For myself, it was my chance to catch up with them.

I set off early in the morning from my camping spot and crept slowly off the clifftop at Mesnil-Val-Plage, ensuring I didn't wake any of the nearby campers, whose young children were still fast asleep. My destination was Dieppe, the second feeding station of Stage 1. Dieppe was going to be a feeding station for myself as well, as I stopped at the local Carrefour and stocked up on supplies for the journey ahead.

*

A large crowd welcomed the 1919 riders into the famous seaport of Dieppe, as they sought much-needed nourishment, after their fight against the strong coastal rain and winds. It was 1.48 p.m., and in a sprint finish Jean Rossius pipped Jules Masselis and Henri Pélissier to the line to secure the first prize being offered by the town of Dieppe. All three were greeted with a standing ovation. They were closely followed by a peloton of ten riders including Michiels, Tiberghien, Masson, Vandenhove, Alavoine, Vandaele, Scieur, Spiessens, Steux and Dhers. Eugéne Christophe followed a mere 15 seconds behind them and Louis Heusghem, who had led in Abbeville, was only three minutes further behind at the back of a group containing Lucien, Lambot, Mottiat and Duboc. There was then a wait of 17 minutes until the rest of the contenders arrived in small groups. Juseret, Engel, Dejonghe were in one group, and Matthys, Anseeuw, Nempon, Ménager, Chassot, Huret and Verdickt, in another. It was another three quarters of an hour before a further group of riders arrived containing Lucotti, Defraye, Roy and Verstraeten. Then, a further quarter of an hour after that, when René Gerwig came in on his own. By now over an hour had gone by since the first group of three had arrived in Dieppe and in rolled a weary Van Waesberghe, Zlenck and Orduna, the bad weather having taken its toll on them. I'm happy to announce that 36 minutes later, at 4.22 p.m., a solitary rider appeared on the horizon. It was none other than the young magician Francis Pélissier. He'd managed to repair his bicycle in Paris, and had set off on his own across the battlefields of the Somme and along the storm-ridden Normandy coast, without the comfort of the peloton or anyone around him. I tried to imagine the willpower needed to cycle 259km on your own, when all seemed lost, for thirteen and a half hours.

Other riders were not made of such stern stuff as the bad roads and adverse weather conditions took their toll. Three French riders abandoned at Dieppe; the Parisian Albert Heux having punctured five times, François Chevalier and André Renard (Fox), who wasn't as cunning as a fox, as he'd run out of spare tyres!

*

Unfortunately, I could not get into the town of Dieppe, as the roads were barricaded for, can you believe it, a bike race. It being a Sunday, Dieppe was hosting the annual 'Randonnée des Trois Vallées' and as it happened, they were passing right across my route. I would like to have stayed to watch them pass, but my schedule didn't allow it, so I headed out to the coast and onto the last 129 clifftop kilometres of Stage 1 into Le Havre. A few kilometres out of Dieppe I passed the coastal town of Varengeville-sur-Mer. Here it was the turn of the Belgian Alfons Spiessens to abandon the race. It showed how tough the conditions were as he'd finished 7th, 6th and 10th in the general classification in the three previous pre-war tours and was not one to abandon lightly. I picked up a cheese and ham baguette and another 'chausson pomme' in a tiny boulangerie in Quiberville, to make sure there were no hints of an abandonment on my part.

The atrocious weather conditions all seemed so incongruous to me, as I passed through each pretty Normandy seaside town, with the sun blazing through my van window. I had targeted Veules-les-Roses as my base for the day's cycle and, with it being a Sunday and a perfect summers day, all the locals were parking up and heading for the beach. I managed to find a place to park on a clifftop road and set off into town. Veules-les-Roses lives up to its name. A quaint picture postcard place, reminding me a lot of the Cotswold villages in England. The narrow streets radiate out from the old church square and down to the seafront. The village itself is bisected by the Veules, the smallest river in France at only one kilometre in length. You can amble alongside it following the pretty footpaths and bridges and admire the crystal-clear beds of water-cress. The Veules gushes through old flour mills and past ancient cottages strewn with window boxes full of blossoming deep red geraniums and, of course, roses.

Still, enough of the niceties, it was now time for me to tackle the coastal route myself, and I cycled out of Veules-les-Roses, along the relatively flat D925 to the port of Saint-Valery-en-Caux. It wasn't long before I was slamming my brakes on full as I sped down to the harbour front and crossed the lift bridge to the marina. To my left, were hundreds of tiny pleasure boats and a few working fishing boats. To my right, was the intricately crafted 'Maison Henry IV'. I had to stop and take a photo of this incredible building. Its façade resembled an intricately carved patchwork quilt of wooden noughts and crosses. The detail is outstanding, and the building is alive with sculpted figures, showing the decorative elements of various plants, animals and objects inspired by the journeys made by the local seafarers, between South America and Normandy at that time.

'Noughts and crosses' Maison Henry IV -. Saint-Valery-en-Caux

I didn't have time to linger and soon I was grinding through the gears and climbing up the coastal road out of the town. After bursting a few blood vessels, I found myself alone on a single-track road, heading in a straight line, over the fields to the distant horizon. As I cycled the wind picked up as if to remind me what the 1919 riders went through. I didn't mind though, this was heaven. The surrounding fields were a blaze of colour. There were crops of deep green barley bowing in the wind, followed by sun-scorched wheat, waiting to be harvested. A dark green carpet of leaves hid the crop of purple and white turnip heads trying to force their way out of the ground. Next, I could see hundreds of tiny white butterflies attracted by the vast expanse of tiny blue flowers on a carpet of flax. This was heaven indeed and I couldn't have been happier. As I rode, I heard the song of skylarks hovering in the blue sky above me and the occasional yellow wagtail bobbed and nodded in my direction. I was wondering why this area was so fertile in produce, when a few kilometres further on, between Le Tot and Conteville,

I came across a massive nuclear production plant. Maybe this was the reason for the abundance of crops? A search on Google maps reveals part of the plant in its majesty but a further, more distant section, has been deliberately blurred and obscured from view. Interesting?

It wasn't long before I was zooming down to the seafront again and into the town of Veulettes-sur-Mer. The entrance to the town is down a long sea road, running parallel to the pebbled beach. As I passed groups of families were sat outside their camper-vans starting to prepare Sunday lunch and raising their glasses of aperitifs towards me and shouting 'Bonjour'. As I passed the road sign announcing the town's name I stopped and took a picture of it and my water bottle. This spot would play a big part in determining the outcome of Stage 1, but to find out why you'll have to carry on reading. As I got further into town, the restaurants were filling up and people were relaxing in the sun and reading the menus over a chilled glass of wine. No such luxuries for me but the cheese and ham baguette hit the spot, washed down with a bottle of Evian.

As I rode further, I could imagine the likes of Eugéne Christophe and the peloton toiling along the exact same roads exactly one hundred years ago to the day. I could picture them jostling from side to side in front of me, bobbing along as the peloton does, waiting for the moment to strike. And this was exactly what happened. The Old Gaul Eugéne Christophe, followed by the Belgian Joseph Vandaele attacked and left the field in its wake, as they headed towards the old fishing port of Fecamp. Again, great crowds lined both sides of this seaport, famous for its salted herrings, and the fact that Charles II fled here from England, after his defeat by Cromwell. The duo managed to put four minutes between them and the chasing pack containing Jean Rossius, Henri Pélissier and Léon Scieur. This was no mean feat as they headed into the last 53km of the race, and a possible first stage win in Le Havre. It was another eight minutes before Alfred Steux and Firmin Lambot passed the control. The Belgian pair of Philippe Thys and Jules Masselis had both been the victims of punctures and were already far behind.

*

After Fecamp, the frequency of steep cliffs dropping down into, and back out of the coastal towns was relentless. At Etretat the cliffs were some of the steepest, and a lightning descent from Jean

Rossius seemed as though it might establish a decisive lead for 'The Eternal Second', as everybody could sniff the big prize of the first stage win. However, the lean Greyhound, Henri Pélissier managed to keep on his wheel. The others were not so lucky; Joseph Vandaele momentarily lost them, and Eugéne Christophe, the victim of a crash was dropped and lost five minutes to the leader. Vandaele somehow managed to find the energy to re-join the front two and it seemed, both he, Rossius and Pélissier were going to deliver a decisive blow to the peloton.

Then and now : The Boulevard François 1st, Photo of arrival of the peloton arriving in Le Havre (1920).

L'Auto announced there was a crowd of 30,000 spectators, spread along the tree-lined Boulevard François 1st in Le Havre, eager to see their first Tour de France stage win since Philippe Thys' win in 1913. Apparently, the organising officials had to call in; 100 men from the army and 30 police on horseback to control the crowds.

It was 6.50 p.m., when the official Tour cars arrived, announcing that the Belgian Jean Rossius was actually out in front on his own. He duly arrived some minutes later to the delight of the immense crowd who gave him, and the others following, a massive standing ovation. 'The Tour de France had triumphed in the Havre! It will be the same everywhere' - L'Auto confidently announced.

After 16 hours of agony in the saddle Jean Rossius got off his bike and exclaimed,

"That was hard, but you must admit it was my turn to win a Stage. The others have always won but never me! I'd had enough". He smiled "The role of Eternal Second doesn't apply to me anymore. All the same, I had better luck than the others, all having lots of punctures. Still, that doesn't prevent me from feeling good, and I will try the utmost to keep the few seconds I have gained. What joy if I came to win the Tour! And, after all, why not?"

Mind you Jean Rossius and the others still could not rest. After riding for 388km they now had to push their bike a further one and a half kilometres up through the town and follow the gendarmes to the Grand Hôtel Moderne, on the Boulevard de Strasbourg, where they proceeded to sign the control sheets in the following order.

Stage 1: Paris – Le Havre (388km)

1.	Jean Rossius	(Eternal Second)	in 15h 56m 00s
2.	Henri Pélissier	(The Greyhound)	in 15h 57m 15s
3.	Joseph Vandaele	(Facing Waterloo)	in 15h 53m 10s
4.	Eugéne Christophe	(The Old Gaul)	in 16h 01m 41s
5.	Léon Scieur	(The Locomotive)	in 16h 05m 22s
6.	Alfred Steux	(The Kid)	in 16h 06m 47s
7.	Lucien Buysse		in 16h 22m 27s
8.	Hector Tiberghien		in 16h 23m 53s
9.	Emile Masson	(The Unknown)	at a length
10.	Firmin Lambot	(The Saddler)	in 16h 23m 59s
11.	Jules Masselis		in 16h 49m 40s
12.	Marcel Buysse		at a length
13.	Félix Goethals	(The Sock Seller)	in 17h 05m 32s
14.	Jean Alavoine	(Gars Jean)	at a length
15.	Paul Duboc	(The Apple)	at a length
16.	René Vandenhove		in 17h 08m 53s
17.	Charles Juseret		in 17h 26m 50s
18.	René Chassot	(Cheeky Monkey)	in 17h 40m 40s
19.	Eugéne Dhers		at a length
20.	Jules Nempon	(The Upstart)	at a length
21.	André Huret		17h 40m 40s
22.	Louis Engel		at a length
23.	Honoré Barthélémy	(Glass Eye)	at a length
24.	Alexis Michiels		at a length
25.	Joseph Verdickt		17h 55m 51s
26.	Urbain Anseeuw		18h 33m 42s
27.	Constant Ménager		at a length
28.	Odile Defraye	(The Unwanted)	18h 51m 35s
29.	Robert Jacquinot		at a length
30.	Alois Verstraeten		18h 52m 50s
31.	Louis Mottiat	(The Man of Iron)	19h 02m 00s
32.	Jacques Coomans	(The Smoker)	at a length
33.	Louis Heusghem		at a length
34.	Luigi Lucotti	(The Italian Job)	19h 11m 07s
35.	Albert Dejonghe		19h 19m 00s
36.	Francis Pélissier	(Young Magician)	19h 54m 55s
37.	Paul Zlenck		19h 57m 55s
38.	Edgar Roy		20h 18m 23s
39.	Napoleon Paoli		20h 37m 42s
40.	Lucien Decour		23h 50m 15s
41.	Léon Leclerc	(Lanterne Rouge)	24h 36m 00s

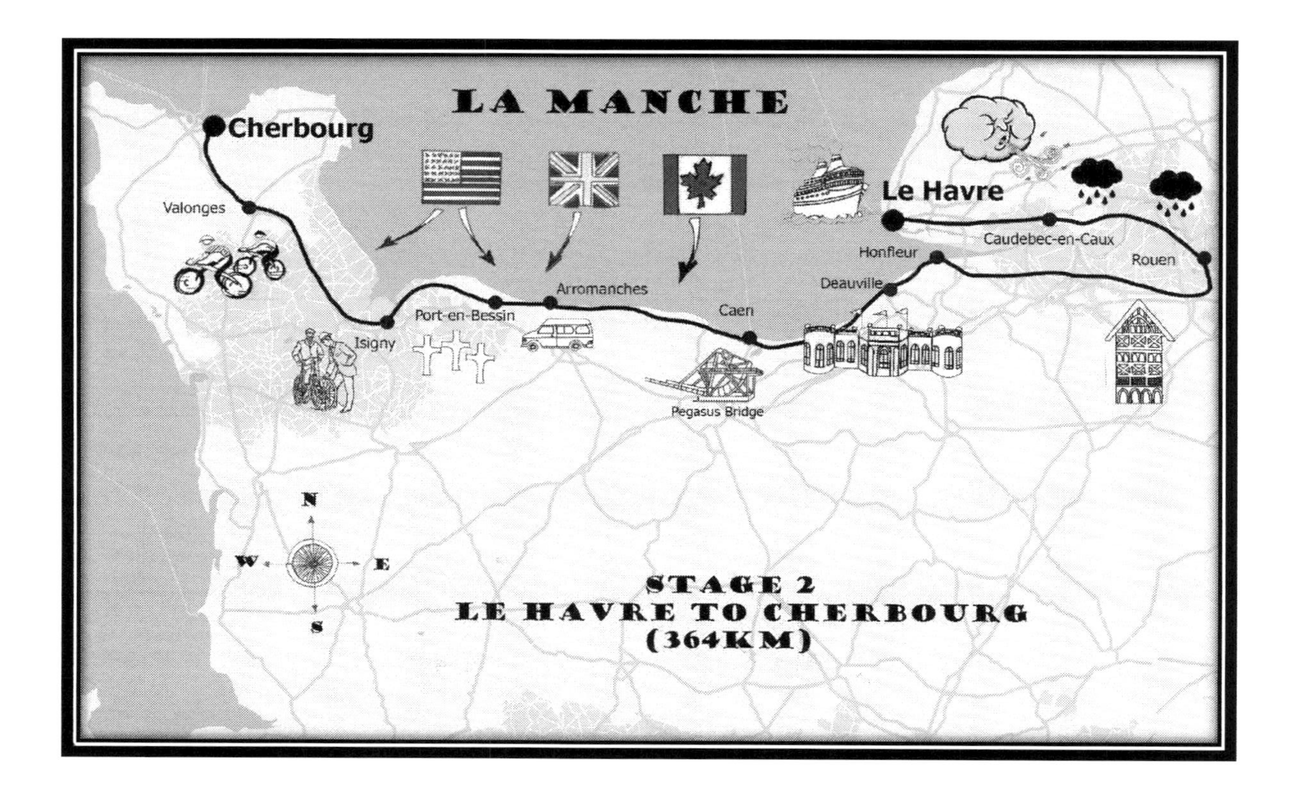
LA MANCHE
Cherbourg
Valonges
Isigny
Port-en-Bessin
Arromanches
Caen
Pegasus Bridge
Deauville
Honfleur
Le Havre
Caudebec-en-Caux
Rouen
N
W
E
S
STAGE 2
LE HAVRE TO CHERBOURG
(364KM)

Chapter 6: Landing on the Normandy beaches

Stage 2 - Tuesday 1st July 1919 (Le Havre - Cherbourg)
Monday 1st July 2019 (Le Havre – Port-en-Bessin)

I stood outside the Grand Hôtel Moderne, on the Boulevard de Strasbourg in Le Havre. The 1919 riders had already departed, having signed in at 2.30 that morning to register for the 364km stage to Cherbourg.

The grandiose hotel of 1919 had all but disappeared and the building had been converted into a plush apartment block. It was Monday morning and soon the local commuters would be arriving at their workplaces in the nearby banks of BNP, Credit Agricole, BRED Banque Populaire and Credit Lyonnais.

Then and now – the Grand Hôtel Moderne – Le Havre.

I gazed at the building in front of me, and tried to imagine the riders spending the night here, and tucking into their plates of 'rosbeef' at dinner. They may well have discussed the previous day's key events over a glass of red wine. The main topic of conversation would have been the bike crash, that Francis Pélissier had suffered in Paris, which took him more than two hours to repair. They would have talked about the multitude of punctures they'd all suffered, travelling over the pot-holed roads of the Somme. They would have whispered to each other 'Did you know Emile Masson (The Unknown), Henri Desgrange's favourite to win the Tour, punctured five times during the stage?' They discussed Odile Drefraye (The Unwanted) and Hector Heusghem's bike accidents and Napoleon Paoli's fall. Certainly, they would have chatted about Charles Juseret suffering a broken pedal, when he tried to avoid an oncoming car. Luckily for Charles, he'd had no major injuries and he'd been able to fix the pedal. They would have been astonished and maybe relieved to hear that the winner of the previous two tours, Phillipe Thys (the Bassett Hound), had to arrive into Le Havre by car. The excellent sprinter had suffered severe stomach cramps, and had to abandon on the advice of the doctor, three kilometres from the finish line. The chat would have been short, and as soon as coffee was served, they all headed for a long soak in a hot bath, had some treatment from their masseurs and retired for a well needed rest.

On the morning of the race, conversations would have raged again. There were only 41 of them left to compete in the second stage. A Tour record number of 26 riders had to abandon after the gruelling first stage. This was of course, of some concern to the organisers, losing forty percent of the competitors after the first stage. Would there be enough to get to Paris? Out of our favourites the following riders were eliminated.

No.	Name	Nationality	Nickname
15	Philippe Thys	Belgium	Bassett Hound
106	Etienne Nain	France	The Dwarf
115	José Orduna	Spain	Sole Spaniard
143	Paul Thondoux	France	Soft Tuna
152	Henri Moreillon	France	The Dean
12	Georges Devilly	France	**
121	Marcel Misserey	France	**

*** The last two riders Georges Devilly and Marcel Misserey had been late for the start and had not signed in at the Parc des Princes. This meant the official number of starters was recorded as 67 not 69. It is assumed that these two riders were eliminated in Le Havre according to Tour rules.*

Mind you, the main topic of the day for the peloton, as they pushed their bikes down the gas-lit Boulevard de Strasbourg, to the official start line at the end of the Boulevard L'Amiral Mouchez, would have been the astonishing fact that yesterday's winner Jean Rossius (Eternal Second) had been given a 30 minute penalty. Originally it had been mooted that the Belgian Jules Masselis was to be punished but this was incorrect. L'Auto defiantly announced.

'During the first stage, the articles 1 and 44 of the rules of the Tour de France 1919, have manifestly been violated by Rossius and Philippe Thys. Rossius has passed a bidon of water to his friend. A minimal fault you may say? A capital fault we say. In fact, it is the core principle, in the heart of our rules, which has been broken here. The first fault and therefore the first sanction and this is relatively light. This example, we are sure, should show all our riders, that any infringement of our rules will be severely punished.'

Poor Rossius, the Eternal Second. He wasn't even that anymore. The 30-minute penalty had pushed him back to eleventh in the field and Henri Pélissier was now declared the winner of Stage 1. The incident had happened in Veulettes-sur-Mer, on the seafront where I had been welcomed by the barbecuing sun-worshippers in their camper-vans and the local diners at the restaurants. Did this cosy seaside town lead the two Belgians to their great mistake? I'd taken a picture of my plastic Tour de France drinks bottle on the town road sign in memory of the harsh treatment that had been handed out to this great young Belgian cyclist.

L'Auto reported that a crowd of more than 2,000 residents of Le Havre had gathered outside the Grand Hôtel Moderne, at midnight, to see off their cycling heroes. It was raining again when at 2.30 a.m. Robert Desmarets, the official starter, gave the call to head out into the night.

*

I couldn't believe my luck, as the sun was shining again on the calm English Channel, and the early morning ferries arriving from Portsmouth, England, docked easily in the port. I had studied my route map in earnest today as I needed to reach the chic seaside resort of Cabourg in time for breakfast with Rob, a good friend of mine, who was arriving on the overnight ferry in Caen and joining me for a couple of days of the 1919 Tour.

*

The river Seine flows from its source south of Paris into the mouth of the English Channel at Le Havre. In 1919 there were none of the splendid bridges (Pont de Normandie, Pont de Tancarville) that carry you across the Seine to the continuation of the Normandy coast. Instead our 40 brave riders, had to head inland and follow the river south for 85km to Rouen before they could cross to the other side and return north for 74km to Honfleur. (Yes, there were only 40 riders left now). Constant Ménager had not arrived for the start of Stage 2. Maybe he had only wanted to cycle through Amiens, his home town. L'Auto reported that when they visited him the previous evening, he was not on Page One! The road to Rouen was quite innocuous, which was good news, as the weather conditions were atrocious for the riders. The rain poured down as they rode through the dark of night, hardly noticing the villages of Harfleur, St. Romain and Lillebonne on the way down to the first control at the riverside town of Caudebec-en-Caux. They arrived here at 4.25 a.m. just as dawn was starting to break. They would not have been able to see the beauty of some of these riverside towns, with their majestic shopfronts, overlooking the tiny river boats moored along the harbour walls. The riders themselves were unrecognisable as they pulled into the control point, covered in mud, and despite their physical efforts some were still shivering and chilled to the bone. It was too much for Alexis Michiels and André Huret who abandoned here sick. No more Tour for them and so the field was reduced to 38.

Paul Duboc (The Apple), who had been fairly quiet in the Tour so far, was keen to make his mark, as the peloton headed down through Duclair, (where Albert Dejonghe was the next to abandon sick – now 37) into his home town of Rouen. The views of the valley of the river Seine were magnificent (like a ribbon in lace) as the riders swept down through Canteleu into the outskirts of the town. Despite the bad weather the crowds were out in force to cheer Paul, their local hero. However, things didn't go to plan as The Apple had a second puncture a few kilometres out and lost touch with the leaders. He was absolutely furious at his misfortune, but still the crowds cheered him as he came in at 6 a.m., nine minutes behind the main peloton of 15 riders, who'd arrived at 5.51 a.m. He was now at the back of a second group in 21st position.

*

As I followed the peloton down to the Quai de Havre, and turned right to cross the river Seine on the iron bridge of the Pont Boieldieu, I took a diversion up to the Gare de Rouen (Rive-Droite), as it was here that I came across the First World War footsteps of my grandfather again. As I mentioned in Stage 1, he'd arrived on the Somme in February 1916 after nine months of fighting in the mud and blood of the fields of Flanders. He'd taken his first footsteps on the Somme, at Longueau train station, to the south of Amiens.

On 15th September 1916, three years previous to the 1919 Tour de France, he had been wounded near to the towns of Flers and Gueudecourt, whilst reconnoitring out in No Man's Land with his Second Lieutenant. This was an extremely historic day for the conflict on the Western Front as it was the first day that the Allied Forces used their new secret weapon in trench warfare: 'The Tank'. The tank got its name because the soldiers believed them to be water tanks as they were transported up to the front line in secret, hidden under tarpaulins. After doing some further research into this historic day, I was astonished to discover that my grandfather's regiment, the Oxfordshire and Buckinghamshire Light Infantry, were actually positioned to the right of tank, D1 'The Dolphin', which was the first tank to set off in combat in World War One. Unfortunately, it wasn't a great success and my grandfather would have witnessed 'The Dolphin' being hit by a shell and exploding into flames, only a couple of kilometres from where it had started out. Nevertheless, the overall deployment of tanks in trench warfare, had startled the Germans and significant territorial gains were made that day. This was the reason why my grandfather was out reconnoitring in No Man's Land, later in the day, as the British Army tried to push on and capture the town of Gueudecourt. I have the letters written by his Second lieutenant, Theodore Rodocanachi, that confirmed my grandfather's wounds to my great grandmother, back in England. He also confirmed that he had seen Emmanuel in the military clearing hospital at 10 p.m. that evening and that by 4.30 a.m. the following day, he had been taken by hospital train to the station in Rouen, and was shipped back to the UK. Just as I felt the history of the 1919 Tour de France vividly as I followed in their cycle tracks, so I felt strong emotions, coming face to face with the heroic deeds of my, by now 23-year-old grandfather. Obviously, he survived these wounds and I believe he had it in mind to propose to my grandmother as he passed wounded through Rouen train station. They were married in the February of 1917 when he was fit enough to walk. Not long afterwards he was sent back to the front and by May 1917, he was deployed in the first battle of Passchendaele. (More of his story in Chapter 14: Nice-Grenoble and Chapter 18 : Metz-Dunkirk)

*

At the control point in Rouen, 85km from the start, the peloton was 11 minutes behind the forecast schedule. After the following 74km, returning back up the Seine to Honfleur, it was suddenly 55 minutes behind. This section had taken an extra three quarters of an hour! What had happened to them en route? There is no official explanation. There was a long slow climb out of the river valley from the Grande Couronne up to the Bourg Achard, but this was nothing compared with what was to come. Maybe they were feeling a 'bit leggy' after the first stage, and the lack of time for proper training after the war, was starting to take its toll. What we do know is that the weather was atrocious and the incessant wind and rain must have been against them as they pulled into the outskirts of Honfleur, covered in mud and completely unrecognisable. It was now 8.51 a.m. and a large crowd lined the cobbled streets in front of the 16th to 18th century houses that surrounded the 'Vieux Bassin' (the old harbour) and welcomed their heroes into the feeding station. The leading group was now starting to take shape and contained some of the favourites, Henri Pélissier (the Greyhound), Eugéne Christophe (the Old Gaul), Odile Defraye (the Unwanted), Urbain Anseeuw, Jean Rossius (Eternal Second), Jean Alavoine (Gars Jean), Firmin Lambot (The Saddler) and Francis Pélissier (the Young Magician). Louis Engel was complaining of a kidney problem and actually wanted to abandon but he was persuaded to soldier on.

*

I pulled into the old harbour in Honfleur on the 'Quai de la Quarantaine' in brilliant sunshine. I stopped to take a photo of the view that had inspired several artists, including the great Claude Monet. Honfleur brought back many happy memories for me, including the time I'd stopped here for the night, with my wife, heavily pregnant, on the way to a wedding near Paris. The only hotel room we could find was in the garret of an old timber-framed house, exactly opposite the belfry of the 15th century St. Catherine's church, which proceeded to chime regularly throughout the night.

I took my photo and I was reversing off the Quai side when a middle-aged man approached, signalling me to wind down my van window. He smiled a toothless grin and I thought 'Here we go'. Anyway, all he wanted to know was whether I needed directions. I didn't really, and in fact, I was in a rush to get to my breakfast meeting in Cabourg. Still, it was an opportunity to practice some French and so I listened to him intently as he told me the best route out of town and along the coast.

*

Funnily enough, L'Auto also insisted on giving the riders some advice on this stretch of the road and gave the following warning,

'Attention! the route along the coast from Honfleur to Isigny is narrow and windy. We recommend the greatest of prudence to the riders and to the people who follow on this route on the first of July. There are sharp turnings and hidden roads and you can suddenly find yourself in front of the oncoming traffic with no warning. You must therefore follow scrupulously the rules of the police and keep strictly to the right.'

*

I too, was going to follow the advice I was given, after all I was still on Stage 2 and didn't want any early accidents.

*

The 1919 journey continued to Deauville and passed largely without incident, apart from the Frenchman Lucien Decour, who abandoned here because of a problem with his tyres. This seemed a bit of a feeble excuse, and it may have been that the Parisian was tempted to see the new 2,000-seater stadium that had just been rebuilt, on the initiative of the wonderfully named Société d'Encouragement, at the famous Deauville race-course. There again, he may have fancied a trip to the seaside casino, where it is believed Ian Fleming played the tables and got his inspiration for the James Bond novel 'Casino Royale'. Whatever, the field was now down to 37.

*

I pulled into the casino on the seafront in Cabourg and telephoned my friend Rob, who'd arrived in Caen on the early ferry from Portsmouth. As I knew it would take some time for me to arrive from Le Havre, I told him to cycle out along the coast, and I'd meet him for breakfast. He said he was only ten minutes away and he had a story to tell me!

Apparently, the previous evening he'd parked at Portsmouth docks and fettled his bike ready for the Channel crossing. Not being an experienced cyclist, he'd boarded the ferry first and proceeded to cycle down the ramp and onto the ship. Within 150m his front wheel got lodged in the gap between the ramp and the boat. Subsequently, he went arse over tit, flew over his handle bars, and ended up spread eagled on the floor much to the amusement of the 50 or so cyclists who were following him, and had read the 'Cyclists must dismount before boarding vessel' sign. Bruised and with his pride battered, he'd arrived at the ferry terminus. He had a choice of two routes from Caen to Cabourg, the busy main road or a quieter gravel track which hugged the coastline. Rob chose the latter and within another couple of hundred metres he had his first puncture, and a couple of kilometres further on he punctured again. Next, a stocky well-built man in a hoody started to walk towards him. Rob could see a knife being pulled and his photo appearing in the following day's Caen Gazette, under the headline 'English Tourist found washed up on the beach in front of Cabourg casino'. I tried to hide my laughter as I choked on my croissant-a beurre. I was now into my fourth day of travelling 1,000km, without incident, and here was Rob only an hour and a couple of kilometres in, and already he might have to abandon!

We headed back on to the 1919 route through Caen, crossed the Pegasus Bridge, and arrived in a coastal area that had been completely decimated during the D-Day landings on the 6th June 1944. En route, we were continually reminded of the 75th anniversary celebrations that had taken place a month ago. In the town of Arromanches, the car park was festooned with the flags and bunting of the Allied forces. Out to sea, across Gold Beach, we could see the concrete remnants of the portable Mulberry harbour, that was tugged over from Southern England on D-Day, to become a temporary port for a staggering two and a half million men, half a million vehicles and four million tonnes of supplies.

*

There was a similar celebration at Arromanches in 1919 for the leading six Tour de France riders. Francis Pélissier, Henri Pélissier,

Jean Rossius, Louis Heusghem, Firmin Lambot and Eugéne Christophe who arrived at the feeding station in front of the town hall at 1.27 p.m., and were welcomed by a group of buglers. It was indeed a time to celebrate, as the food had been organised by one of the correspondents of L'Auto, a Monsieur Boquet, whose family owned the café next door to the town hall, and to keep everything in the family his mother, Madame Boquet, had prepared all the home cooked food, throughout the night before.

The leading group of six had escaped from a second bunch of three riders, who arrived three minutes later, and included Emile Masson, Honoré Barthélémy and Jacques Coomans. Everybody was complaining about the poor inner tubes and the number of punctures they were getting. The two Buysse brothers had suffered badly, with Marcel puncturing five times and Lucien three. Léon Scieur had crashed badly on the coastal road, just before arriving into Arromanches, and was busy patching up his bike. All three of them wanted to abandon, but after feeding copiously, on Madame Boquet's delicious spread, they were persuaded to continue. However, the Belgian Joseph Verdickt had been seen pushing his bike along the tramway into the town of Ver-sur-Mer, just before Arromanches, and it was here he had to abandon. (36 riders left)

*

The plan for myself and Rob was to cycle along Juno Beach to Omaha Beach and visit the American war cemetery at Colleville-sur-Mer. Along the route there were further reminders of the recent 75th anniversary celebrations. There were roadside flower beds, grown to represent the stars and stripes of the national flag of the United States of America. Barns and farm outbuildings were adorned with red, white and blue bunting and large black and white photos of the D-Day landings hung from their sides. Signposts had been specially constructed, displaying photos and stories of ordinary American soldiers, who had sacrificed their youth for the protection of mankind.

A visit to the American war cemetery is a time to reflect on the incredible sacrifice of humanity, as you look out at 9,387 white crosses all laid out in symmetrical lines. Each cross represents the lost life of a soldier who had fallen in the D-Day landings. On the 'Walls of the Missing', constructed in a semi-circular garden on the east side of the memorial, are inscribed another 1,557 names. Rosettes mark the names of those since recovered and identified. I looked out from the cemetery, through the overhanging trees onto the deserted Omaha Beach. It looked peaceful and tranquil in the glow of a summer's day and I couldn't begin to imagine the horrors it had witnessed on that day in 1945. Rob and I had a solemn and reflective return to our campsite, in the picturesque Port-en-Bessin. Here we retired for a meal of moules-frites washed down with a refreshing bottle of Muscadet-sur-Lie plus a glass of the local Calvados (Apple Brandy).

'Tanks for the memories' D-Day 1945, Coleville-sur-Mer

Stage 2 - Wednesday 2nd July 1919 (Rest Day)
Tuesday 2nd July 2019 (Port-en-Bessin - Cherbourg)

It was another glorious summers' morning, as Rob and I headed off in the camper-van, along the coastal road which led through Grandcamp Maisy into Isigny-sur-Mer.

*

This was where the unfortunate Léon Scieur had punctured again. He had now used up his supply of four inner tubes. On the way he had already used his original two but luckily, he'd managed to purchase two more. Now, he'd run out of money and was obliged to stop and make repairs. In those days, this involved undoing the stitching around the tyre, replacing the punctured inner tube, and resewing the tyre back up again. To escape the pouring rain, Léon sat huddled in a doorway, trying to escape the driving rain. His fingers were so cold he could barely stitch up his tyres. A woman took pity on him and offered to help, but Léon knew the rules, and mindful of the penalty that Jean Rossius had incurred on the previous stage, he politely declined her offer.

The route itself now turned inland, and headed directly through the Côtentin Peninsula, to the seaport of Cherbourg. Our brave riders had to cross this peninsular, cycling into violent headwinds and incessant rain, and at the rural village of Carentan, the contenders for the stage win became clear. It was 6 p.m. and the leading group of eight now consisted of Honoré Barthélémy, René Vandenhove, Emile Masson, Jean Rossius, Firmin Lambot, Francis Pélissier, Eugéne Christophe and Henri Pélissier.

25km from the finish at Valonges, the Pélissier brothers decided to race for the line, despite the violent headwind. Could this not be seen as some form of collusion between the two brothers? They were still neck and neck when on the outskirts of Cherbourg, an L'Auto official appeared with a red flag signalling there was one kilometre to go. In the previous day's newspaper, it had been announced. 'The competitors are alerted to the fact that at the approach to each stage finish there will be a signal, from one of our men carrying a red flag, indicating that we are exactly one kilometre from the finish line' This was the precursor to the now ornate 'Flamme Rouge' which consists of an inflatable red arch carrying a sponsor's name emblazoned on each support, aimed at the vast TV audience that the Tour can command these days.

The arrival in Cherbourg was scheduled to take place on the climb from Octeville, near the Pont Martinvast, in the place known as ' The White Stream'. And so, the two brothers fought it out for the stage win, vying neck and neck to the finish line, where Henri beat his younger brother Francis by three-wheel lengths. Under the thick layer of mud that covered him, Henri Pélissier appeared radiant though extremely tired.

"It's really too hard," he said to us. "the rain you saw was terrible! Hey, I haven't stopped shivering since this morning! Really, I need a good hot bath to give me back my feelings. However, would you like me to tell you what has given me the greatest pleasure today? Well! It is the great finish made by my brother! And even I would have let him win, if the rules were not the rules and Papa Desgrange, not the least amenable of course directors! On this, goodnight I'm going to relax."

The Pélissier brothers had arrived in Cherbourg at 6.21 p.m., nearly three hours after the scheduled finish time of 3.25 p.m. This didn't allow the L'Auto writers that much time to get their copy in for the following day's edition covering Stage 2. The riders, who had managed to survive the stage, headed down to the Café de Paris, on the Quai de Caligny to sign in. Here, an orchestra played live music all evening in celebration of the day's events. The last to arrive was Joseph Vandaele who had broken his chain three kilometres out and had to push his bike through the crowds to the finish line. Bravo to him.

*

The Café de Paris on the Quai Caligny still exists as a working restaurant, and Rob and I were tempted to eat here but unfortunately, we still had some travelling and cycling to do. I did go up and peer inside through the front door and wondered if the diners realised that exactly one hundred years ago, on this day, a group of 27 (yes, that's all that had registered in the Café de Paris) extremely dirty and hungry riders had entered the café to a tremendous ovation from the large crowd, waiting outside, after cycling for 16 hours through violent wind and rain.

Then and now : Café de Paris – Quai de Caligny - Cherbourg

Stage 2: Le Havre – Cherbourg (348km)

1. Henri Pélissier	in 15h 51m 13s
2. Francis Pélissier	in 15h 51m 14s
3. Honoré Barthélémy	in 15h 55m
4. Jean Alavoine	in 15h 55m
5. Jean Rossius	in 15h 55m 53s
6. Emile Masson	in 16h 00m 07s
7. Eugéne Christophe	in 16h 06m 38s
8. Firmin Lambot	in 16h 08m 50s
9. Félix Goethals	in 16h 47m 16s
10. Urbain Anseeuw	at a length
11. Jacques Coomans	at a length

General Classement (G.C.)

1. Henri Pélissier (The Greyhound)	31h 48m 28s
2. Eugéne Christophe (The Old Gaul)	32h 08m 19s
3. Jean Rossius (Eternal Second)	32h 21m 53s
4. Emile Masson (The Unknown)	32h 24m10s
5. Firmin Lambot (The Saddler)	32h 32m 49s
6. Jean Alavoine (Gars Jean)	33h 00m 32s
7. Alfred Steux (The Kid)	33h 13m 55s
8. Félix Goethals (The Sock Seller)	33h 22m 48s
9. Joseph Vandaele (Facing his Waterloo)	33h 28m 41s
10. Honoré Barthélémy (Glass Eye)	33h 35m 40s
11. Jules Masselis	34h 14m 38s
12. Léon Scieur (The Locomotive)	34h 27m 06s
13. Urbain Anseeuw	34h 50m 58s
14. Odile Defraye (The Unwanted)	35h 01m 51s
15. Jacques Coomans (The Smoker)	35h 19m 16s
16. Jules Nempon (The Upstart)	35h 22m 59s
17. Odile Defraye (The Unwanted)	36h 01m 51s
18. Charles Juseret	36h 18m 33s
19. Paul Duboc (The Apple)	36h 21m 44s
20. Louis Mottiat (The Man of Iron)	36h 23m 34s
21. Luigi Lucotti (The Italian Job)	37h 18m 42s
22. René Chassot (Cheeky Monkey)	37h 26m 52s
23. Louis Engel	37h 53m 25s
24. Louis Heusghem	37h 53m 43s
25. Paul Zlenck	39h 44m 07s
26. Alois Verstraeten	40h 13m 35s
27. Léon Lecelrc (Lanterne Rouge)	**49h 35m 00s**

STAGE 3
CHERBOURG TO BREST
(405KM)
LA MANCHE
Cherbourg
'bocage'
Coutances
Granville
Pontorson
Dinan
St. Brieuc
Guingamp
Morlaix
Roscoff
Brest
Pontanezen
US Army camp
N
E
S
W

Chapter 7 – You're all carthorses!

Stage 3 - Thursday 3rd July 1919 (Cherbourg - Brest)
Wednesday 3rd July 2019 (Cherbourg - Granville)

After falling behind the forecast schedule on Stage 2, and with continuing bad weather forecast on the northern coast of France, Henri Desgrange took the decision to bring the start of the next stage forward by half an hour. So instead of starting out at the unearthly hour of 2.30 a.m., this was brought forward to 2 a.m., and therefore an extra 30 minutes of cycling in the dark and gloom for the 27 lucky (?) riders that were left. Henri was not too impressed that after just two stages, he had now lost sixty percent of the riders that had started in Paris. In today's edition of L'Auto he was quite dismissive of the 14 riders that had abandoned on Stage 2, and announced that amongst the **dead** were:

Alexis Michiels (who abandoned sick early on at Caudebec-en-Caux) said: "I was cold, but cold inside, not knowing if I could get back in the race! Rather than doing less well than I did in the Paris to Brussels race, I prefer to abandon." Henri thought that Alexis was still too young to really compete in his Tour.

Of Albert Dejonghe, Henri stated that he had such great hopes of the Belgian rider. "It seemed to us that he had the makings of a Petit-Breton (the winner of the Tour de France in 1907 and 1908). We doubt it today. In any case, he does not have the heart of our late Lucien." Albert had abandoned early in the day at Duclair, before even reaching Rouen.

Hector Tiberghien had also abandoned. "Does the winner of Paris-Tours have only one race in his belly? Was he the victim of an accident? I don't know but his compatriots will be saddened by his departure."

The two Buysse brothers had also given up, Lucien and even the bulldog Marcel. René Vandenhove, Eugéne Dhers, André Huret (who abandoned sick with Michiels at Caudebec-en-Caux), Joseph Verdict and Robert Jacquinot were also among the victims.

"It's a shame, but the first two, had just taken part in the Tour of Italy (which had finished only three weeks previously), and like the common man they could not repeat their effort. On the other hand, Vandenhove lacks chest, whereas Dhers, Huret, Verdickt and Jacquinot, have just been released from their regiments, and with the lack of preparation and training their abandoning was understandable!"

Four further French riders didn't deserve a mention, Constant Ménager (who didn't start Stage 2 as he wasn't on page one), Edgar Roy, Lucien Decour (who we know had abandoned at Deauville) and our poor Napoleon Paoli, who seemed to have disappeared completely.

With only 27 riders left Henri must have been getting quite concerned. Particularly as a lot of riders were abandoning due to punctures and problems with their tyres. Not being one to rest on his laurels, Henri announced immediately that the official cars following the race would carry a selection of spare tyres and inner tubes, that could be used by the riders facing severe difficulties. What kindness indeed!

And so, the magnificent 'twenty-seven' signed in at the Café de Paris in Cherbourg at one a.m. in readiness for the official departure on the Avenue Carnot, a short distance across the harbour, on the Canal de Retenue. As they wheeled their bikes across the swing bridge to the start line it was raining again. Would this weather never cease!

*

The area to the north-west of the Port of Cherbourg, called the Cap de la Hague, is an area of outstanding natural beauty and is an absolute treat for any cyclist. Quiet country lanes take you through the picturesque flower-strewn, sandstone hamlets that hug this dramatic coastline. Small fishing ports with tiny seafood restaurants tempt you on each section of your route. At every corner there is a photo opportunity, and it is tempting to wile-away a few hours, relaxing on deserted sandy beaches, or walking across the ancient stone-walled fields, through megalithic stone circles, to sit and wonder at the dramatic towering ancient lighthouses, built to protect this rocky coast.

The beautiful coastline around the Cap de la Hague and a French prisoner escapes from 'the Tower' at St. Germain des Vaux.

All of this Rob and I did, as we cycled a circular route of the cape, whilst the 1919 riders took their rest day and recuperated in Cherbourg. This was Rob's last day, as reluctantly he was heading back to the port, to catch the fast ferry back to Portsmouth.

I headed south and re-joined the peloton, south of Cherbourg. The 1919 route now took me through a region that had been heavily occupied by the Germans in the Second World War. The intense fighting, that had followed the D-Day landings in June 1944, led to the destruction of many towns and villages on the Contentin Peninsular, as the Americans liberated each town, one by one, and pushed the Germans further inland. The area is agricultural and was known as ***'bocage'*** country, because of the vast amounts of hedgerows and sunken lanes crisscrossing the terrain. These hedgerows made combat difficult, as they could conceal the enemy at every corner. Many of the buildings, that the 1919 riders would have seen on their way down through this peninsula, were later destroyed during Operation Overlord, and their place taken by modern twentieth century equivalents.

However, there were still many key historic buildings on view. The ruins of the Chateaux at Briquebec, Saint-Sauveur-le-Vicomte and La Haye-du-Puits, and the reconstructed abbey of the Holy Trinity at Lessay which had been completely destroyed in 1944. I pulled into the car park in front of the abbey, to pay my respects, not to the Benedictine monks, but to the young Belgian, Jean Rossius (Eternal Second), whose bike broke down here.

*

Jean managed to push his bike 20km to the next major town at Coutances, but soon realised that it was irreparable and that this was the end of his Tour de France. The inconsolable Rossius sat down on the kerb and wept. Without the harsh 30-minute penalty for the water bottle incident he was still the fifth best rider in the Tour, and, with 13 stages still to go, that could easily have been recovered.

*

As you approach Coutances, the magnificent Cathedral Notre-Dame, towers above the surrounding buildings and at 80m high it can apparently be seen from as far away as the island of Jersey. The fact that it was still standing is, in itself, a miracle as the town was heavily bombed in the intense fighting of Operation Cobra, which followed on from Operation Overlord and the D-Day landings in July 1944, and most of the buildings around the cathedral were razed to the ground. The town of Coutances was a key strategic target for the Allied forces, as its capture meant that they had escaped from the difficult terrain of the 'bocage' landscape and secured the peninsular.

The cathedral of Coutances in 1945 and as it is today.

I pulled in to try and take a photo of this imposing Roman Catholic cathedral. You can tell the magnitude of any building when you have to disappear down a nearby side street to get the whole structure into the frame.

I came across a fromagerie and purchased some of the local soft cream cheese. Looking a bit like a Brie, Le Coutances du Contentin is an intensely rich double-cream cow's milk cheese and tastes delicious squashed inside a crusty freshly-made baguette.

*

The leading group of 24 riders, pulled into Coutances at 5 a.m. precisely, in advance of the time predicted by L'Auto. They had battled through the night, down tiny narrow lanes, where the atrocious weather had turned the roads into a quagmire. At the head of the peloton was Jean Alavoine (Gars Jean), the Pélissier brothers (Henri-The Greyhound and Francis-The Young Magician) and Emile Masson (The Unknown). They were immediately followed by Honoré Barthélémy (Glass Eye), Urbain Anseeuw, Firmin Lambot (The Saddler), Eugéne Christophe (The Old Gaul), Jacques Coomans (The Smoker), Jules Nempon (The Young Upstart), Odile Defraye (The Unwanted), Louis Engel and Paul Duboc (The Apple). Half an hour later, the poor Jean Rossius pushed his bike into the control at 5.32 a.m. and as we know, abandoned. He arrived with Léon Leclerc, who had been the lanterne rouge at the end of the second stage (some 18 hours behind the leader). Finally, Paul Zlenck passed at 5.38 a.m. He was tired and soon joined Rossius and abandoned. The Lanterne Rouge (red lantern) was the name given to the rider who was sitting in the last position of the General Classification. The name came from the red-light on the back of French passenger or freight trains. It was not seen as a derogatory term, but rather the rider was treated with some respect, as the 'lanterne rouge' on the last day of the race, had actually completed all the stages of the Tour and got to Paris.

*

I now turned towards the coast and headed for Granville, my chosen spot for today's cycle. This area is famous for its apple production, and all along the route there were roadside signs for Pommeau (apple juice and apple brandy mixture), Cidre and Calavados (apple brandy). The funny thing was I didn't see a single apple orchard, or even a sole apple tree, all the way to the coast. As I neared, I got stuck behind numerous tractors pulling low-hung trailers, with young lads dressed in fishing overalls, either standing or sitting on the back. Granville Bay is famous for its seafood, in particular it's scallops (coquilles-Saint-Jacques) and whelks, but also, it's magnificent blue lobster. I had chosen Granville as my starting point for the day's cycle, because of my vivid memories of the 2016 Tour de France, and the stunning aerial shots of the fortified coastal town, as the peloton swept through here on Stage 1. They'd started on the magical island of Le Mont-Saint-Michel, almost following the 1919 route in reverse, but instead of heading up to Cherbourg, they veered off to the finish line, on Utah Beach. This was to be Mark Cavendish's twenty-seventh career stage victory and the Manxman's first ever chance to pull on the yellow jersey. He couldn't have been happier. He couldn't prevent a cheeky grin from bursting across his face as he blurted out,

"It's phenomenal, it really is phenomenal. We really wanted this. To win a stage is always incredible but to wear the yellow jersey is an honour I've never had before. I'm really emotional."

I booked into my campsite at Donville-les-Bains, to the north of Granville and cycled out on the coastal road that leads down to the town. I tried to imagine the leading group of riders, still headed by Gars Jean, flying down the steep road, in the driving rain, into the town. The first building they would have come across would have been the elegant 'Casino de Granville' which stretched out along the cliffs overlooking the bay. For me, it looked resplendent in the mid-afternoon sun. Mind you I was now feeling the wrath of the strong winds that can hit this coast, as the wind whistled through the narrow alleyways as it blew unhindered from the west across Mont Saint Michel bay. Granville was the home of the famous fashion designer Christian Dior, who grew up in these parts, and used to design and make the costumes for the annual regatta. The family house is now a museum and the Belle Époque style villa stands proudly on a clifftop overlooking the sea. As I passed through the town there was still evidence of the recent 75th anniversary D-Day celebrations and one town house window was wonderfully decorated in tribute to the American soldiers, who had liberated France. Old photos and newspaper cuttings were interspersed with a recreation of the war, complete with tiny model soldiers, in tanks and jeeps, following tiny road signs pointing to Cherbourg and Caen.

I stopped to wander through some of the narrow-cobbled alleyways that connected the old part of the town. I turned a corner and stumbled across the bar 'La Rafale' in the Place Cambernon where a group of middle-aged ladies seemed to be having a great time. Their chatter echoed around the square as they consumed their glasses of Stella Artois, whilst clicking away with their knitting needles. The quicker they drank, the quicker they knitted, Purl, Plain , Stella, Purl, Plain, Stella. Knit One, Drink One.

The Captain's Cabin - Shop frontage – Granville

Leaving Granville on the more exposed coastal road, heading south to Saint Pair-sur-Mer, I was almost blown off my bike. It was one of those winds, into which you need to turn your front wheel constantly, to maintain a forward direction. The 1919 riders had been struggling with these fierce cross winds on top of driving rain all day. So, in the mid-afternoon sun under a clear blue sky, I had no room for complaints. There were quite a few hardy souls braving the conditions and sunning themselves behind wind shelters on the Plage de la Piscine. Out in the bay, there were hundreds of windsurfers flying across the choppy waters, like shooting stars crossing a watery galaxy. After Jullouville-les-Pins, I turned inland to Sartilly and the surrounding pine trees gave me some respite from the wind, and also offered me a stunning view of Le Mont-Saint-Michel, rising majestically from the water like a scene from the Arthurian legend of the mythical island of Avalon. The existence of Mont-Saint-Michel in Normandy, and its mirror image

Saint Michaels Mount, off the shore of Penzance in Cornwall has always fascinated me. It is as if the two coasts were once connected in ancient times and the two islands somehow floated off in different directions. The French claimed they built their island commune first and that the English version was modelled on theirs at the time of William the Conqueror, around 1066 AD. Both were a place of pilgrimage for Benedictine monks and it was I who also made a pilgrimage there in 2013 to witness the 100th edition of the Tour de France.

I'd chosen to watch Stages 10, Saint-Gildas-des-Bois to Saint-Malo, and the Stage 11-time trial, Avranches to Le Mont-Saint-Michel. The race was set up well for the British riders, and thousands of cycling fans, had made the short hop across the Channel to see if their heroes Mark Cavendish and Chris Froome could continue the British impact on the Tour following Bradley Wiggins historic first win in 2012. There had been two British stage wins so far, Stage 5 for Mark Cavendish in Marseille and Stage 8 for Chris Froome in Ax 3 Domaines, where he donned the yellow jersey for the first time in the race and was wearing it into Brittany. Stage 10 and 11 were to become difficult stages for Mark Cavendish, who was accused of deliberately causing an accident, as the bunch sprint raced across the cobbles, into the fortified town of Saint-Malo. It looked on camera, as though Cavendish veered into the Dutchman Tom Veelers, causing him to fall. The Amaury Sports Organisation (A.S.O.) reviewed the incident and took no action, but for some spectators this was not enough. The following day I cycled out to Le Mont-Saint-Michel to witness the time trial coming in from Avranches. A time trial is a better overall spectacle for the roadside spectator, as the crowd get to see each individual pass through, as opposed to the blur of the peloton. It was a close stage, won narrowly by the German Tony Martin followed by Chris Froome, who extended his lead over his yellow jersey rivals. Froome would now wear the yellow jersey all the way into Paris. However, Stage 11 itself was overshadowed by an incident where a spectator threw a bottle of urine over Cavendish, and the Manx-man was whistled and catcalled all along the route. The act was roundly condemned by Froome and the stage winner, Tony Martin. "It was really disappointing," Froome said. "One of the best things about our sport is that the spectators can get close to the top riders in the world and feel the excitement and the colour. It's disappointing that one individual should ruin it for Mark. He's one of the great personalities of the sport – some people love him, some hate him – but to do something disrespectful like that is sad. It leaves a bad taste in the mouth."

Yes, Spot on, Chris.

Stage 3: Friday 4th July 1919 (Rest Day)
Thursday 4th July 2019 (Granville to Brest)

There was a bunch of 24 riders in the 1919 peloton as it reached the feeding station in Pontorson, south of Granville. It was 8 a.m. and, given the cold and rain, the crowds were a lot less than had been seen previously in 1914. Still, this was rectified when the race reached the halfway stage in the beautiful hill top town of Dinan. The riders crossed into the town by way of the magnificent Lanvalley-Dinan viaduct, it's ten arches spanning the River Rance and headed into the Place Duclos.

*

Dinan, really is worth a visit if you get the opportunity. It is only a short ride inland from the ferry port of Saint Malo, and easily accessible from the UK. In fact, if you travel over as a foot passenger with your bike, you can catch a ferry across to the chic seaside resort of Dinard, and from there take a beautiful cycle ride down the River Rance into Dinan itself. The town of Dinan is on two levels, with the lower town, mainly consisting of busy riverside restaurants where, over a relaxing lunch, you can watch the local boats sailing along the River Rance. To get to the upper town you have to take a steep climb up the cobbled Rue du Petit Fort to get to the medieval town itself. Here tiny narrow streets spill forth timber-framed restaurants of all descriptions, from Breton Crêperies to top gourmet seafood restaurants. A particular favourite of mine was 'La Mère Pourcel', housed in a fifteenth century building and listed as an historic monument. It was one of the restaurants my wife and I had visited on our first trip to France many moons ago, and we returned here recently to celebrate a special wedding anniversary. I say, it was a favourite, as just over a week before my arrival on the 22nd June 2019, a fire had ravaged part of the old town and 'La Mère Pourcel' was one of the victims. What a tragedy!

The medieval town of Dinan and the restaurant La Mère Pourcel ablaze.

Meanwhile, at 9.55 a.m. on the 3rd July 1919, it was as if the whole town of Dinan was out in force, and it was almost impossible to walk around the control area. The organisers soon realised that the size of the crowd could be an issue and took extra care to make sure there were no accidents or incidents as the peloton, still largely together, stopped to sign in.

René Chassot arrives first into the control at St. Brieuc after his cheeky attack.

The first half of the third stage had been over fairly rolling terrain as it crossed from Normandy into Brittany. However, after Dinan and Lamballe, on the road to the port of Saint Brieuc, the gradient increased sharply. It was here that the Parisian René Chassot (The Cheeky Monkey) cleverly made his attack and gained two minutes on the peloton as he raced into Saint Brieuc to sign the control sheet alone, in sight of the 13th century cathedral. This attack was short lived and Chassot was soon reeled in by the main group at the next control point in Guingamp.

*

I stopped in Guingamp to pay homage to the local football club, who won the Coupe de France (French FA Cup) in 2009, whilst being a Ligue 2 club. This marvellous achievement becomes even more incredible when you realise that the population of the town is only around 7,000 and the gloriously named Stade de Roudourou boasts a capacity of 18,000 spectators. 'En Avant de Guingamp Côtes D'Armor FC' are, as their name suggests, wonderful.

The same cannot be said for the 1919 route itself, which since leaving Dinan, cut boringly across the centre of Brittany, missing out the spectacular 'Pink granite coast' and the 'Coast of legends'. At Morlaix, the last coastal control, I had decided I couldn't miss out on a cycle around one of the most beautiful peninsulas in the region, before heading inland to follow the route to Brest. I pulled up and parked near the harbour, under the shadows created by the magnificent viaduct that towers over the town, carrying the Paris to Brest railway. From Morlaix, I cycled north on the Route de Carantec, which hugs the tidal Rivière de Morlaix. The sun shone brightly on the multitude of tiny white boats out in the estuary, as here, at the small town of Locquénolé, the river immediately widened into La Manche, (The English Channel). Given the wide-open expanse of water in front of me, the strong coastal winds were gusting across the bay, trying to blow me back towards the 1919 route.

I persevered and soon I could see the prize I was waiting for. In the distance were a series of tiny islands, strung across the entrance to the magnificent bay of Morlaix. The larger of these islands were used as strategic defences against any attempts of invasion, usually by the British. One such island, contains the imposing Chateau du Taureau which was built in 1544 occupying every inch of the rocky crag it is sat on. A second island, the Île Louet, contains an ancient lighthouse and a tiny residence for the lighthouse keepers. If you have the money, and the inclination, you can now rent this unique property in its stunning secluded location. There was no chance of visiting these islands today due to the severe gales that were whipping the surrounding sea into a dangerous frenzy. The woman in the ticket office, offering daily boat trips to the Chateau du Taureau, gave me the thumbs down sign, as she passed me a timetable for another day, from behind the shelter of her window.

I continued my Tour of the Carantec peninsular, and on the western side, I took shelter in a cove that looked out onto the 900-metre-long causeway, which leads to the stunning seahorse-shaped island of Île Callot. At five kilometres long, the island can boast a few small houses, a tiny school and a church. It's long sandy beaches and rugged landscape make it popular with walkers and tourists, but you have to be aware of the times of the tides, to ensure you don't get cut off from the mainland. In the distance, I could see the large passenger ferries cutting across the horizon, and docking at the terminal in Roscoff. This was the end of my sightseeing Tour and it was time to cut across the region of Finistère (Land's End) and head for the Stage 3 finish line in the port city of Brest.

The entrance gates to the US Army camp at Pontanezen in Brest. Sleeping quarters for all but two of the 1919 riders.

I arrived in Brest at around the same time as the 1919 riders at 6.15 p.m. I tried to locate the official finish line of Stage 3, which was in front of the American First World War Camp at Pontanezen, two kilometres outside the city of Brest. The camp had been established here, because of the size and depth of the harbour, and over 791,000 American troops had been landed there, since the Spring of 1918, and in 1919 it was still being used as a debarkation point for their return.

Francis Pélissier winning Stage 3 in Brest, 1919.

The American camp had long disappeared and all I could find was a tram stop bearing the name Pontanezen. L'Auto described the finish as being at the summit on the side of Pont Neuf. I found a 'Bar-Terrasse café' called Pont Neuf on the Rue de Paris and imagined that the finish took place here. It took a bit of imagination to conjure up the scene of hundreds of Americans in khaki, lining the route, some sitting on the roofs of the local houses and some hanging from the nearby trees. I counted a row of six trees and five bushes on this suburban street and decided this would have to do. I tried to imagine the band of the American navy, all stood in position, instruments ready to welcome the arriving peloton.

*

At 6.15 p.m. the official car appeared announcing the first arrivals. Then at 6.30 p.m., the crowd saw the appearance of two riders battling for the stage win. It was the two Pélissier brothers again, fighting as if they were enemies. Francis Pélissier managed to come out on top this time by three lengths. The enormous crowds cheered the two champions and the American naval band struck up the tune of the Marseillaise and Francis collected his bouquet of flowers for the stage win.

The applause had barely died down when the peloton appeared. There was a bunch sprint, in which Jean Alavoine (Gars Jean) came out on top before Goethals, Masselis, Masson and the rest. Apparently, Francis Pélissier (Young Magician) had a face, beaming like a child in a beautiful soap advert, as he went up to sign the control sheet.

"Finally, I won a race." he says. "What a beautiful revenge after the jinx of my first Stage! But what a pity all the same, when you think that without my accident, I would today be the most dangerous challenger to my brother Henri! The two brothers as enemies! That would be funny, wouldn't it? Still that does not prevent me from delivering a blow to him as often as I can, as I cannot resist the beauty of a victory! Apart from that, I'm well, physically and morally and I firmly believe that I will soon repeat my success of today."

The ornate wrought-iron kiosk in the Place President Wilson, Brest.

L'Auto reported that when all the 24 remaining riders had crossed the finish line, they were given tram tickets and escorted by the Velo Club de Brest (V.C.B.) to the Grande Café du Commerce in the square named the 'Place President Wilson'. This square had recently been renamed in honour of the great American diplomat, President Woodrow Wilson, who had arrived in Brest harbour on 13 December 1918, on his way to attend the Paris Peace Conference. It is worth noting that there were actually 25 riders that finished Stage 3.

The Licence 'B' rider and 'lantern rouge' Léon Leclerc actually made it, arriving at midnight, two hours and fifty minutes after the previous rider, and he missed being reported in the following day's edition of the paper. He was now sitting in twenty-fifth position in the General Classement, a glorious 12 hours and 12 minutes behind everyone else. Did he shout on arrival 'Allo, Allo, I've arrived? It's me, Leclerc!!'

All the riders spent the night in an annex of the American barracks at Pontanezen, due to an unfortunate lack of hospitality from the hoteliers in Brest. All that is except for the Pélissier brothers who somehow managed to get a room in a hotel in the city. On being visited by the Tour de France marshal, Alphonse Baugé that night, Henri Pélissier, who was not quite as great a diplomat as Woodrow Wilson, was blowing his own trumpet.

"You know that I am a thoroughbred racer and the rest of them are all just carthorses!" he started. His arrogance knew no bounds. "I am not out to provoke anyone. It's just simply that I am the best. The race will go to the strongest!"

Well he may not have wanted to provoke the others, and what he had said may have had an element of truth in it, but I tell you what, there were now 23 angry riders out there, probably chatting amongst themselves in the army barracks, all with a burning desire to see Henri fail.

Bring on Stage 4 !!!

Stage 3: Cherbourg – Brest (405km)

1. Francis Pélissier	16h 30m 5s
2. Henri Pélissier	at 3 lengths
3. Jean Alavoine	16h 33m 24s
4. Félix Gœthals	same time
5. Jules Masselis	same time
6. Emile Masson	same time
7. Eugéne Christophe	same time
8. Alfred Steux	same time
9. Louis Mottiat	same time
10. Honoré Barthélémy	same time

General Classment (G.C.)

1. Henri Pélissier (The Greyhound)	48h 18m 23s
2. Eugéne Christophe (The Old Gaul)	48h 41m 43s
3. Emile Masson (The Unknown)	48h 57m 34s
4. Firmin Lambot (The Saddler)	49h 16m 27s
5. Jean Alavoine (Gars Jean)	49h 33m 56s
6. Alfred Steux (The Kid)	49h 47m 19s
7. Honoré Barthélémy (Glass Eye)	50h 09m 04s
8. Félix Goethals (Cheeky Monkey)	50h 26m 12s
9. Jules Masselis	50h 48m 02s
10. Léon Scieur (The Locomotive)	51h 03m 20s
11. Urbain Anseeuw	52h 01m 15s
12. Francis Pélissier (Young Magician)	52h 16m 14s
13. Joseph Vandaele (Facing his Waterloo)	52h 51m 46s
14. Charles Juseret	52h 51m 57s
15. Louis Mottiat (The Man of Iron)	52h 56m 58s
16. Jacques Coomans (The Smoker)	53h 07m 00s
17. Jules Nempon (The Upstart)	53h 10m 43s
18. René Chassot (Cheeky Monkey)	54h 24h 21s
19. Louis Heusghem	54h 27m 07s
20. Luigi Lucotti (The Italian Job)	55h 05m 26s
21. Odile Defraye (The Unwanted)	55h 24m 56s
22. Paul Duboc (The Apple)	56h 14m 49s
23. Louis Engel	56h 49m 40s
24. Alois Verstraeten	59h 36m 40s
25 Léon Leclerc (Lanterne Rouge)	**71h 48m 32s**

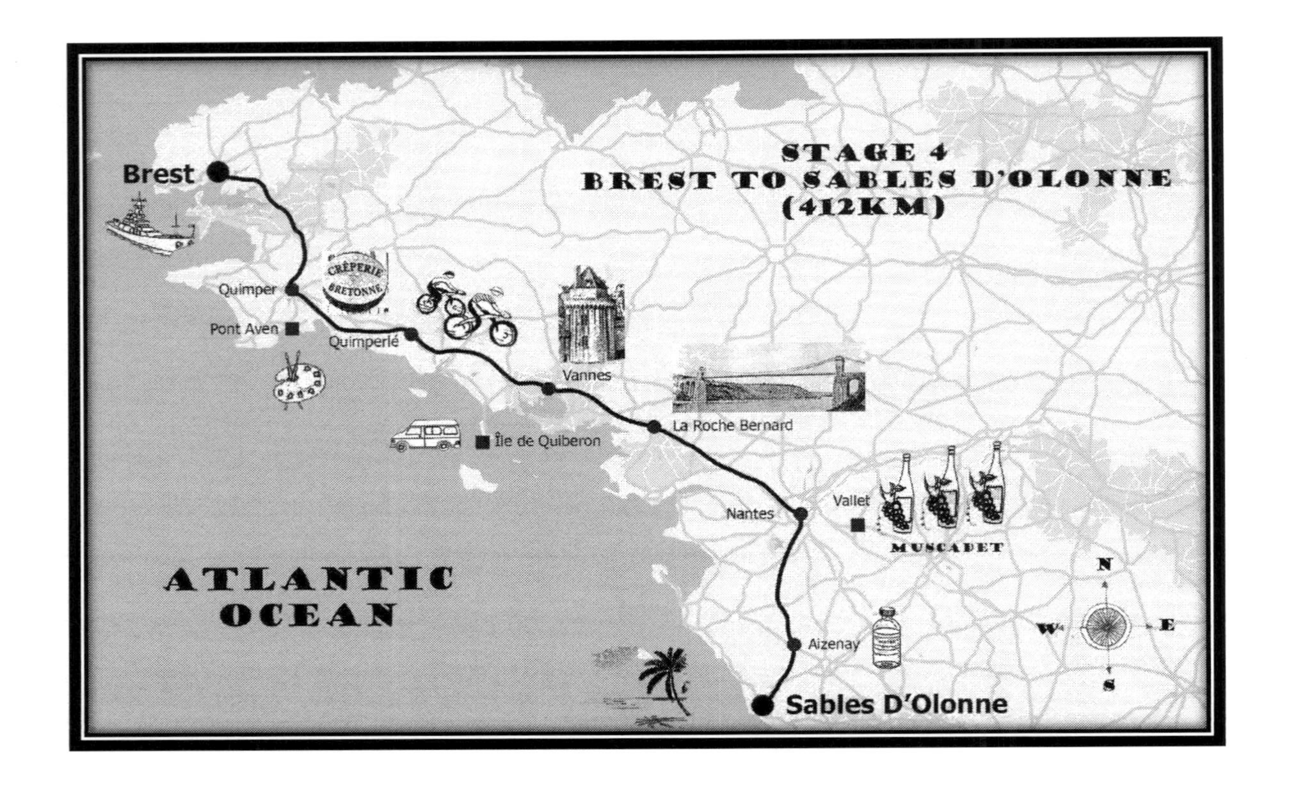
STAGE 4
BREST TO SABLES D'OLONNE
(412KM)
Brest
CRÊPERIE BRETONNE
Quimper
Pont Aven
Quimperlé
Vannes
La Roche Bernard
Île de Quiberon
Nantes
Vallet
MUSCADET
ATLANTIC
OCEAN
N
W
E
S
Aizenay
Sables D'Olonne

Chapter 8: Convicts of the Road

Stage 4: Saturday 5th July 1919 (Brest - Sables D'Olonne) Friday 5th July 2019 (Brest – Île de Quiberon)

It was raining again!

Not only that, but a thick dense fog had come down and settled around the Grand Café du Commerce, in the Place President Wilson in the centre of Brest. In fact, the fog was so thick, L'Auto reported that the headlights of their wonder car 'Le Brasier' could only pierce ten metres in front of them, as they drove into the square. It was still only 12.30 a.m. The official start time had been pulled forward by an hour to 2 a.m., but despite the unearthly hour and terrible weather, there were still considerable crowds outside the café. Only 23 of the 25 riders, that had completed Stage 3, signed in. Odile Defraye (The Unwanted) had reported that he was sick and unable to continue when he had been visited by the L'Auto team the previous night, and the youngster Charles Juseret, who had been suffering with a bad right knee, also pulled out.

*

I arrived in the port city, basked in the early morning sunshine, and crossed the River Penfeld by the Pont de Recouvrance. The mouth of the river flows into a large natural bay, which can only be accessed from the Atlantic Ocean, through a narrow channel, called the Goulet (bottleneck) de Brest. As I parked in front of the fortified walls of the imposing Chateau de Brest, I could see why the Americans had chosen this safe haven to land their troops in 1918.

It was a short walk from the chateau to the starting place in the Place President Wilson, but on arriving I could find no sign of the Café du Commerce. I'd looked at some old photos of the square from 1919 to try and locate it without success. What was noticeable was that the magnificent ornate wrought iron music pavilion, which had stood in the centre of the tree-lined square, had now been replaced with a circular concrete structure, looking more like a stranded Starship Enterprise, than a place for the celebration of peace.

The Starship Enterprise lands in the Place President Wilson, Brest.

The beginning of the 1919 route was a repeat of the end of Stage 3, heading back out east for the first time, and arriving back in Landerneau. It was now 5 a.m. and dawn was breaking as a group of 15 riders, containing the Pélissier brothers, rode into the riverside town. No attack had been made by the carthorses on the brothers as yet!

It was still misty, when the leading group headed down into the town of Châteaulin, along the banks of the River Aulne, arriving at the Quai de Brest. They passed the Café de Bretagne and carried along the riverside to cross the bridge at the control. They then turned left, and continued on the other side of the river at the Quai de Carnot before hitting the steep climb back out of the town. The main group were followed by a second group of seven riders three minutes behind. Last but not least came the 'lanterne rouge' Léon Leclerc, thirty minutes behind, but still riding bravely on his own. He received great applause for his efforts. After Châteaulin, there was no more fog, but the roads were in an awful condition. A recent heavy downpour had created lakes of thick muddy water, which was flowing down from the fields and straight across the roads. Our cycling heroes were covered from head to toe in thick mud and the crowd couldn't tell them apart.

It was the same at Quimper at 5.55 a.m., when the now leading group of 20 of the 23 riders, sailed down the steep incline into the ancient capital of the Department of Finistère (Land's End). However, there were two further abandonments here, as Louis Engel and Louis Heusghem both reported to the control that they were sick, and could continue no longer. This was not the case for the omnipresent Léon Leclerc, who carried on even though he was now an hour and ten minutes behind. The fog had cleared and the bunch just had time to lift their heads to catch a fleeting glimpse of the imposing gothic cathedral of Saint Corentin, towering over the neat timber framed houses. They filed past the cathedral, turned left and headed out of town towards the railway station, to pick up the steep road to Rosporden.

*

I decided that I needed more than a fleeting glimpse of this ancient town and so I treated Quimper as a 'ravitaillement' and walked through the narrow-cobbled streets to the Place Saint-Corentin to partake in a 'Formule Petite Dejeuner €9.00' at the café brasserie Le Finistère, which looked out onto the cathedral square. As I munched my way through two croissants and two baguettes, washed down with a café au lait, I sat and watched the day unfold around me. It was a Friday morning and it seemed to me that the students of Quimper had a Freedom Day where they were allowed to head downtown and socialise. As each student arrived, the obligatory two kisses were given to each friend, before they were able to carry on with their conversation. The art of greeting people with a number of kisses had always been a mystery to me, whilst living and working in France. Was it one, two, three or four kisses that were required, alternating cheeks as you pecked? Actually, the truth is that it depends on the region you are in and apparently there is a coloured map of France in existence which shows how many kisses you are expected to give in each region. Never sure, I used to start with two kisses and if that didn't seem enough, I'd ask. As an Englishman working abroad, I could see some sense of greeting people properly as you started the day or met for the first time. In our offices everybody would take the time to come up to you and say 'Bonjour', and either shake your hand or give you a peck or two. On returning to England, I found it strange that people you knew, sometimes long-standing colleagues, could walk past you without so much as a look in your direction, or sometimes greet you with a gruff 'Morning'.

As I sat refuelling, in readiness for the days cycle ahead, I overheard one discussion in the café about the 2019 Tour de France and the French hopes for Romain Bardet and Thibaut Pinot to break Team Ineos' stranglehold on the yellow jersey. The race was due to start in Brussels tomorrow. After a whole week in France, this was the first mention I had heard of the 'La Grande Boucle'.

It was time for me to move on, and as I headed back through the lanes, underneath the overhanging timber houses, each one painted in a different pastel colour, I stopped in the aptly named 'Place au Beurre' (Butter Square) and counted eight Crêperies in the vicinity. After devouring that many pancakes I'd have thought a visit to a 'craperie' might have been the order of the day. Mind you I was slightly embarrassed when, arriving back at my camper-van, I realised that I'd left last night's washing festooned across the interior working surfaces of my camper-van, in full view of the Quimperois residents. Most of the laundry were my specially made yellow jerseys I'd had printed for the ride, but in amongst these were boxers and socks. They were now dry, so I sheepishly folded them and put them away, out of sight. My cycling itinerary for the day was to take the scenic route between Quimper and the similarly named Quimperlé, both on the 1919 route, but going via the coastal towns of Concarneau and Pont Aven, and then catching the train back to base.

Anyone who watched the TV chef Keith Floyd's 'Floyd on France' in the 1980's will know of Concarneau. The sight of Keith in a bulbous crash helmet, wobbling down the cobbled harbour front on his trusty moped, on his way to cook in a local fish restaurant, was something to behold. Concarneau is a town with a surprise. The main town is built around the harbour and is famous for its fish, in particular tuna, and its Festival of the Blue Nets, held each August. However, hiding out in the harbour on a tiny island, accessible only by a narrow stone bridge, is the original fortified town. Crossing over the water, and entering through the ramparts, one is suddenly thrown into a medieval jewel, with its tiny main street, thronging with people dining at the numerous fish restaurants, or browsing at the occasional Breton gift shop.

Back on land, in the main town square, it was market day, and the variety of produce on sale, was overwhelming. I came across one stall that was devoted to cherries. Did you know there were seven different varieties?

Cycling down the Avenue de la Gare, I got the first recognition of my self-made yellow jersey, and a shout from a passing van. 'Maillot Jaune - Allez, Allez !!'. You could tell the start of the real Tour was approaching.

Paul Gaugin's painting 'Breton women dancing' displayed in Pont Aven.

My next stop was Pont-Aven which, as its name suggests, is a town with numerous bridges that straddle the River Aven. Pont-Aven is well known for its contemporary art school, and in particular the post-impressionist, Paul Gauguin, who resided here for a number of years and painted many pictures of the region and its people. Reproductions of some of his paintings such as 'Breton women dancing' and 'Breton women taking tea' can be seen displayed on local buildings and in art galleries in the town. Gauguin's use of vivid colours in his scenic paintings was inspired by his trips to Tahiti and were said to have been an influence on such notorious artists as Van Gogh, Picasso and Matisse.

I continued on to Quimperlé, where for the first time in a week, some clouds gathered and would you believe it a few spots of rain started to fall. But that was it, a few spots and the clouds were gone and the sun burst through again. I rested in the Place Saint Michel, in front of the church of the same name. This seemed to be a bit of a one-horse town, and I couldn't find the horse! A couple of old women chatted on a bench across from me. They sat as only old women can, with their legs akimbo, as if in need of a through draught to keep the old blood circulating. I soon found out that there were two parts to Quimperlé. This was High Town, the more modern area. The Lower Town, the old historic centre, was down the steep hill running along the river valley.

*

It was on this section of the 1919 stage, that the inclement weather improved at last, and in Quimperlé, Henri Pélissier stopped for a second to take off his raincoat (*) and tighten the handlebars which had come loose on his bike. That was it! All as one, the enraged peloton sensed their opportunity and took flight, much to the disgust of Henri. By the time they got to the first feeding station at the seaport of Lorient it was 8.20 a.m. and the peloton had gained five minutes on Henri. Mind you, his younger brother Francis, had gone with the peloton and was actually in the lead, winning the prize for the first rider to cross the line. Henri came in all alone at 8.25 a.m., a minute behind the Italian, Lucotti.

I looked at the map and studied the rest of the route. Was this a preordained move by the peloton? After all, the terrain from here to the Sables D'Olonne was now largely flat, and the incident in Quimperlé had provided a perfect opportunity for them to put the blinkers on this thoroughbred racehorse, and teach him a lesson.

Stage 4 - Sunday 6th July 1919 (Rest Day) Saturday 6th July 2019 (Île de Quiberon – Sables D'Olonne)

Saturday 6th July 2019 was the start of the 106th edition of the Tour de France. The 21 stages of the 3,460km race were due to finish on the same date as the 1919 Tour on the July 28th in Paris. This year's Grand Départ was to be staged in Belgium, starting and finishing in Brussels, and passing through the suburb of Woluwe-Saint-Pierre, where the great Eddy Merckx grew up. It was the organisers' idea to celebrate the one hundredth year of the yellow jersey by commemorating the man who had worn it the most (111 times on 96 days. In some years there could be two or three stages held in one day). This year was the 50th anniversary of the great Belgian rider's first Tour win in 1969. He was known throughout the cycling world as 'The Cannibal', because of his ruthless nature and the way he seemed to eat up the road and the riders in front of him. This seemed a bit odd to me, to celebrate the 'maillot jaune', the greatest single symbol of the Tour de France, in the country of their fiercest rivals. But hey, who am I to pass judgement? C'est La Vie! The first stage of the 2019 Tour was a mere 192km in length, less than half of today's 1919 stage between Brest and Sables D'Olonne. Also, the 176 riders starting out and finishing today, were already 1,400km behind the carthorses of 1919 and myself, of course.

After my afternoon cycle, I'd spent the night at a campsite on the magical Presqu'Île de Quiberon, which as its name suggests is not quite an island but more an elongated crooked finger, attached to the mainland, clawing its way out from the Baie de Quiberon, and pointing directly at the Belle-Île and Île-d'Houat, out in the Atlantic Ocean. I was up early as I wanted to do a tour of the 'Nearly Island', and as the sun started to lift its head, I reached the island's tip. I stopped for a while to watch dawn break from behind the distant islands. A flock of linnets flitted around in the tufted hare-tail grasses, which surrounded the paths leading down to the bay. I soon found out that the gravel track I'd ridden along was none other than the 'Promenade Louison Bobet' and there was a plaque dedicating the route to the champion French cyclist who had won three consecutive Tour de France titles between 1953 and 1955. He had also created a Centre for Thalassotherapy (the improvement of health through the use of sea water, seaweed, algae and mud) on the island. The reason for the early start time was not to catch up with the peloton as Henri needed to do but to keep a lunch date with a French family from my home town's twin-town of Vallet, which was on the other side of Nantes.

*

How was Henri Pélissier coping after the nasty trick that had been played on him? At the end of Stage 3, he had a healthy 23-minute 10 seconds advantage, over his nearest rival Eugéne Christophe (The Old Gaul) and this was what he needed to protect. After 154km, he was only 5 minutes behind the main peloton, so it was not too disastrous as yet, but he was now riding solo, something he had not had to do since leaving Paris. This would be a test for 'The Greyhound' to see how he coped without the protection that can be offered by a surrounding peloton, and without the support of his brother, Francis who was sticking with the main peloton as they took the sharp turn in front of the crowds outside the Café Gloux in Lorient, and flowed across the bridge suspended over the River Scorff. It must have felt strange for him to be now cycling alone in amongst his brother's greatest enemies, knowing they were going all out to distance themselves from Henri, and were trying to drop Francis as well.

French soldiers waiting to be demobbed, on the cobbled streets of the old town of Vannes.

In Vannes, after cycling 208km, the riders reached the halfway point of Stage 4 and it was the same story. Francis was still in amongst the main peloton, as it pulled into the Place de La Madeleine, at the entrance to the town. It was now 10.25 a.m., and Henri had lost a further 11 minutes, after suffering a puncture moments before arriving at the control. His lead over the Old Gaul was now down to seven minutes and he was getting worried. Also, Vannes was an old medieval town, full of pavé (cobblestoned) streets, so this was not the place to make up any lost time. Henri rode gingerly down the narrow Rue Hoche, passing 'La Caserne des Trent', the barracks of the French 116th Infantry Regiment. Several soldiers in uniform cheered him on from the sentry box on the street, outside what was a converted convent. They were still in celebratory mood after the signing of the Peace Treaty the previous weekend, and they were looking forward to being demobbed.

The route instructions given in L'Auto for the riders to follow through Vannes were pretty convoluted. After the Rue Hoche, they were to enter the Place L'Hôtel -de-Ville, take a left in Rue du Mene by the Credit Lyonnais bank, in full view of the Cathedral Saint Pierre. Working their way around the Hôtel de L'Epee, they would come to the butcher's shop 'Jacquet', where they needed to turn at a right angle, and straightaway, turn left into Rue Allaric-le-Grand and pass in front of the Prefecture, crossing a small bridge over the tiny Lizier stream. Finally, at the crossroads, they could take the right turn in front of the Herve-Moizant restaurant and head out towards Nantes!!

*

I was struggling with the aid of a Satnav and it did cross my mind how could so few riders, attempt a 5,560km race around France, without getting lost or going in the wrong direction. I guess the crowds would have kept most of them on the right track and if they were in the peloton, they would have the safety of knowing that the official cars would keep them on the right path. However, if they were riding alone or even worse, riding alone in the dark or fog, as this morning, then there must have been plenty of opportunities to go astray. Henri Pélissier was now on his own, and his mind had to be focused on following the correct route, and at the same time looking for an opportunity to catch up with his enemies.

There was not much chance of this as Henri headed for the control point at La Roche-Bernard, 248 km from the start. The route was horrendous with lots of tight bends and sharp turnings. It was a tough job for Henri to keep in touch with the leaders. Fortunately, a beautiful new steel suspension bridge, had been built over the River Vilaine in 1911, to carry the riders into the fortified town of La Roche-Bernard, built on the rocks that gave the town its name. As they crossed the new bridge, the peloton could see the stone buttresses of the original suspension bridge, laying in ruins down below them. The bridge I crossed was yet a further replacement bridge, that was constructed in 1960 following the destruction of the 1911 bridge after the German occupation in the Second World War.

It was now midday, and after the morning fog, the heat of the sun burst through to make it even harder for Henri. He soon found out at the control, that he was now 20 minutes behind Francis and the others, and his overall lead in G.C. was now down to three minutes.

Something peculiar happened before the second feeding station in Nantes. Somehow, during the 70km between La Roche-Bernard and Nantes, Henri had managed to catch up with Félix Goethals and Honoré Barthélémy, and when the threesome arrived at the control, they were only 15 minutes behind the leading group.

Strangely, Henri's younger brother Francis had disappeared from the leader board. Henri Desgrange reported that, from the top of his car 'Le Brasier', he had seen the two brothers riding together, but on arriving in Nantes, Francis was suddenly an incredible 27 minutes behind his brother. He'd somehow lost 42 minutes in total. Extraordinary!

Francis explained that he had been sick but thankfully he was feeling much better now. A more plausible explanation (but not a verifiable one) was that the younger brother, who had no real hope of winning the 1919 Tour, because of his broken bike at the start of the race, had dropped back to assist his elder brother, who had been riding alone.

L'Auto reported, that following the outbreak of the scorching sun at La Roche-Bernard, the riders had then encountered some severe thunderstorms as they headed inland to Nantes and due to the adverse conditions, most of them were again covered from head to foot in baked mud.

All the riders initialled the control sheet at the feeding station in front of enormous crowds. Nantes was after all the sixth largest city in France. Gentlemen in plus-fours or waist-coated suits, wearing bowler hats or ribbon straw boaters, sat and applauded their magnificent efforts. As each rider departed, they received a standing ovation as they headed towards the River Loire and the Île de Nantes, crossing the two bridges, the Pont de La Madeleine and the Pont Rousseau.

*

I, too headed off to my own feeding station and the lunchtime date with my French friends, the family Gastineau, from my home town's twin-town of Vallet. Vallet lies to the east of Nantes and is in the Muscadet region of France. The town itself is surrounded by acres and acres of vineyards, growing the Melon de Bourgogne grape from which, their famous wine is made. Every available space in the area is used to grow this sacred grape. I saw one house with a side alley leading down to a garage and the grass verges on each side of the track bore vines.

I dined graciously with the Gastineau's and we recounted stories of the family's recent football exchange trip to the UK and my current 1919 Tour de France trip, over a chilled glass of the finest Muscadet Sevre et Maine sur Lie.

It was soon time for me to catch up with Henri Pélissier, and discover what had happened to him and his younger brother, at the race finish at Sables D'Olonne. I climbed back into my camper-van, waving goodbye to the Gastineau's, and discovered I could not hold the steering wheel, because of the heat. The outside air temperature was now 35 degrees, and the heat wave wasn't showing any signs of diminishing.

*

I re-joined the 1919 route at Les Sorinieres, a road exit to the south of Nantes, and learned that Henri had suffered yet another puncture and lost even more time. From here though, it was a flat ride all the way down to the finish at Les Sables (the Sands) D'Olonne, on the Atlantic coast. At Azenay with just 23km left to go, he had caught up again and was only 15 minutes behind the leading group, meaning he was still ahead in the G.C. by 8 minutes. After dropping Goethals, he had caught up with René Chassot, who was weary and a wreck, and then Chassot punctured, leaving Henri all alone. Although weary, the thoroughbred racehorse caught up with Masselis and Verstraeten, and Henri still had hopes of getting back to the head of the peloton. In a final burst of energy, he furiously tried to drop Masselis and Verstraeten, as he had been dropping other riders all day.

With only five kilometres to go, he was exhausted and stopped, leaning his bike against the wall of a cottage, asking the owner for a drink. Soon he was gulping down a cool refreshing drink and he searched in the pocket of his jersey, with one hand trembling, for some small change to pay the local peasant. The local man was dismayed at Henri's offer, and with eyes full of tears, he tried to refuse the payment. Henri screamed with rage. "I have to pay; I have to pay you. It's the rules. This Tour de France of Henri Desgrange makes all the riders, feel like convicts on the road **(truc du forcat).** We do not deserve to have to cope with all this misery."

This was the first time that the seaside town of Sables-D'Olonne had welcomed a stage of the Tour de France and the finish line, in front of the train station, was bedecked with flags. The local municipal sports club, the V.C.S., had put up barriers to control the crowds stretching along the road. It was 5.30 p.m. before a leading group of five riders appeared at the top of the Avenue de la Gare. Much to the crowd's excitement there was a bunch sprint to the line, won by a length by Jean Alavoine (Gars Jean), recording the seventh stage victory of his career. He was followed closely by Alfred Steux (The Kid), Eugéne Christophe (The Old Gaul), Emile Masson (The Unwanted), and Jacques Coomans (The Smoker).

Then and now – the train station at Sable D'Olonne.

I pulled into the train station at Sables D'Olonne and the scene had not changed much from 1919. The station entrance was still sheltered by a large wrought iron and glass canopy and the ornate station clock still warned passengers if they needed to run for their trains. The only difference was, instead of hiring a horse and carriage to take you to your final destination, you could now rent a Peugeot 208 from Avis car rentals.

The Avenue de la Gare, now the Avenue Jean Jaures, is still lined with trees and I could imagine Jean Alavoine, leading the bunch of five riders down this final straight to the finishing line. Mind you, the massive crowd were struggling to identify who was in the lead, as they cheered the five brown, muddy and dusty shapes jostling for the win. After their time was recorded, the cyclists were driven up to the Café du Commerce, on the Rue Nationale, to sign in. Jean Alavoine was ecstatic with his victory.

"Well, Yes. I am perfectly happy. Happy to have won the stage! I'm glad I didn't get any bad luck! And I'm happy to at last be able to show my buddies that I was not bluffing or boasting when I told them before the start, I was going well. I did the whole stage today without anyone noticing me. No great shouts from "Alavoine"! Nothing! But always the smile! If I have only a little bit of blood left in my veins in the Pyrénées, you will see that the 'youngsters' will not be able to compete with this old crab. I'm going to teach them to climb properly and how to arrive in Luchon and Perpignan in the best condition."

Jean Alavoine (Gars Jean) looks as fresh as a daisy after cycling 412km and winning the 4th stage of the Tour de France 1919 (Sables d'Olonne)

Henri somehow managed to finish in tenth position, after his brave effort to catch back the peloton, and arrived an astonishing

35 minutes and 42 seconds behind the winner 'Gars Jean'. Somehow, he'd lost an additional 20 minutes 42 seconds over those last 23km into Sables D'Olonne he was now 12 minutes 42 seconds behind Eugéne Christophe who was leading the G.C. I wonder what the hell was in the drink he had received from that peasant! Francis fared even worse, coming in last with three other riders, nearly three and a half hours behind the winner 'Gars Jean'.

As for Eugéne Christophe (the Old Gaul), he had quietly snuck to the top of the G.C. and must have been overjoyed with his lead of over 12 minutes after four stages.

"I know perfectly well that I can't fight with young riders, who are quicker sprinters than me, but the Tour can equally be lifted by a rider who has never won a stage. The slightest breakdown of a bike may depress a young rider, but not an old tramp and a mechanic like me. Do you think, that if Rossius' accident had happened to me, I would have abandoned? Never! Remember the Tour de France, 1913!"

I have some bad news to report, somewhere between Quimper and the finish line, we had lost our 'lanterne rouge' the brave Léon Leclerc. He was reported by L'Auto 'to have disappeared from the traffic' during the stage. Maybe he took a wrong turning and got completely lost. He was after all, cycling all on his own. Who knows, he may still be out there cycling around France! What we do know is that he was never seen in professional racing again. Alois Verstraeten, one of the two remaining Licence B riders left in the Tour, along with Jules Nempon, graciously assumed the mantel.

Well, after all that drama, tomorrow is another day. It's only Stage 5 – Sables D'Olonne to Bayonne, which at a distance of 482 km (300 miles) is the longest and most boring stage ever to be held in the history of the Tour de France.

*It must be noted that each rider bought a raincoat to take with them on the Tour de France. They had to purchase these from the offices of L'Auto, the day before the race for the princely sum of 1FF. This sum would be returned to them when they reached Paris and handed the raincoat in (assuming they made it!).

Stage 4: Brest – Sables D'Olonne (412km)

1. Jean Alavoine	in 15h 51m 45s
6. Alfred Steux	at a length
3. Eugéne Christophe	at a length
4. Emile Masson	at a length
5. Jacques Coomans	at a length
6. Léon Scieur	in 16h 02m 09s
7. Firmin Lambot	in 16h 04m 50s
8. Jules Masselis	in 16h 23m 04s
9. Alois Verstraeten	in 16h 23m 05s
10. Henri Pélissier	in 16h 26m 37s
11. Félix Goethals	in 16h 33m 12s
12. René Chassot	in 16h 33m 13s
13. Honoré Barthélémy	in 16h 44m 06s
14. Luigi Lucotti	in 17h 34m 10s
15. Urbain Anseeuw	at a length
16. Joseph Vandaele	at a length
17. Francis Pélissier	19h 17m 12s
18. Louis. Mottiat	at a length
19. Paul Duboc	at a length
20. Jules Nempon	at a length

Le Classement General (G.C.)

1. E. Christophe	(The Old Gaul)	64h 32m 28s
2. H. Pélissier	(The Greyhound)	64h 45m 10s
3. E. Masson	(The Unknown)	64h 49m 19s
4. F. Lambot	(The Saddler)	65h 21m 17s
5. J. Alavoine	(Gars Jean)	65h 25m 41s
6. A. Steux	(The Kid)	65h 39m 04s
7. H. Barthélémy	(Glass Eye)	66h 53m 10s
8. F. Gœthals	(The Sock Seller)	66h 59m 24s
9. L. Scieur	(The Locomotive)	67h 05m 29s
10. J. Masselis		67h 11m 06s
11. J. Coomans	(The Smoker)	68h 58m 45s
12. U. Anseeuw	)	69h 35m 25s
13. J. Vandaele	(Facing his Waterloo)	70h 25m 56s
14. R. Chassot	(Cheeky Monkey)	70h 57m 34s
15. F. Pélissier	(Young Magician)	71h 33m 26s
16. L. Mottiat	(Man of Iron)	72h 14m 1s
17. J. Nempon	(The Upstart)	72h 27m 55s
18. L. Lucotti	(The Italian Job)	72h 40m 36s
19. P. Duboc	(The Apple)	75h 32m 01s
20. A.Verstraeten	**(Lanterne Rouge)**	**75h 59m 45s**

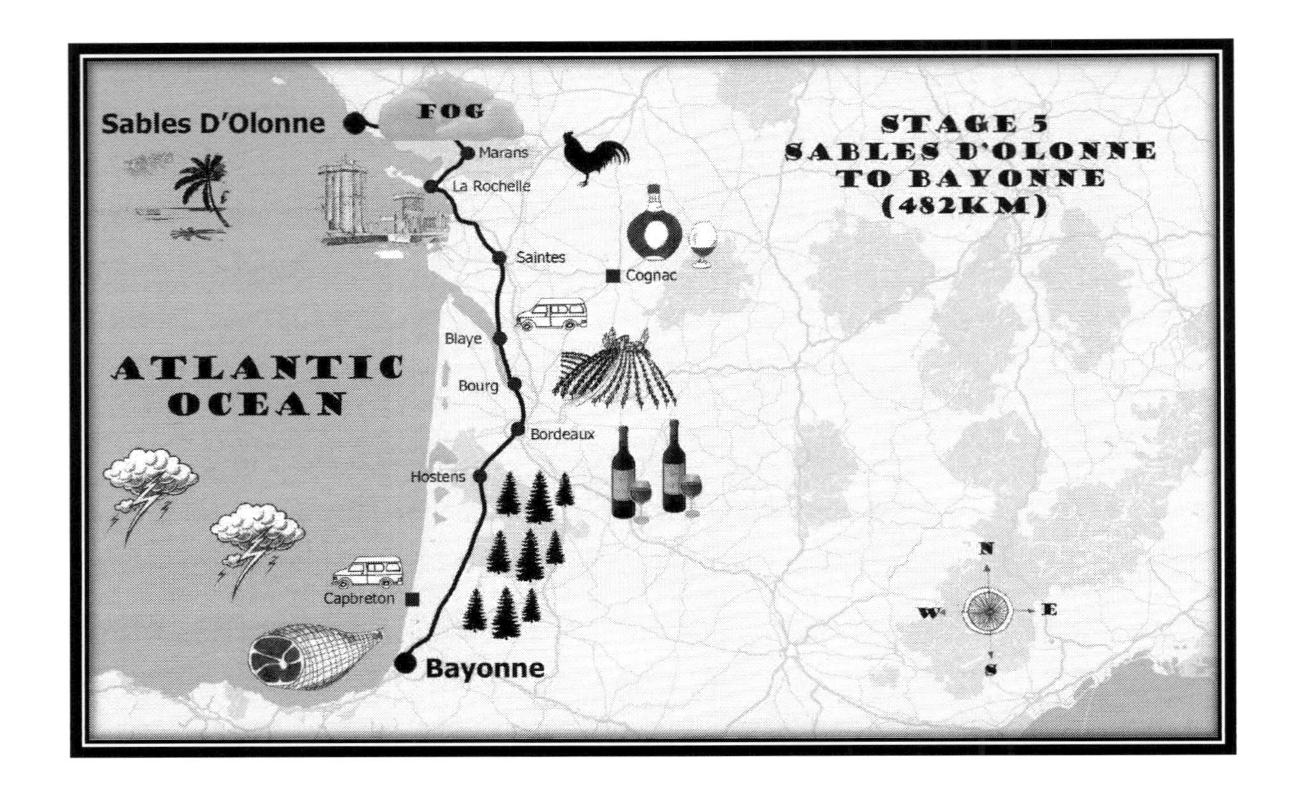
STAGE 5
SABLES D'OLONNE
TO BAYONNE
(482KM)
Sables D'Olonne
FOG
Marans
La Rochelle
Saintes
Cognac
Blaye
Bourg
Bordeaux
Hostens
Capbreton
Bayonne
ATLANTIC
OCEAN
N
W
E
S

Chapter 9 : To Infinity and Beyond

Stage 5 - Monday 7th July 1919 (Sables D'Olonne-Bayonne)
Sunday 7th July 2019 (Sables D'Olonne–Blaye)

"You're all against us! The hotels we stay in are rubbish, and do not befit a star such as myself. On top of this, last night the Maître d'Hôtel refused to serve me with a high-quality red wine.

WE QUIT!"

And so, at the registration desk for Stage 5, Henri and Francis Pélissier, turned up in plain clothes with their bags packed, ready to catch the train back to Paris. The brothers' petulant abandonment meant only 18 competitors were now left to tackle the 482km stage to Bayonne. This was longest stage that Henri Desgrange had ever devised (it remains so to this day) and to ensure his precious publishing deadlines were met, he'd brought the official start time forward by two hours to 10 p.m., the previous day. This meant, for the first time, the remaining 18 heroes would actually be cycling throughout the entire night. The sun was still shining on the famous stretch of sand, arching around the sparkling Atlantic Ocean, that gives Sables D'Olonne its name, as they signed in at the Café du Commerce, around 9 p.m. They stared at the impetuous brothers with a wry smile on their faces. Hadn't they taught the arrogant Henri a lesson? Hadn't they proved to him they were not the carthorses he thought they were? Victory to the peloton! Still they had a lot to prove to themselves on this stage to beat all stages. Each and every one of them knew they were going to be pushed to the limits of their endurance on today's marathon ride.

*

I managed to find the location of the Café du Commerce, which still exists at Number 79, Rue Nationale, but this modern green steel and glass café, complete with concrete terrace, was not the glorious place where I imagined the Pélissier Brothers quitting the Tour. My only regret as I stood outside the café this morning was that I'd come all the way to Sables D'Olonne and not seen the famous sandy beach. The tide was in!!

The functional Café du Commerce in Sables d'Olonne, signing in point for Stage 5. Maybe the state of this café is what caused the Pélissier brothers to abandon.

I headed out of town, in the early morning sunshine, to the official start line at the Porte de Talmont, 500m from the café. 'Talmont-sur-Hilaire' was my first destination, and it was quite an impressive one, as it boasted the great military leader, Richard the Lionheart, as one of its previous residents. As I passed the now ruined walls of the Chateau de Talmont, I thought the home of this great warrior was an appropriate starting point for my own personal 482km crusade, over the flat terrain of the Vendée, to the south-west corner of France. The route instructions in L'Auto told me that it was impossible to go wrong, as the road was completely straight. All I had to do was follow the telegraph poles strung out on my left-hand side. They were right. In front of me, as far as the eye could see, stretched the expansive wheat fields of this fertile part of France. To pass the time I'd started counting the number of zebra crossings in each small town. I passed through the tiny village of Les Magnils-Reigniers and counted a total of nine. It had always amazed me as to why so many villages in France were overloaded with crossings, particularly when most French motorists tended to ignore them anyway. On my first ever business trip to France, I stayed in the town of Fontainebleau, south of Paris. I set off in my hire car and soon came to my first zebra crossing on the High street. A middle-aged lady was about to step onto the crossing with her dog, so naturally I stopped. She was so surprised, that instead of crossing the road, she reversed back up onto the pavement. The cars behind me started pipping their horns frantically, so I drove on. I couldn't understand why they would be so impatient. After a number of months of living and driving around France, I soon discovered why. It was due to the number of zebra crossings that could appear in any single town. For example, if a school was moved to another building in the town, a new zebra crossing would be put in place to serve it. However, the old one wasn't removed, as this was seen as an unnecessary expense. Consequently, motorists took little notice of them.

Far away in the distance, I could make out the spire of the wonderfully named 'Cathédrale Notre-Dame-de-l'Assomption de Luçon' which measuring 85 metres in height, dominated the skyline. Luçon is the gateway to the beautiful region and national park of 'Le Marais Poitevin', an area of marshland, similar to the Fens or the Norfolk Broads in England.

*

However, this was a gateway, through which the 1919 rider, Urbain Anseeuw, would not pass. For some unfathomable reason the Belgian decided to abandon here, 50km from the start. The previous night he had been in good spirits, and he was laughing and joking with the rest of his fellow riders, as he always did. He may have been feeling the effects of his recent exploits a few weeks earlier in 'Le Circuit des Champs de Bataille' (the Tour of the Battlefields), where he had battled through snow, ice and rain to finish second in a race over the bloody battlefields of the Somme and Flanders. (For an excellent read, try Tom Isitt's 'Riding the Zone Rouge'- Weidenfeld & Nicolson, 2019)

It was still a puzzle though. Why abandon here, so early? I tried to put myself in the position of the rider. It would have been around midnight and the roads would have been plunged into darkness. A thick fog had descended on the town of Luçon, rising up from the marshlands beyond. Urbain may have lost contact with the leaders, and as a result, he was now cycling alone over the open countryside in complete darkness with no one to guide him. 'Le Marais Poitevin' is a region with an abundance of wildlife and I'm sure there would have been many strange and eery noises emanating across the dark flat fields and out of the watery ditches surrounding the marshes. There may have been a sudden flapping of wings as a large startled marshland bird flew out of the bushes and passed immediately overhead. It may also have been that enough was enough. This was Urbain's first Tour de France and maybe he had misjudged the continual effort that needed to be sustained to challenge the leaders. Also, the thought of this marathon stage, plus the daunting prospect of the Pyrenean mountain stages to come, had made him realise he had reached his limit. Whatever the reason Urbain abandoned. He would now be known as a 'Shadow', the name the peloton gave to any rider abandoning during the night. In the following year's Tour de France in 1920, Urbain did actually manage to complete Stage 5 and the mountainous Stage 6 from Bayonne to Luchon. However, that was enough for him and he abandoned again. It would be his final attempt to complete the Tour de France.

With his abandonment, the field was now down to 17 riders, meaning a total of 50 had abandoned since the start. They had only completed four stages and not even got to the mountains. I know the perfect race for Henri Desgrange was one where only one rider made it to the Parc des Princes in Paris, but this was getting too close for comfort.

*

I entered the garden gate of 'Le Marais Poitevin', and headed for my destination; the canal-side town of Marans. Here hundreds of tiny canals crisscross each other, hiding wildfowl such as swans, herons and little egrets, fishing for their breakfast. This region is also famous for the 'Poule de Marans', a black chicken, which unusually lays a deep red egg with an excellent flavour, much sought after by top chefs. As I drove, I saw numerous signs advertising 'Strawberries, Raspberries, Cherries, Melons, Potatoes and Tomatoes' for sale. This area is known as 'La Venise Verte' (The Green Venice) and it is easy to see why. My cycle route today was to be along a section of 'La Velo Francette', a 600km cycle route from the seaport of Caen in the north, to La Rochelle in the south-west. The last section from Marans to La Rochelle follows the 1919 route, along the Canal de Rompsay. At my start point in Marans, I was stopped by a number of French people in cars, leaning out of their car windows, and gesturing 'Boulangerie?' It was Sunday, and no true French family could start their day without a crispy baguette, pain au chocolat or croissant washed down with a strong espresso and a glass of fresh orange. Marans itself looked beautiful in the morning sun, and I wondered around the narrow streets to the market place, overlooked by the church with its unusual glass bell tower, topped with an ornate steel webbed spire.

I cycled off along the canal and headed over the numerous canal bridges, which festooned with pretty flower boxes, linked the town together. The restauranteurs were in the process of putting out the tables and chairs onto the canal side in readiness for the Sunday lunchtime diners.

The canal side restaurants of Marans, in Le Marais Poitevin,

Cycling out of town, along the quiet canal paths, I was in my element. The sky was an iridescent blue contrasting beautifully with field upon field of deep yellow sunflowers. I followed the canal path over bridges of varying types of construction, and passed large concrete structures and lock gates, whose aim it was to control this vast network of water. People walked their dogs and families cycled together, enjoying the summer sun. Those more energetic jogged or skateboarded along the paths, and those less inclined took newspapers and books to read under the trees, to sit and relax in the dappled sunlight.

One of the many canal fortifications aimed at controlling the flow of water in Le Marais Poitevin.

Suddenly, one section of the path soared high above the canal, as the canal itself disappeared into a deep ravine far below. The cycle path became dusty, as it cut through an area of rocks and entered some woods. The noise of the cicadas was intense, as they sang their song in unison, in the heat of the day. I looked at the weather app on my iPhone and it registered 31 degrees, so not quite as hot as the 35 degrees I'd experienced yesterday.

Soon, houses started to appear through the trees and it was evident that I was approaching La Rochelle. As luck would have it, the canal flowed into the Quai Duperré and the Quai Valin, the same spot where the 1919 peloton had arrived at 2 a.m. that morning. I soon realised the 17 riders, who all arrived together, would not have seen any of the beauty I had witnessed, as for them, it was still the middle of the night. The quayside in La Rochelle was buzzing and thousands of tourists were either heading for the beach, or heading for lunch at one of the many top restaurants to be found in the narrow-cobbled streets of this fortified port.

As much as I wanted to do both, I needed to return to Marans and continue south with my journey. I stopped on the harbour wall and bought a large glass of freshly squeezed orange from an old lady, dressed in traditional costume, bedecked with a large straw hat. She served the drinks from a Heath-Robinson machine that sat under a parasol attached to her bike. She put two or three oranges into a large copper container, and with a number of turns of her pedals. Voila, beautiful fresh orange! She asked me where I was from and where I was going. She could cope with the fact that I was from England, but struggled with the concept that I had travelled 1,657km around France and still had 4,000km to go.

The towers protecting the entry the harbour at La Rochelle, built mainly to protect the town from the attacks of the English.

"Tout en velo? - All on your bike?" she asked.

"Non, un partie par velo, un partie par camping car"' I replied, to which she smiled and looked at me, mightily relieved.

It was time for me to leave Le Vendée and head south along the coastal road, following the Charente river inland to the town of 'Saintes', famous for its Roman ruins and in particular it's impressive amphitheatre. The medieval town looked stunning as the ancient town houses, overlooked by the dominating domed cathedral, cast reflections onto the River Charente, turned blue by the afternoon sunshine.

*

At last, the 1919 riders would have been able to see something of their surroundings. It was 4.51 a.m. and after seven hours of riding in the pitch dark and fog, dawn was staring to break on a new day. The riders were still largely together. After yesterday's exploits, and the length of this stage, I think they were happy to stay in a group, lit up partially by the weak headlamps of the official cars following them through the night. It was the same situation when they arrived at the first feeding station at Pons, all 17 arrived huddled together for comfort. This was cognac territory, and with the town of Cognac and its distilleries only 24km down the road, I'm sure some of the battle-worn riders would have hoped that perhaps a drop of the locally produced Hennessey, Martell or Remy Martin, had found its way into their bidons.

*

Soon after leaving Pons, the straight open Roman roads lead southwards, through fields of vineyards, their vines flowing like parallel lines of braided hair, over the surrounding clay and limestone hillsides. I soon came across signs enticing me into the local Chateaux. 'Vignobles Bourcier – Premier Côtes de Blaye – Vente de Rosé Vrac en Bag in Box'. I was approaching the town of Blaye on the banks of the River Gironde. Blaye is listed as a UNESCO heritage site because of its ancient citadel and its fortified walls. This was the halfway point of the stage and my stopping point for the night. I'd done some research into campsites in the area and discovered that the nearby 'Chateau Marquis de Vauban' allowed camping cars to stay in the grounds absolutely free of charge. The only problem was that you couldn't book in advance and all available pitches were allocated on a first come, first served basis. It was getting quite late in the evening, and I thought that I may have missed my chance to camp here, but as I approached the outskirts of the town, I drove past a sign indicating the 'Citadelle de Vauban 17'eme Siecle'. I reversed back to the turning and headed down a narrow track which brought me to the impressive gates of the chateau, resplendent with its flying tricolours. I felt a bit nervous, heading into the grounds, but I was soon being directed into my place for the night, by a welcoming girl from the chateau. She showed me where I could take on water and also the nearest electricity point to hook up for the night. I couldn't believe my luck as I set up camp looking out at row upon row of vines. I got chatting to my neighbours, Jean Paul and Anne Marie from Brittany, and I said "Can this be true, free camping and all the facilities as well?"

Waiting for the Chateau bell to sound for aperitifs - Citadelle de Vauban.

"Yes", they said "and now you must listen out for the chateau bell. It will ring at 5.30 p.m. and that's the time for all campers to meet outside the chateau for aperitifs! "

What a great idea and what a great way for you to meet everybody. As I tucked into some cooked meats, washed down with a glass or two of the chateau's red wine, I swapped stories with my fellow campers. They were only moderately impressed with my 1919 Tour de France journey, as most of them were on a travelling adventure themselves. Jean Paul and Anne Marie had spent a month touring Spain and were now heading back to their home town of Rennes in northern France.

Stage 5 - Tuesday 8th July 1919 (Rest Day)

Monday 8th July 2019 (Blaye - Bayonne)

I was up early this morning to cycle the 1919 route along the River Gironde and not wanting to disturb my Breton neighbours, I pushed my bike quietly out of the campsite and cycled into the town of Blaye. The UNESCO citadel of Blaye is indeed a sight to behold, although my view of it was slightly tarnished by a fun fair, which had been set up outside the town's walls. Of course, it was now the week leading up to the 'Quatorze Juillet' or 'Bastille Day' and 'Les Fêtes Foraines' (fairgrounds) would be held all over the country.

*

In 1919 at 7.51 a.m., the 17 remaining riders had ridden together into the control in Blaye in intense fog. As if to give me a real sense of what they were going through, I was greeted by an intense mist lying over the River Gironde. I say River Gironde, but in fact this is not true, as the Gironde is actually an estuary, which takes the River Dordogne and River Garonne, to their destiny in the Atlantic Ocean. The mist was so thick I couldn't see the impressive islands of Île Bouchaud and Île Nouveau, which lay in its centre. For all that, the estuary had a majestic feel to it, and the overhanging mist seemed to lend a sense of mystery to the vast expanse of water. I stopped on the banks to take a shot of the tiny fishing boats which floated gently out in the ghostly mist. This could have been a scene from 1919.

'Play Misty for me' – early morning mist lies on the Gironde estuary.

Upon reaching the next town of Plassac, I headed down to the Corniche de la Gironde, a tiny road that runs parallel to the estuary, offering good views of the river on a clear day. This narrow country lane took me through tiny hamlets, such as Marmisson and Gauriac, which revealed ancient 'Maisons (houses) Troglodytes', built into the rocks overlooking the estuary.

At Bayon-sur-Gironde, I came across an imposing church sat plum in the middle of the road. As I approached, the road deviated around this mini cathedral, topped with a gigantic statue of the Blessed Virgin Mary, carrying her new-born baby. After Bayon, I picked up the coastal road again down to the citadel of Bourg. On the way I had seen beautiful birds, such as the Woody-Woodpecker hoopoe, and a number of kites circling the clifftops. What had amazed me was the lack of vehicles along my route. I know I had started off early in the morning but I was expecting to encounter a lot more Monday morning traffic.

I stopped at Bourg and pushed my bike down the cobbled street and under the arch of the stone gateway leading into the old town. Again, it was quiet and the shopkeepers seemed to be content to amble along and have a chat with their neighbours, as they proceeded to open their shops for the day's trading. I sat for a while under the large wrought iron structure which served as the market place dominating the Place de la Liberation, as Bourg woke up to the day ahead. I bought a copy of today's L'Èquipe to find out what had happened in the first stage of the 2019 Tour de France. The headlines revealed the Dutchman Mike Teunissen had managed to steal the stage win and took the first yellow jersey from the favourite Peter Sagan.

By now, the morning mist had lifted, as I headed back to the Chateau in Blaye. The coach trips following the 'Route des vins de Blaye et Bourg' were out in force, and I stopped where they stopped, to admire the now picturesque views of the Gironde Estuary. As I rode back along the water's edge, I could see numerous quaint stilt fishing huts that jutted out into the estuary. These operated a square-shaped pulley net (or 'filet carré') which was lowered into the river to trap the fish. The large nets gave the humble shacks their French name of "carrelets"

I also noticed a lot of people, wild camping in tents and camper-vans on the water's edge, either as tourists or as expectant fisherman, who were up early to stake their rods and try their luck in the Gironde. It occurred to me that this was maybe the reason the Chateau offered free camping on their grounds. It was a relatively cheap way of attracting tourists away from wild camping and tempt them into their vineyard to sample their wine and hopefully depart with a case or two of their finest red.

After my invigorating ride, I was now back in my camper-van and heading to the wine capital of the region, Bordeaux. I passed through the village of La Lustre, which true to its name was pretty lacklustre and then through the wonderfully named village of Pont de Moron, which was a stupid name as there was no bridge and I couldn't see any morons! After crossing the Dordogne river, I immediately joined the traffic queuing on the autoroute (A10) into Bordeaux, only to be greeted by the sight of smoke billowing across the motorway. It was soon evident that up ahead there was a car on fire and the 'pompiers' would soon be on their way. The traffic was backing up quickly and I had a decision to make. I could either follow the 17 riders, who were still altogether, down into Bordeaux and witness Paul Duboc (The Apple), the first rider to sign the control sheet at the Café de l'Avenue; or I could head off, out of the danger area, over the River Garonne and towards the Landes Forest . Given the potential long delays, it was an easy decision to make, although I was slightly disappointed that I wouldn't be visiting one of the wine capitals of the world.

*

It was only 9.43 a.m. when the Magnificent Seventeen crossed the mighty river Garonne, cycling over the Pont de Pierre into Bordeaux. They immediately took a left and followed the railway that runs parallel to the river, along the Quai des Salinières, filing under the steel rail bridge and back out of the city, in the direction of Bègles. They had been in the saddle for 12 hours and were about to reach the most challenging part of the route, heading south-west through 10,000 km2 of pine forest. The peloton still had to cover 180km, through an unchanging, never-ending landscape of pine trees, which was more of a mental challenge than a physical one. The millions of pine trees that cover ninety percent of this region were planted in the mid-19th century to help convert the marshland into a habitable place to live. Prior to this the locals had to walk around on stilts to attend their goats and sheep, giving the impression of giant swamp creatures, straight out of a H.G. Wells movie.

Inhabitants of the Landes, Jean Louis Gintrac (1800-1850)

The peloton and I soldiered on along the infinite straight roads, where the horizon never seemed to get any closer. I could imagine the peloton, laughing and joking with each other, sticking together to keep their spirits up. However, it wasn't long before this changed, and a series of punctures near to the town of Hostens, caused the peloton, that had been together for so long, to break up. There were 146km to go. Jules Nempon was the first to suffer a series of punctures and he dropped back all alone. Then, it was the turn of Félix Goethals and Honoré Barthélémy, who both punctured. To make matters worse, it was raining again and thunder and lightning lit up the dark grey skies, just visible over the tops of the pine trees.

*

As if to give me a sense of the atmosphere and weather conditions the 1919 Tour riders experienced, I too, could see storm clouds gathering out in the Bay of Biscay to the west of me. I needed to get to my campsite quickly and set up before the forecasted storms arrived later that evening.

*

After 20 hours in the saddle, the peloton flowed down the steep hill, entering Bayonne from the Côte de Moulin Neuf, to the north of the town. With the train station on their right, they crossed the long Pont Saint Esprit that arched over the River L'Ardour and soon they were in sight of the finish line at the Brasserie Schmidt, (now the Café du Theatre) on the Place de la Liberté. The sun broke through to dry up the roads, giving the enthusiastic crowd the chance to see a decent sprint finish. As the trumpets sounded there were now ten remaining riders crossing the river. Once again, Jean Alavoine found some extra energy from somewhere to break from the bunch and win by a length from René Chassot, closely followed by Scieur, Vandaele, Coomans, Verstraeten, Lucotti, Christophe, Masson and Lambot. It was Gar Jean's second consecutive stage win. An admirable feat given the conditions. As in the Tour de France today, the stage winner could not escape the press, who descended on him before he could even catch his breath.

"Yes, I don't want to make you suffer, I will give the obligatory interview. After all, I want to commit to come and see you every day if it means that I'm going to win all the remaining stages. In any case I'm fine! I am as well as I can be after five tough stages and I think I'll do well in the Pyrénées. Today, apart from during the night, which wasn't much fun with the fog, everything went well for me and I was lucky not to have any punctures. I was only happy, when at last, I was done with pedalling as if I was in a box of cotton wool! With this salute, I will entrust my legs to 'Pano' (Panozetti was his elegant masseur)

Emile Masson (The Unknown) had done well to finish in the final sprint as he got his musette (food bag) stuck in his chain, on the approach to Bayonne. This gallant effort meant that, given Henri Pélissier's withdrawal at the start of the stage, Henri Desgrange's favourite for the Tour had now jumped up to second place in the G.C. Others were not so lucky, Paul Duboc had a fall and several punctures in the last 50km and Louis Mottiat and Honore Barthélémy had some bad luck in the Landes Forest. It was not clear what had happened, but maybe they'd seen some of the locals walking around on stilts and shit themselves!

All the riders were weary and covered from head to toe in mud and after the bad weather and long distances they had covered, nobody could tell them apart. The ten that had arrived all wore the same grey jerseys issued by La Sportive and the thick mud helped to conceal their identities. Alphonse Baugé whispered to Henri Desgrange,

"See for yourself, Henri, people are trying to pick out the race leader. But there's no way of picking him out. It's odd. The rider in first place should have a special jersey."

"How could we go about that?" replied Desgrange.

"'What about a jersey that's yellow in colour like your newspaper L'Auto?'

"You're right. Let's do it, order some yellow jerseys for me immediately" came the reply.

Then and now: 'Brasserie Schmidt, Place de la Liberté, Bayonne

Stage 5: Sables D'Olonne – Bayonne (482km)

1. Jean Alavoine	in 18h 54m 7s
2. René Chassot	at a length.
3. Léon Scieur	at a length.
4. Joseph Vandaele	at a length.
5. Jacques Coomans	at a length.
6. Alois Verstraeten	at a length.
7. Luigi Lucotti	at a length
8. Eugéne Christophe	in 18h 54m 20s
9. Emile Masson	at a length.
10. Firmin Lambot	at a length.
11. Alfred Steux	in 19h 05m 39s
12. Paul Duboc	in 19h 09m 28s
13. Jules Masselis	in 19h 20m 39s
14. Louis Mottiat	in 19h 48m 43s
15. Honoré Barthélémy	in 20h 35m 37s
16. Félix Goethals	in 20h 35m 37s
17. Jules Nempon	in 21h 54m 15s

General Classement (G.C.)

1. E. Christophe	(The Old Gaul)	83h 27m 48s
2. E. Masson	(The Unknown)	83h 45m 39s
3. F. Lambot	(The Saddler)	84h 15m 37s
4. J. Alavoine	(Gars Jean)	84h 19m 48s
5. A. Steux	(The Kid)	84h 48m 32s
6. L. Scieur	(Locomotive)	85h 59m 36s
7. J. Masselis		86h 31m 45s
8. H. Barthélémy	(Glass Eye)	87h 28m 47s
9. F. Gœthals	(The Sock Seller)	87h 35m 01s
10. J. Coomans	(The Smoker)	87h 52m 52s
11. J. Vandaele	(Waterloo)	89h 20m 03s
12. R. Chassot	(Cheeky Monkey)	89h 51m 31s
13. L. Lucotti	(The Italian Job)	91h 34m 43s
14. L. Mottiat	(The Man of Iron)	92h 02m 53s
15. J. Nempon	(The Upstart)	94h 22m 10s
16. P. Duboc	(The Apple)	94h 41m 29s
17. A.Verstraeten	**(Lanterne R)**	**94h 53m 52s**

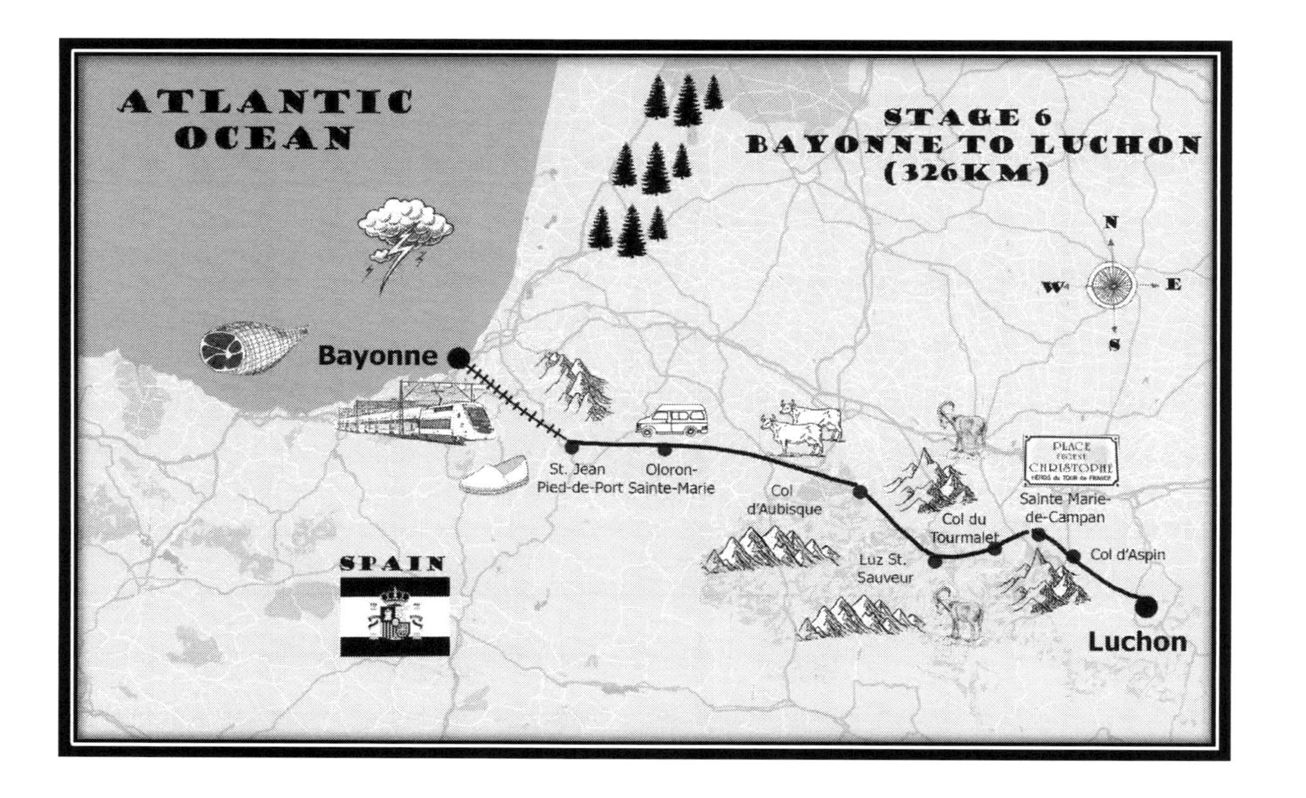
ATLANTIC
OCEAN
STAGE 6
BAYONNE TO LUCHON
(326KM)
N
W
E
S
Bayonne
St. Jean
Pied-de-Port
Oloron-
Sainte-Marie
Col
d'Aubisque
Luz St.
Sauveur
Col du
Tourmalet
Sainte Marie-
de-Campan
Col d'Aspin
Luchon
PLACE
CHRISTOPHE
SPAIN

Chapter 10: Climb every Mountain

Stage 6: Wednesday 9th July 1919 (Bayonne- Luchon) Tuesday 9th July 2019 (Bayonne–Oloron-Sainte-Marie)

Who needs television? I certainly don't!

I'd arrived at my campsite at Capbreton the previous night, and had managed to get set up under the pine trees, before any prospective thunderstorms came my way. What I didn't realise was that a human whirlwind was about to hit me, before the meteorological storms came in. This storm took on the form of a French family of three in a tiny camper-van. Within two minutes of arrival, the father came over to ask me if he could share my 'embranchement électrique' as his connection wasn't working and it would save him a long trip back to reception. "Bien sur", I replied, trying to be helpful.

Whilst he was hooking up his van, his two teenage children, brother and sister, emerged looking thoroughly pissed off. They brought out a young excitable dog that had obviously been going stir crazy for a number of hours, and was now running around like a 'chien-lunatique' (a brilliant 'Beware of the Dog' sign, I had once seen on a French garden gate). Meanwhile the siblings started emptying the van of all its contents, setting up a plastic table and covering it with packets of cheap crisps and one litre bottles of fizzy drinks. They tied the dog's lead to the leg of the plastic table, and of course the dog proceeded to drag the table all around the campsite, scattering the contents that were on top of it. The father eventually emerged. He was in holiday mode and had removed his T-shirt to display his magnificent pot belly which must have taken a few years and a few bottles of Stella Artois to cultivate. I thought this was all a bit odd given imminent storms were forecast.

Within seconds of sitting down to munch on the spread of 'e-numbers' that were laid out before them, they were arguing. The father clipped his daughter around the ear and shouted "Tu me respecte!" The brother came to the aid of his sister and the dog, not wanting to feel left out, went ballistic. Brilliant!

The children were ordered off and headed for a walk around the campsite. The father, unwisely decided to let the dog off the lead so it could have a wander around and let off some steam. This was bad luck for an elderly French lady who was taking her tiny chihuahua for its nightly stroll and toilet rituals. They had just come within striking distance of our pitch, when the chien-lunatique decided to go on the attack for its supper. Clouds of dust rose into the air from the gravel path, and the lady trying to protect her beloved dog from being devoured, twisted and fell to the ground.

Well by now the whole site was alerted and numerous well-meaning campers appeared and came to her aid. Someone sent out a call from their mobile phone. Monsieur Pot Belly was most apologetic and brought a wobbly plastic chair out for her to sit on as she was obviously in some discomfort. The wind picked up and it started to rain. Other campers brought some umbrellas out to shelter the old lady and looked at Monsieur Pot Belly as if he had a large sign saying 'Dickhead' on his forehead. His daughter, having returned, looked completely embarrassed by the whole event and after a heated exchange of words with her father she stormed off into the woods.

By now it was getting dark and the wind and rain were getting stronger when a large red van with flashing lights turned up with the words 'Vehicle de Secours et Assistance aux Victimes' written down the side. It seemed a bit over an overkill when six yellow helmeted firefighters came to the aid of the little old lady and her chihuahua still sat on her plastic chair. Well, I suppose I could have helped, I hear you say, but I think there was enough assistance available and anyway, what a great evening's entertainment, far better than any episode of Eastenders or Casualty!

During the night the storm really took hold and I was woken around 2 a.m. to cracks of thunder and flashes of intense lightning. I lay in the dark and thought of the following day's stage through the mountains of the Pyrénées and realised that, at this exact moment, the 17 remaining riders were already signed in at the Brasserie Schmidt and had walked to the official start, in front of the old Bayonne-Anglet-Biarritz (B.A.B.) train station (which no longer exists) on the Allées Paulmy, in readiness for the signal to head for the mountains. Robert Desmarets gave them the final call. A pistol was fired and the riders headed off with shouts of 'Vive Desgrange' ringing in their ears.

Today's mountain stage is one of the cruellest stages in the Tour de France. Introduced in 1910, by Henri Desgrange's right hand man Alphonse Steines it was mooted as an idea to 'pep' up the Tour. The riders were coping too easily with the small passes that had previously been made through the Alps. Alphonse was sent out on a mission into the Pyrénées to investigate whether the roads over the mountains could actually be used. Apparently, when he got there, he found the roads completely impassable and covered in snow. He proceeded to get lost, and had to pass the night in a hut on the Col d'Aubisque with a group of local miners, before he could descend from the mountain in the morning. When asked by Henri Desgrange whether the Tour could actually be staged over the Pyrénées, he replied that everything was fine, and the Col du Tourmalet was quite feasible, even for an average cyclist.

In 1910, Octave Lapize was the first cyclist to reach the highest point in that year's race, the Col du Tourmalet, and he is famous for shouting 'Vous êtes des assassins, oui, des assassins' (You are murderers, yes, murderers) at the L'Auto officials as he pushed his bike wearily over the summit.

*

So in 1919, Stage 6 would be 326km in length and feature seven brutal climbs, the Col d'Oschquis (582m), the Col d'Aubisque (1,748m), the Col de Tortes (1,650m), the Col du Soulor (1,550m), the Col du Tourmalet (2,122m), the Col d'Aspin (1,497m) and the Col de Peyresourde (1,545m) on, what can only be described as stony tracks. Some of these roads were not even recognised on the national network, as they were intended for farmers driving animals across the mountain ranges, or for foresters to pull timber down to the sawmills in the valley.

*

To give some idea of what these riders were about to attempt on 'fixed wheel' bikes, it is interesting to compare this stage with the 2019 Stage 14 featuring the Col du Tourmalet. Tarbes to Tourmalet-Bareges measures a mere 117.5km in length and features two climbs, first the Col du Soulour, followed by a tactical race up to the finish line, on the summit of the Col du Tourmalet. So, a third of the distance and a third of the number of climbs. No comparison at all really!

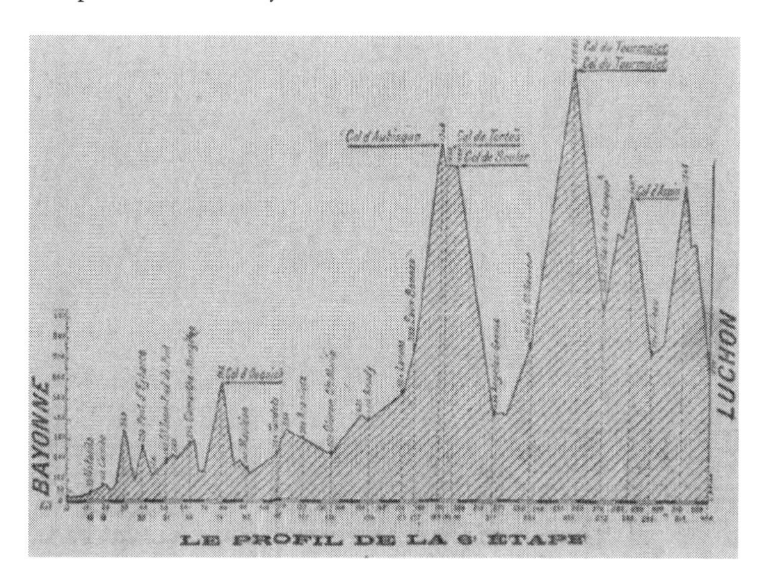

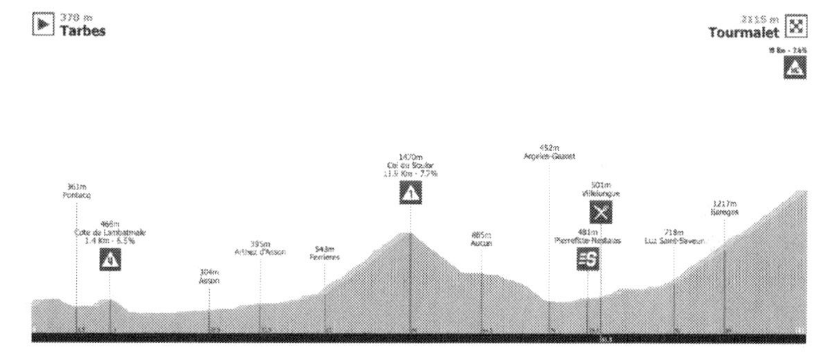

The 17 riders had already been told to ensure their brakes were well tested and fit for purpose for the mountains. On top of this L'Auto also gave them the following advice,

'Competitors are invited to be cautious on all the roads in the mountains. There will be a number of horses, mules, donkeys, oxen, cows, calves, goats, sheep and pigs, walking freely out along the route. We particularly call for the riders to pay attention on the long descents and the winding passes, which are narrow and sometimes in a bad condition. Some of these passes are cut from deep channels in the rocks, and the soil is crumbly and falls into the gullies. The descents will become dangerous for any rider who is careless. They will often run between rock walls on the mountain side and a low man-made wall, separating the road from the edge of the precipice. Some bends are tight and abrupt and can be hidden by trees. The utmost caution is recommended, not only to the riders, but also, to all the car drivers which follow the race. It is also quite common to encounter on these paths unforeseen problems, such as wood timber convoys whose movement is slow. In this case, it is wise for cyclists to put their feet to the ground, and for the cars to stop and even switch off their engine, in order not to scare the animals, which are not used to being disturbed.

SHIT!!!!!!!!!!!!!!!

*

As I stood on the platform at the Gare de Bayonne, the rain continued to fall heavily. It was a cold and misty morning but at least the previous night's thunderstorms had cleared. I was waiting for the midday SNCF train, to St.-Jean-Pied-de-Port, which followed the first section of the 1919 route of Stage 6. My fellow passengers were a mixture of tourists, young families and hikers. The latter were catching the train to St.-Jean-Pied-de-Port, as this is the gateway through the Pyrénées, for the famous catholic pilgrimage (Santiago de Compostela), to the tomb of one of the holy apostles, buried in the cathedral of Saint Jacques de Compostelle in Galicia, north-west Spain.

I had been delayed by the overnight deluge. I'd had to clean and remove a mixture of pine-cone debris and storm water, from the pop-up section of my camper-van. Consequently, I'd missed the earlier 8 a.m. train and this was the next one available, as there were only four trains per day. As I'd left the campsite in Capbreton, I'd seen Monsieur Pot Belly taking his teenage children on a route march through the damp and mist into the nearby town. I had a feeling he was going to have another stressful day on his hands.

The train eased through the outskirts of Bayonne, and soon we were in open countryside, heading along a lush valley, crisscrossed with a network of dykes and reed-beds. I realised that for the first time in a long while, I was leaving the French coast and heading inland in an easterly direction. It seemed strange not to have the sea, at my side, as my constant companion. The River Nive flowed to the right of the train, parallel to the 1919 route. Meanwhile the Pyrénées-Bas could be made out a long way off in the distance. At Cambo-les-Bains, the route passed the grand Villa Amarga, home to the playwright Edmond Rostand who brought the story of Cyrano de Bergerac to the theatrical stage. Next, the train passed under a road bridge and the 1919 route was suddenly on the left-hand side of the train and close to the tracks. As I looked out of the rain splattered train window, I could imagine the riders struggling along the narrow lanes, in total darkness, as the gradient of the road gradually increased. Suddenly, the valley narrowed and the mountain scenery seemed to close in, as the road and river came ever closer. You could see the transmitter on top of Mount Baygoura (Baigura), in the distance, which at 897m above sea level, is the highest point of the Lower Pyrénées. The local houses were in the style of Swiss chalets, with white painted walls and red shuttered windows, crowned by a long sloping roof as a protection against the snow. The surrounding countryside had a feel of the Yorkshire Dales about it.

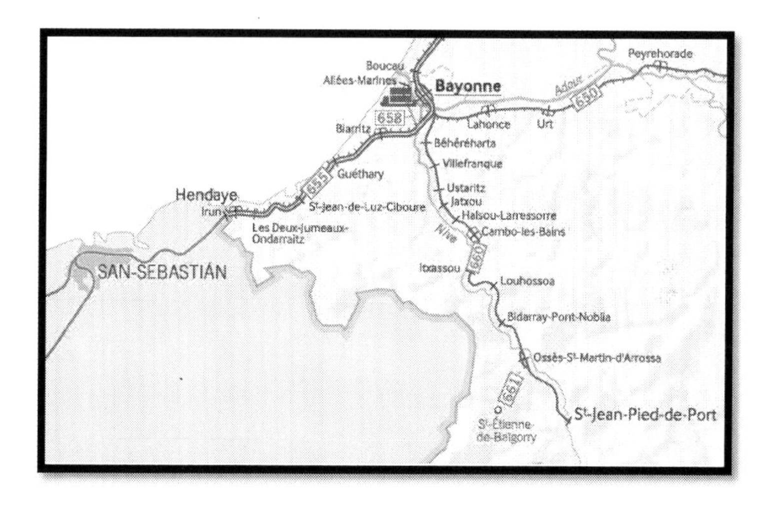

At the Pont d'Eyharce, before the level crossing, I spotted 'Don Quichosse', an espadrille factory. Espadrilles were created in this area of south-west France and northern Spain, and were typical peasant footwear in the 14th century, made out of a canvas upper and a seamed rope sole. Mind you, I couldn't see many of my fellow passengers wearing them as they headed for a hike in the local mountains.

Soon the train was pulling into its final destination in the old town of Saint-Jean-Pied-de-Port. 'Pied de Port' means 'Foot of the Pass' in Pyrenean French, and has already been mentioned, it is the gateway from France into Spain, the border being only 8km away. It's a quaint old town with a skyline dominated by its ancient fortress. From here, narrow-cobbled streets run downhill through the 15th century town gates, the Porte St-Jacques and the Porte d'Espagne and over two ancient bridges crossing the River Nive. From the bridges, there are fine views of the old town houses whose balconies overhang the river. Many of the buildings are built of pink and grey sandstone (schist), and retain many distinctive features, including unusual inscriptions over their doors. One, a bakery called 'André Fiterie' lists the varying prices of wheat that were paid in 1789.

Unfortunately, I didn't have time to linger as I needed to return directly to Bayonne to pick up my camper-van. I re-joined the train, and the passengers had changed from mountain hikers to afternoon shoppers, heading into the city for a bit of shopping and maybe to pick up a cured Bayonne ham.

I now had to catch up with the 1919 riders who had passed through Saint-Jean-Pied-de-Port altogether at 4.37 a.m. as it was getting light. It was just as well that dawn was breaking as they were about to face their first test of the day, the Col d'Osquich, which at 582m high and an average ascent of 5.2%, was a mere warm up for what was to come.

*

By 6 a.m. they had reached the town of Mauléon-Licharre, where they received some bad news. René Chassot, who had been the life and soul of the party, had a terrible fall and had broken his collarbone. Exactly where this fall had taken place, it is not clear, but the doctor advised him that there was no point of him signing in at the control, his race was over.

At 7.52 a.m. the peloton arrived at the refuelling station in front of the Hôtel de la Poste in Oloron-Sainte-Marie. Jules Masselis was the first to sign in out of the group of 15 riders who had arrived together. Only Félix Goethals had been dropped and he was only 3 minutes behind.

*

I also stopped for refreshments and pulled into an Intermarché to stock up on supplies. Henri Desgrange would not have been impressed with me though. After the disrupted sleep in the storms last night, and after driving and cycling 2,200km in ten days, I pulled over and fell asleep in the supermarket car park, with my seat belt still on!

Stage 6 – Thursday 10th July 1919 (Rest Day)
Wednesday 10th July 2019 (Oloron-Sainte-Marie - Luchon)

I pulled up the blinds of my camper-van to be greeted by the dawn of another beautiful day and a stunning view. In the distance, I could see a range of imposing mountains. My campsite was on the edge of the Pyrénées National Park and I was about to embark on the toughest section of my journey so far. My plan for the early morning cycle was to take a circular route close to the two torrential rivers that flow into Oloron-Sainte-Marie; the Gave d'Ossau and then return by the Gave d'Aspe.

Then and now : Feeding station, Hôtel de la Poste – Oloron-Sainte-Marie.

I started at the 1919 refuelling point in Oloron-Sainte-Marie, the Hôtel de la Poste in the Place de Resistance, and crossed the flower laden bridge of the Gave d'Ossau. A sharp turn took me up the steep Rue de Biscondau, and out of town. Two old women stood chatting together, arms folded, on their front doorsteps. They looked me up and down and seemed to be critically appraising my slow progress. It was still early in the morning and the town was beginning to awaken. Soon I'd reached the summit and I looked back to see an impressive view over the valley, towards the Église de Notre Dame. I was now out into open countryside and following the Route des Crêtes, which I hoped meant something other than the obvious translation. As I hit the main road a panoramic view opened up and there they were.

The forbidding sight of the 'Haute-Pyrénées' mountains to come.

Over in the distance I could see the mountains through which, both I and the 16 remaining riders, would travel. I wondered what was going through their minds as they approached these imposing mountains. It was a form of Chinese water torture as gradually minute by minute the road took them nearer and nearer and the mountains loomed larger and larger. For myself, I was in my element, marvelling at the pastoral view. The sun was beginning to rise and the cold chill of the day was starting to fade. Farmers and sons were busy working in the fields, amongst mountains of cow dung, and firing up their tractors ready for the day's work ahead. I could hear birds singing in the nearby woods. I saw blue jays flitting from branch to branch and grass warblers dancing and catching flies in the morning sunshine. A bit further on I saw a dead bird on the roadside. I stopped and saw it was a beautiful nuthatch. Such a waste of such a rare bird. Soon I was passing through local Pyrenean villages such as Soeix, Eysus, and then in Lurbe-Sainte-Christau, I came to an abrupt halt. Out of a side road came two lumbering bulls followed by their harem of lady friends (Blondes d'Aquitaine) and the farmer. The leading bull gave me a look as if to say "This is our road, buddy, we come this way every day. You can sit and wait". So, I did.

Traffic jam - Lurbe-Sainte-Christau, Lower Pyrénées.

On the way back to Oloron-Sainte-Marie. I passed numerous signs, pointing the way to white water rafting clubs, which were obviously good business along this stretch of river. By now, groups of cyclists were heading out for their morning ride and I took some satisfaction from the fact that I had probably already completed their route. I crossed the Gave d'Aspe at Bidos and saw a sign outside a hairdresser saying 'Fanny, Coiffure Esthetique' and thought 'Perhaps not today!' As I arrived back in the narrow lanes of the town, I caught the smell of hot chocolate, wafting through the open shuttered windows, a sign that the children's breakfast was being served. I would eat my breakfast of croissants en-route, as I needed to head for them thar' hills!

The town of Laruns is situated at the foot of the Col d'Aubisque and is the entrance to a large Tour de France cycling theme park. The local train station is adorned with large images of the four race jerseys, yellow, green, polka-dot and white and a poster reading 'Tour de France 2018 - Lourdes to Laruns'. The town had been a ville d'ètape for Stage 19 of the 2018 Tour, and as such it was the last mountain stage, prior to a team time trial, and the processional finish in Paris. That day, Team Sky did a professional job on protecting their man in yellow, Geraint Thomas, shepherding him over the Col du Tourmalet and the Col d'Aubisque, enabling him to finish second into Laruns, all but confirming the Welshman's first Tour de France triumph. Again, this Pyrenean stage had been critical in deciding the Tour de France winner.

In the centre of the town numerous lycra-clad cyclists were limbering up by the pavement cafés that circled the ornate water fountain at the heart of the square. This was the starting point for the Col d'Aubisque challenge, a 1,200m climb over 18km, at an average ascent of 7%.

*

The 1919 riders would have approached Laruns in trepidation. It may have even given them a dose of La Runs! They knew that over the next two demanding stages the Tour could be won or lost. Eugéne Christophe's strategy was damage limitation. He knew that the younger climbers could steal some time from him, but he hoped his experience of tackling this mountain stage would give him enough advantage, so as to not concede too much time to his rivals. It must be remembered that the remaining 16 riders had already been in the saddle for nearly seven and a half hours to complete the 170km through the Lower Pyrénées. It was only 9.35 a.m. when they hit the first town on the climb, Eaux-Bonnes (Good Waters), perched on the side of a mountain 'S' bend. As you enter the town square you can't fail to notice 'La Bulle', a massive modern glass bubble that sits on top of the old thermal baths, giving the impression that R2D2 from Star Wars has crashed landed into the building.

It was here, at the control, that the 12 leading riders stopped to flip their back wheels over to the other cog to obtain a lower gear ratio to tackle the mountains. However, Luigi Lucotti and Léon Scieur thought differently and saw an opportunity to get ahead of their rivals. They decided not to swap their wheels over and sped off up the mountain. However, the gradient of this section of the route changed suddenly from around 8% to a lung wrenching 13%

and it wasn't long before Jean Alavoine and Louis Mottiat caught up with them. Would this tactical decision come back to haunt the 'Italian Job' and the rider known as 'The Locomotive'?

The first section of the route clings to the mountain side, as the riders hug the sharp rocks on their left, climbing out of their saddles, straining to complete each bend. To their right, they could see glimpses of the up-coming mountain peaks through the towering pine trees strung out along the roads edge.

Driving in this area is treacherous. Today, small groups of cyclists, largely cycling clubs, are taking on the mountain challenge, and as the road twists and turns, they dominate the road on both sides as they either wind their way slowly up the mountain, or fly down on the opposite side. Overtaking can only be made on certain straight sections of the road and any move has to be made quickly and decisively. Certain sections of the road are protected from rockfalls by overhanging cantilever concrete roofs and tunnels.

*

Soon the 1919 riders reached the hamlet of Gourette at the base of the next ascent. Originally, it consisted of a number of hovels, lived in by miners, that worked the local zinc mines. It was here, with these miners, that Alphonse p had sought refuge from the constant snowfall, on his exploratory mission of the Pyrénées in 1910. Well, Gourette was no longer a small mining town, as the popular pastime of skiing has transformed it into a mixture of large functional block hotels, bars, restaurants and shops selling and renting all types of ski wear.

From here, the ascent to the summit varies from between 8 and 16%, and Luigi Lucotti knew he would have to be at his best if he was going to gain any advantage from his tactic not to stop and change his gear. He would not have been encouraged by L'Auto reporting that during large snow-melts, parts of the road could disappear down the mountain! I pulled over in the car park of the Hôtel Les Crêtes Blanches, that appeared to be hanging on the precipice overlooking the valley. I made sure the handbrake of the van was pulled full on as I wandered over to look back down the mountain at the, by now, tiny LEGO ski resort of Gourette. From here to the summit, the scenery transforms into open mountain prairie and I passed a few cyclists struggling with the final few kilometres to the top. Even though the ascent was flattening out, each pedal turn was excruciatingly painful, after the effort of what had gone before.

The signpost declaring that you have reached the Col d'AUBISQUE at 1,748m above sea level is illegible and covered in a mosaic of Moto-Bike stickers; proof that different bike clubs had managed to reach the top. I could see only one sticker representing cyclists, whose achievements in reaching the summit, were something more to be admired. The modest cyclists seemed to be content to take selfies in front of three giant steel cycles (painted green, yellow and polka-dot) on the summit, or in front of the statue of Lucien Buysse who, although he abandoned after Stage 1 of the 1919 tour, went on to win the Tour de France in 1926, after a legendary victory over the Col d'Aubisque.

The summit of the Col d'Aubisque - 1748m above sea level.

Luigi Lucotti was the first to sign the control at the summit, and as such became the first Italian to lead a peloton over a mountain pass. It was an incredible effort by the Italian in the lower gear. He was closely followed by Jean Alavoine fifty seconds later and two great climbers, Honoré Barthélémy and Firmin Lambot, came in only three minutes further behind. The first 'hors-categorie' mountain was complete, just three to go!

Henri Desgrange was not one to give the riders much comfort as he reported that the descent from a 'col' could be as tough as the climb. Apparently, a one-kilometre section of the descent from the Col d'Aubisque, was only 3 metres wide, and at its peak it overlooked a precipice where the soil had collapsed and was only held back by a fragile wall.

Luigi Lucotti : the first Italian to lead the peloton over a mountain pass, Col d'Aubisque, Stage 6, 1919.

This was a new experience for me as well and it was with a sense of trepidation that I set off down the mountainside in my camper-van. I could see the narrow limestone ledge of the Cirque de LiTour which I had to drive along and I felt like an intruder, getting in the way of the cyclists hurtling, at the same speed as me, down to the valley floor. Soon a flock of sheep appeared, reminding us all who the road really belonged to, as they wandered slowly across our path and skipped down the mountainside. Also, high in the deep blue sky, I could see some black eagles soaring on the winds, searching for some prey. I could imagine an Englishman, served in a tin van, would probably do for starters.

As I approached the Col du Soulor, I was reminded of the 2019 Tour de France, currently in progress. At the roadside, I came across a sign, warning that the road from the Col du Soulor to Argelès-Gazost would be closed on the 20th July, in eleven days' time as Stage 14 Tarbes to Tourmalet-Bareges joined the 1919 route for the 19km climb to the summit of the famous Col du Tourmalet (The Distance Mountain).

Roadblock warning signs for the 2019 Tour about to arrive in 11 days' time and the torrent that is the River Bastan flowing through Luz-Saint-Sauveur.

Before attempting the climb, I pulled into the town of Luz-Saint-Sauveur for a commercial break. After the cool and light cloud of the mountains, the heat of the midday sun in the valley hit me, as I parked opposite a van advertising bike hire. On the rear doors was a photographic depiction of the winding, snaking route that I was about to follow. The other thing that struck me, as I climbed out of my van, was the intense noise generated by the River Bastan, as it crashed down from the mountains and flowed over the river bed of rocks and boulders and under the bridges connecting the town.

The journey up to the summit of the Distance Mountain is a joy to behold as looking back you can see a silvery snake, twisting and turning on itself, all the way down the mountain. I arrived at the summit and there it was. The impressive silver statue, which towers above you, depicts the cyclist Octave Lapize, straining up the mountain to cross it for the first time in 1910. If you listen carefully you can hear him shouting 'You are murderers, yes murderers' at the watching officials.

I stopped and took a peek in the obligatory souvenir shop and contemplated whether to buy a Col du Tourmalet T-shirt, an edelweiss table mat or a Marmot (an oversized mountain squirrel) shaped rucksack. As I did so I tried to imagine the 1919 riders struggling up these rocky tracks on fixed wheel bikes. The effort required was phenomenal and I know that, because of the terrible conditions of the roads, they had to push their bikes up certain sections of the route. In fact, when they got to the top of the Tourmalet, they were greeted by two walls of snow, which were so thick, they had not melted in the midday sunshine.

Statue of Octave Lapize – Col du Tourmalet

Honoré Barthélémy (Glass Eye), the great climber was the first to arrive, all alone at the summit of the Distance Mountain. There is a great photo of both himself and Firmin Lambot toiling up the dirt track of the Tourmalet. They both look identical in their cloth racing caps and their standard issue thick woollen jumpers. You can see how difficult it would have been for the spectators to tell them apart. I believe it is actually Lambot who is leading Barthélémy at this point. Both have a number of rubber inner tubes wound around their neck and shoulders, as well as the ones tied under their saddles in case of emergency. On top of this a canvas musette (food bag) is slung over their shoulders, showing how restrictive their cycling action would have been. Firmin Lambot (The Saddler) arrived at the summit in second place, and was now some ten minutes behind Honoré, showing the Parisian's prowess as a climber.

Luigi Lucotti (The Italian Job) arrived in third place a full 16 minutes behind the leader. His tactics of not changing gear hadn't worked and he was now beginning to tire from his earlier efforts. Luigi was followed two minutes later by Jean Alavoine. (Gars Jean).

Firmin Lambot (The Saddler) leads Honoré Barthélémy (Glass Eye) up the Col du Tourmalet on stage 6, 1919. The crowds are slightly different from those that will be seen in 2019.

The race leader Eugéne Christophe (the Old Gaul) was worried about not losing too much of his current lead in the mountains. His key rivals were Emile Masson (+18 mins), Firmin Lambot (+48 mins) and Jean Alavoine (+52 mins). At the top of the Tourmalet he'd lost 16 minutes to Lambot and 8 minutes to Alavoine. So far, so good for Eugéne's tactic of damage limitation and now there were just two more mountain climbs to go.

Next up was the Col d'Aspin, an area of the Pyrénées which brought back some painful memories for the Old Gaul. It was on this stage in 1913 that he had forced himself into first position, ahead of Odile Defraye, and he was now heading to the Col du Tourmalet to try and extend his lead. At Sainte-Marie-de-Campan it all went horribly wrong. I'll let Eugéne Christophe take up the story.

"I plunged full speed towards the valley. According to Henri Desgrange's calculation, I was leading the general classification by 18 minutes. All of a sudden, about ten kilometres from Sainte-Marie-de-Campan down in the valley, I felt that something was wrong with my handlebars. I could not steer my bike any more. I pulled on my brakes and I stopped. I could see my forks were broken. Well, I tell you now that my forks were broken, but I wouldn't say it at the time because it was bad publicity for my sponsor. And there I was left alone on the road. When I say the road, I should say the path. All the riders I had dropped during the climb soon caught me up. I was weeping with anger. I remember I heard my friend Petit-Breton shouting as he saw me, 'Ah, Cri-Cri, poor old lad.' I was getting angry. As I walked down, I was looking for a short cut. I thought maybe one of those pack trails would lead me straight to Sainte-Marie-de-Campan. But I was weeping so badly that I couldn't see anything. With my bike on my shoulder, I walked for more than ten kilometres. On arriving in the village at Sainte-Marie-de-Campan, I met a young girl who led me to the blacksmith on the other side of the village. His name was Monsieur Lecomte."

It took two hours to reach the forge. Lecomte offered to weld the broken forks back together but a race official and the managers of the rival teams would not allow it. The rules stated that a rider was responsible for his own repairs and any outside assistance was prohibited. Christophe set about the repairs as Lecomte told him what to do. It took three hours, and the race judge penalised him 10 minutes, later reduced to three, because Christophe had allowed a seven-year-old boy, Corni, to pump the bellows for him. Filling his pockets with bread, Christophe set off over two more mountains and eventually finished the Tour in Paris, in seventh place.

The memorial to Eugéne Christophe, and Cri-Cri repairs his forks at the forge at Sainte-Marie-de-Campan, 1913.

*

I stopped to admire the statue and plaque on the side of the forge, which had been laid to commemorate the episode. I was surprised to find that I was the only one paying homage to this giant of French cycling. There were plenty of people around, but they were either zooming past on their bikes, or heading to eat in the local restaurants.

*

The Gods were with Eugéne this time and he reached the plateau on the summit of the Col d'Aspin (1,497m) in fifth position. He was two minutes ahead of his nearest rival and Henri Desgrange's favourite, Emile Masson (The Unknown), who had been second in G.C. at the end of Stage 5. Even better still he'd only lost a further 4 minutes to his other two main G.C. rivals, Firmin Lambot (The Saddler) and Jean Alavoine (Gars Jean). So, all was looking good for the Old Gaul, as he headed into the final climb over the Col du Peyresourde (1,545m).

*

After the severity of what had gone before the Col du Peyresourde was like crossing the surface of the moon. The summit today is practically anonymous. There is a sign post indicating that you have reached an altitude of 1,569m, (an extra 24m higher than in 1919) on a wide section of road near a large wooden shack, which serves a delicious crêpe covered in regional honey.

*

Things weren't going quite so well for Henri Desgrange's favourite, Emile Masson, as it was on this section that he crashed, damaging his front wheel.

Bagnères-du-Luchon, to give its full name, was decked out with flags and banners to welcome the riders. It was as if the town was having a party to celebrate a national festival. It was around 5.30 p.m. in the evening when the official cars arrived, announcing that Honoré Barthélémy was still out in front and due shortly. The noise of the crowd increased as 'Glass Eye' came down the Main Street leading to the 'Allées d'Etigny' and the finish line in front of the thermal baths and the casino. It was 5.41 p.m. The crowd had to wait a further 20 minutes before they could cheer Firmin Lambot (The Saddler) into the finish and then a further quarter of an hour before Jean Alavoine (Gars Jean) arrived in the third place. The front three were followed shortly afterwards by Luigi Lucotti (The

Italian Job), who looked shattered after his earlier heroics. Then it was the turn of the Old Gaul, Eugéne Christophe, who was relieved to still be at the head of the G.C. after completing this arduous stage. He'd lost 19 minutes to Firmin Lambot but only four to Jean Alavoine and he'd actually gained 14 minutes on the unfortunate Emile Masson, who now dropped to third in the G.C., after losing time cycling with a bent wheel.

Thermal baths at Bagnères-du-Luchon. The building looks the same today.

After signing in at the Central Café, the exhausted riders were pleased to find out that the thermal baths had opened their doors for them to have a deep hot soak and they were able to wash out the stresses and strains of the mountains. Not only this but there was a little surprise in store for them when they returned to their hotel. 'La maison de Cinzano' had left a sample of their well-known vermouth in each rider's bedroom. Sleep well chaps, only another six mountains to climb tomorrow.

Stage 6: Bayonne -Bagnères du Luchon (326km)

1. Honoré Barthélémy	in 15h 41m 51s
2. Firmin Lambot	in 16h 00m 28s
3. Jean Alavoine	in 16h 15m 28s
4. Luigi Lucotti	in 16h 17m 31s
5. Eugéne Christophe	in 16h 19m 54s
6. Léon Scieur	in 16h 19m 59s
7. Jules Masselis	in 16h 29m 26s
8. Emile Masson	in 16h 33m 17s
9. Louis Mottiat	in 17h 10m 32s
10. Paul Duboc	in 17h 26m 15s
11. Jules Nempon	at a length
12. Jacques Coomans	in 17h 46m 30s
13. Joseph Vandaele	at a length
14. Félix Goethals	in 17h 59m 37s
15. Alfred Steux	in 19h 30m 40s
16. Alois Verstraeten	in 21h 05m 28s

General Classement (G.C.)

1. E. Christophe	(The Old Gaul)	99h 47m 42s
2. F. Lambot	(The Saddler)	100h 16m 05s
3. E. Masson	(The Unknown)	100h 16m 50s
4. J. Alavoine	(Gars Jean)	100h 35m 16s
5. L. Scieur	(The Locomotive)	102h 19m 35s
6. J. Masselis		103h 01m 11s
7. H. Barthélémy	(Glass Eye)	103h 10m 38s
8. A. Steux	(The Kid)	104h 19m 12s
9. F. Gœthals	(The Sock Seller)	105h 34m 38s
10. J. Coomans	(The Smoker)	105h 39m 22s
11. J. Vandaele	(Facing his Waterloo)	107h 06m 33s
12. L. Lucotti	(The Italian Job)	107h 53m 14s
13. L. Mottiat	(The Man of Iron)	109h 13m 25s
14. J. Nempon	(The Upstart)	111h 48m 25s
15. P. Duboc	(The Apple)	112h 07m 44s
16. A. Verstraeten	(Lanterne Rouge)	115h 59m 20s

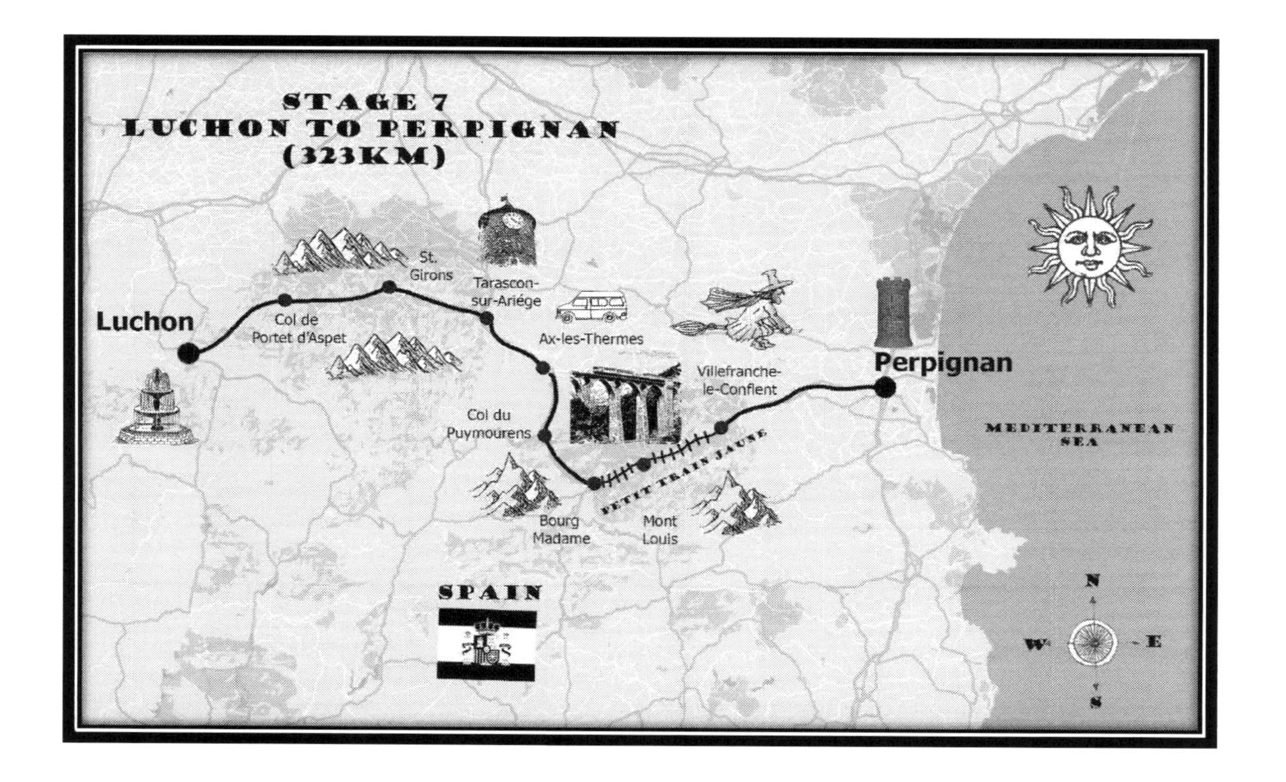
STAGE 7
LUCHON TO PERPIGNAN
(323KM)
Luchon
Col de Portet d'Aspet
St. Girons
Tarascon-sur-Ariége
Ax-les-Thermes
Col du Puymourens
Bourg Madame
Mont Louis
PETIT TRAIN JAUNE
Villefranche-le-Conflent
Perpignan
MEDITERRANEAN SEA
SPAIN
N
W
E
S

Chapter 11 – 'Ford every stream'

Stage 7 – Friday 11th July 1919 (Luchon - Perpignan)
Thursday 11th July 2019 (Luchon – Ax-les-Thermes)

Just as in 1919, the townsfolk of Bagnères-de-Luchon (Luchon), were preparing themselves for the visit of Stage 12 of the 2019 Tour de France in a week's time. The 210km route, from Toulouse to Bagnères-de-Bigorre, was due to pass through the town the following Thursday (18th July) afternoon around 3 p.m. Although not a ville d'étape this year, the people of Luchon were pretty accustomed to the 'Grande Boucle' starting and finishing in their town, as it has now been used 59 times since the Tour's inception in 1903. In fact, Luchon is the fourth most used town in the history of the Tour de France after Paris (141), Bordeaux (80) and Pau (70). The 2019 banners were already in place, hanging from the street-lamps and flag posts around the town. I walked up the tree lined 'Allées D'Etigny' looking for the start point of Stage 7 at the Central Café. The old café and hotel are long gone, but I found the location, and although it was now a bakers and chocolatiers, the scene didn't look that different from the one the 16 riders would have viewed, when signing the control sheet in 1919.

Then and now : The Central Café in Luchon is now a bakery and chocolatier.

I popped into a 'Bar Tabac' to buy a copy of the daily sports paper L'Équipe and the front page was blazoned with yellow. The French had a new cycling hero to cheer, in the shape of Julian Alaphilippe, who since winning Stage 3 from Binche to Epernay, had remained in the yellow jersey going into today's Stage 6 from Mulhouse to the infamous Vosges mountain finish, at the ski station of 'La Planche des Belles Filles'. The 2019 Tour had already caught up with the 1919 Tour in terms of the number of stages completed, as it was running every day. However, it had only completed 817km versus the 2,377km of the 1919 Tour so was still 1,560km behind.

L'Èquipe is today's reincarnation of L'Auto. Following Henri Desgrange's death in 1940, the paper had been run by a consortium of Germans during World War II, and published articles that showed sympathy to the Nazis. After the end of the war in 1945, Jacques Goddet became editor and organiser of the Tour de France. He was the son of Victor Goddet, the original Financial Director, who had okayed the funds for the original 1903 Tour. The French Government allowed Jacques to run the paper from some offices, opposite L'Auto's on the Rue Faubourg in Paris, on condition that he changed the paper's name and the colour of the paper from the current yellow to white.

As usual, Robert Desmarets had fired the gun for the start of Stage 7 outside the Central Café at 2 a.m. I too, was early as I wanted to avoid a repeat of last night's fiasco when I had nearly been locked out of my campsite. Given the fact that I had crossed the seven cols of the Hautes-Pyrénées with our intrepid riders, I arrived at my pre-booked campsite a few minutes after 7 p.m. I jumped out my van, only to find the reception closed and the barrier firmly down. What was I to do? I'd noticed that the other sites in the town all looked full, and I suppose people were arriving for the big festival at the weekend 'Le Quatorze Juillet', 'la Fête Nationale' or Bastille Day as we know it. I started to panic. The only solution was to enter the site and see if I could find someone still working. I found a wooden cabin where a chef appeared to be preparing some pizzas. I explained my predicament and asked if there was anyone around who could help. He smiled and said 'Bien sur, c'est l'heure d'aperitif!' Apparently, the owners had invited all the campers on the site to a large marquee for an aperitif and some 'hors d'oeuvres' prior to settling down for the night. I felt rather embarrassed at interrupting their social event but soon I had been checked in and was downing a cold glass of the local wine with them, thinking 'I could get used to this'.

I lay in bed that night, going over what I had accomplished in the last two days, since leaving the train station in Bayonne. I pictured the incredible views I witnessed on each of the summits I had crossed. I thought about my train journey to Saint-Jean-Pied-de-Port and my cycle through the Lower Pyrénées at Oloron-Sainte-Marie and marvelled at the fact that the 16 remaining riders had accomplished all of this in one day. I wondered what was going through the mind of Eugéne Christophe (the Old Gaul) at the top of G.C. as he embarked on this second mountain stage through the 'Pyrénées-Orientales' to Perpignan on the Mediterranean coast. He would have been reasonably happy to know Henri Desgrange's favourite for the Tour, Emile Masson (The Unknown) had lost time, due to his bent wheel, but he would have been wary of the threat of Firmin Lambot (The Saddler). If Eugéne lost a similar amount of time to him today, as he did on Stage 6, he would be close to losing the leadership of the race. Today's stage, was on paper, slightly less challenging. Henri Desgrange called it a mini

Bayonne-Luchon. However, given the efforts that had been exerted in the previous stage, the Col des Ares (at 839m), the Col de Portet d'Aspet (at 1,074m), the Col de Port (at 1,249m), the Col de Puymaurens (at 1,931m), the Col de Rigat (at 1,622m) and the Col de la Perche (at 1,579m) should not be underestimated. Also, on studying my route map, I spotted that there was a Courtel de Bastard, and noted that Mont Louis was also known as Pic Bastard, so there was no doubt a very good reason for this.

Ironically, the first 20km of this stage is downhill as you approach the mountain ranges on the D125 out of Luchon. Then it's an immediate right turn off the main road at the Pont de Chaum, and once you have passed through the tiny village of Antichan des Frotignes you are at the foot of the first climb, the Col des Ares. After taking the first sharp bend outside the village, you are treated to a magnificent panoramic view, stretching down the valley, back to Luchon. Then as you tackle the Col des Ares, you suddenly find yourself in a channel of pine trees all the way to the top. There is an occasional break in the trees on some bends, where a few trees have been felled for wood, but other than that there is not much to disturb your concentration as you grind your way to the summit. You only realise you are near the summit when you come across a sports-adventure business, and you notice the green sign, indicating 'Col des Ares 797m'

There is a bar at the summit, but there was no time for a drink's break for our 16 riders as they head off for Col number two, the Col de Portet d'Aspet. Not long after the tiny hamlet of Henne-Morte, you are reminded of how dangerous these roads can be, as at the base of the climb, there is a memorial to the Italian rider, Fabio Casartelli. Killed on the descent of the Col de Portet d'Aspet on Stage 15 of the 1995 Tour de France, the youngster was involved in a crash with a few other riders. Unfortunately, the un-helmeted Fabio hit his head on the concrete blocks on the side of the road, knocking him unconscious. With considerable bleeding from his forehead, he was airlifted by helicopter to the nearest hospital at Tarbes, where he unfortunately died 30 minutes after arrival. Later, a doctor concluded that his death had resulted from a brain haemorrhage, and that the wearing of a hard helmet could have significantly have reduced the injuries he sustained. This incident changed the riders view on the wearing of cycle helmets whilst racing, and they became mandatory in 2003.

I arrived on the summit, to be greeted by a pastoral scene, and stopped to take a photo of the altitude sign, which at 1,069 metres was some 5 metres lower than the 1919 measurement. Obviously, a sign of global erosion! Two young cyclists were sitting and chatting on the picnic tables under the shade of two trees. Fully resplendent in their red Cofodis shirts, helmet and cycling shoes. I said 'Bonjour' as I passed and I got a reply in an unusual French accent. It could have been an accent from the south of France, but I thought it was more probably from the north. To be more precise it was the north, the north of England, Yorkshire. It turns out the two lads were on holiday for a couple of weeks and were taking on a few of the climbs before watching the Tour pass through in a few days' time. We talked about the Tour de France, and the impact it had on the county of Yorkshire, after they had hosted the first two stages in 2014. I had watched it with some friends, camping near Muker in Wensleydale. We cycled part of Stage 1 and loved the way the Yorkshire towns and villages had embraced the spirit of the Tour. In Skipton, the local school children had taken part in painting competitions, depicting their own visions of the race that was about to arrive.

We saw bicycles in shop windows painted completely in yellow, from tyre to saddle, plus a dummy yellow cyclist sat in a yellow wheelbarrow. In the countryside we passed fields of sheep brightly painted in yellow, green and even pink polka dots. Perhaps the crowning glory was watching the peloton come up the steep climb over Buttertubs on Stage 1, when a gentleman arrived, dressed in a blue striped Breton jumper plus French beret, with a string of Yorkshire puddings around his neck instead of onions. Brilliant! We all agreed that Yorkshire had done the country proud in hosting the Tour and the Tour de Yorkshire is now a permanent fixture on the cycling calendar. We said our goodbyes and the two lads headed off down the valley.

*

For the 1919 riders, it was getting light as Jean Alavoine (Gars Jean) came over the 'Col' with the Belgian Jules Masselis on his wheel, closely followed by the rest of the peloton. Again, they had stuck to the principle of remaining together in a group whilst cycling in the dark. By the time they reached the feeding station in the town of Saint Girons on the valley floor it was 5.45 a.m. and things had changed. A new leading group emerged, comprising the Licence 'B' rider Jules Nempon (The Upstart), Jean Alavoine (Gars Jean) and Firmin Lambot (The Saddler). They had an advantage of two minutes over the main group, containing Eugéne Christophe (Old Gaul), Léon Scieur (The Locomotive), Honoré Barthélémy (Glass Eye), Louis Mottiat (The Man of Iron), Félix Goethals (The Sock Seller) and Jacques Coomans (The Smoker). The other seven filed in a few minutes later.

Eugéne Christophe is relieved to descend the Col de Port. Stage 7, 1919

Also, the 1919 weather had changed, and after the miserable conditions of the first six stages the riders were now facing the burning heat of the south-west sun. No doubt they would have made sure that they took on plenty of liquid at the control, and ensured their bidons were topped up for the remaining mountain challenges. At the bottom of Col number three, the Col de Port, there was confusion as everybody stopped to change gear. The young climber Barthélémy and the Old Gaul Christophe sprinted off together in an effort to catch the front three. As we know Eugéne couldn't afford to let them get too far ahead and damage limitation was still his tactic. Soon the youngster, Honoré Barthélémy (Glass Eye) started to power ahead from Christophe (Old Gaul), climbing the mountain as if he was on the flat. At the summit, he was 3m 12s behind the front three, and 1m 10s ahead of Christophe. The peloton had now fractured and Emile Masson (The Unknown) and Louis Mottiat (The Man of Iron) arrived together at + 5m 13s, but the other riders came in alone, Jacques Coomans (The Smoker) at + 5m 25s, Léon Scieur (The Locomotive) at + 6m 50s, Félix Goethals (The Sock Seller) at + 11m 35s, Paul Duboc (The Apple) at + 12m 00s, Jules Masselis at + 12m 45s and Joseph Vandaele (Facing his Waterloo) + 15m 18s. Next up was the Col du Puymaurens which at an altitude of 1,931m, and with a gradient of 8% over 10km, was the toughest peak of the day. Could this be the stage in the Pyrénées that decides the race winner, as is so often the case in the Tour de France?

*

The answer would have to wait until tomorrow. I needed to head down the valley to my overnight stop at Ax-les-Thermes, the last feeding station and halfway point of the stage. On the way down the valley, I passed more signs indicating the arrival of the 2019 Tour de France in a few days' time. At Tarascon-sur-Ariège there were road blocks in place in readiness for Stage 15, Limoux to Foix. The 2019 cyclists would pass under the watchful eye of the Tour de Castella, a watchtower overlooking the town from the top of a rocky crag. Here, there would be a sprint section, where the top riders would be trying to earn some points towards the green jersey.

That evening I cycled into Ax-Les-Thermes to try and find the location of the 1919 feeding station in front of the Hôtel Villa Rose Marguerite. I followed the route, past the train station and along the l'Avenue Theophile-Delcasse to arrive in front of the casino and the Place du Breilh. Whilst the casino looked the same as it would have done in 1919, the Place du Breilh was unrecognisable. There were a few old buildings left around, what was now effectively a roundabout, and the old church and the Hospital Saint-Louis remained. However, most of the other buildings had been replaced by modern equivalents and the nearest I could find to the hotel was the 'Villa Marguerite', an apartment for two people available on booking.com. I pictured the five leading riders, Honoré Barthélémy, Jean Alavoine, Firmin Lambot, Jules Nempon and Eugéne Christophe signing the control sheet at 9.04 a.m. L'Auto noted that, whilst the riders looked as 'fresh as blossoms', they were complaining about the amount of dust they were experiencing coming up from the mountain tracks. The stop at the feeding station gave them an opportunity to wash the dust off their faces, wipe their racing goggles and double-check their bidons were full, as this was the last chance for them to take on the liquids required to see them through the next 152km to the finish.

My visit to Ax-les-Thermes would not be complete without a visit to the 'Bassin des Ladres' (the Lepers Pond) in front of the Hospital Saint-Louis. I bet there were a few of the cyclists who would have loved to have soaked their feet in the hot thermal waters, particularly at a temperature of 25 degrees celsius. Whether any of them had a touch of leprosy was anybody's guess!

Stage 7 – Saturday 12th July 1919 (Day of rest)
Friday 12th July 2019 (Ax-les-Thermes - Perpignan)

Ding- Dong – Ding-Dong!! The chimes of the bells of L'église Saint-Vincent in Ax-les-Thermes, ring out incessantly each hour from dawn. This was good news for me as I needed to be up early as I had a busy day ahead. I crept around the campsite not wishing to awaken the young families and a group of Dutch cyclists who had pitched up next to me during the evening. I'd had a brief chat with the men in orange, and they told me of a beautiful cycle along the mountain floor in the Vallee d'Orlu. This sounded good to me so I headed to the bathroom to do my ablutions and hit the road. The facilities in the campsite were clean, but full of large insects and spectacular moths attracted by the fluorescent night lights. This was fine, when standing up to wash and clean one's teeth, but rather disconcerting when sitting down to do what nature intended.

At Ax-Les-Thermes, the River Ariège is fed by two similar sounding tributaries, l'Ariege and l'Oriège. My route took me up alongside the l'Oriège and it was a sheer delight for cyclists. A few kilometres out of the town, the babbling stream turns into the 'Lac de Campauleil', which captures the ice-cold mountain water, before it rushes down through the rocks to feed the modern spa baths. On the other side of the lake is the pretty hamlet of Orgeix, followed by a steep climb to the village of Orlu. Here, you are at the foot of the mountain range, and you can hear the almighty din of a waterfall crashing down the mountainside, feeding a tiny EDF

Hydroelectricity plant, built to capture its energy. Opposite the plant I was surprised to discover 'La maison des Loups', a wolf sanctuary, dedicated to showing off these wild mountain animals in their natural habitat. Soon the road petered out into a hiking mountain track and I could go no further. It was time for me to head back to my campsite and pick up my camper-van. I had a train to catch.

My first task was to tackle the Col du Puymaurens (1,931m), now spelt Col du Puymorens (1,915m), which even with a reduction of one letter of the alphabet and 16m of altitude, was going to be no less daunting a challenge. The start of the ascent of the Col du Puymorens is at L'Hospitalet, (or L'Hospitalet-près-l'Andorre to give it it's full name) a town which conjured up images in my mind of a pure, pristine village, nestling quaintly on the side of the mountain, it's church bells ringing out proudly along the valley. The reality is far removed from my quaint image, as the town serves as an important transport route from France into the nearby principality of Andorra, and as such, is bisected by the N20 autoroute and the TER Midi-Pyrénées railway line. In fact, this railway was in the process of being built as the 1919 riders passed L'Hospitalet, and they were warned that due to the railway's construction, some of the road may have been moved. A great start to the climb!

The hospital sounding part of the name could well be due to the number of serious avalanches which have occurred here over the years. These avalanches had caused consistent roadblocks during severe weather and the French have now built a five-kilometre tunnel, under the Col du Puymorens, to keep the traffic moving. You'll be glad to know that I ignored the temptation to take the quick and safe route through the Tunnel du Puymorens, and followed the 1919 riders over the mountain, saving €13.70 into the bargain.

*

The mountains of the Pyrénées-Orientales are wilder and more barren in comparison to those of the Haute-Pyrénées climbed on the previous stage. Luckily for the riders there were no major headwinds to contend with, as they fought their way up the 'Col' in bright sunshine. The first section is the steepest, and for 1.5km it rises at a gradient of 7.7% and then it drops to a steady 5% for the remaining 8km to the top. Unfortunately, this section started to take its toll on the young Licence 'B' rider Jules Nempon. The Young Upstart from the lowlands of Calais had ridden an incredible race so far, keeping up with the four 'Aces' of the Tour for 186km. He was now starting to tire and drop back from the field. By the time he'd gone over the top of the Col du Puymorens, he was in joint seventh position and 16 minutes behind the leaders. Jean Alavoine, Firmin Lambot, Eugéne Christophe and Honoré Barthélémy having passed together, at 11.38 a.m. Given the good weather, the crowds had come out in force and were strung out all over the mountain roads, down to the control point at Bourg-Madame. Here the news broke that Louis Mottiat (The Man of Iron) had gone rusty and abandoned sick at Saillagouse, 10 km from Bourg-Madame. There were now only 15 riders left.

*

Bloody Hell, I'm late for my train!

After driving around the mountain village of Font Romeu (one of the oldest ski stations in France) for ten minutes, the only other station I could locate was the bus station. Starting to panic, I decided to ditch the Satnav and use the Chat-nav instead, and ask somebody for directions. To my surprise I discovered the train station was over two miles away. The full name of the town was Font-Romeu-Odeillo-Via, and it consisted of three villages, and the train station was located outside the furthest village. I arrived at the ticket office in a mild state of panic because if I missed the 11.06 a.m. train, the next departure was not until 3.40 p.m., and my day would be ruined. When I was doing the planning for the 1919 route, I checked to see if there were any unmissable train journeys that I could incorporate into my itinerary. I was excited to discover that one of the most beautiful train journeys in the world covered part of the final section of Stage 7. 'Le Petit Train Jaune' (the Little Yellow Train of the Pyrénées), built in 1909, takes over three hours to complete the 63km journey from Latour-de-Carol, high in the mountains in the west to Villefranche-de-Conflet, at the bottom of the valley in the east. I was catching the train at its highest point at Font Romeu, as there was no way I could have arrived in time to catch the 8.28 a.m. train from Latour-de-Carol.

Given the paucity of trains that cover the route, the queue for tickets stretched to the door. I tuned into the conversations of the tourists in front of me, and was discerned to find that they were asking for information on the train service and the local area. Didn't they realise the train was about to go in ten minutes? I started to break out into the uncomfortable sweat of a traveller seeing his best laid plans going up in smoke. To make matters worse, the SNCF staff seemed fairly relaxed about a whole line of customers missing the train. When I eventually got in front of the glass ticket booth, I realised why. The train on the platform was the original 8.28 a.m. from LaTour that should have left an hour ago. It had broken down in the station and would now be departing in fifteen minutes time. I felt relieved in one sense, i.e. I was going to catch my train on time, but on the other hand, I was also a bit apprehensive about hurtling down Mont Louis (Pic Bastard), a drop of over 1,000m in altitude, in a knackered train.

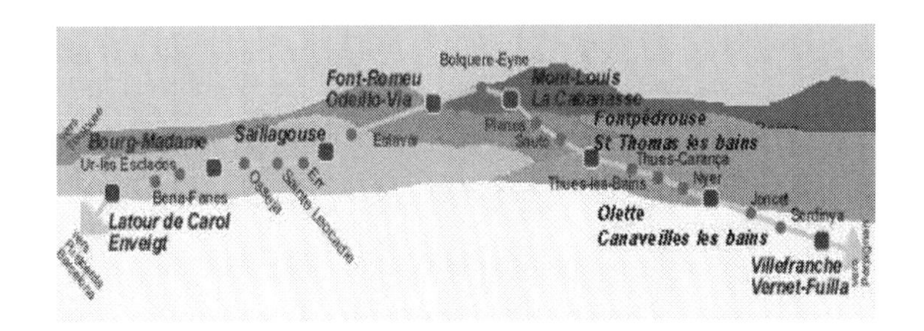

As the train set off across the prairie of the high mountain slopes, the morning stress disappeared. The sun was blazing down on the open meadows of the Pyrénées-Orientales as butterflies danced on top of fragile yellow orchids, bright blue gentians, delicate pink lilies and white spiky asphodels. It wasn't long before we reached the highest train station in France. At 1,592m above sea level in Bolquere-Eyne, we stopped to drop off some intrepid hikers and started the descent. This was like stepping onto the Big Thunder Mountain rollercoaster at Disneyland Paris. Soon we were hugging the steep sides of the deep valley of the River Tet, winding between forests, chasms and gushing streams. The mountainous scenery included many tiny villages, two historic fortresses, and a precariously perched hermitage. The line, begun in 1903, is a spectacular feat of civil engineering, and apart from the dozens of short tunnels, it includes many bridges and a series of large and small viaducts, such as the remarkable Pont Gisclard and the Pont de Cassagne, which is the only railway suspension bridge in France.

Shortly after starting the descent, we passed the halt at Fontpedrouse. Here the leading four 1919 riders, Honoré Barthélémy, Jean Alavoine, Eugéne Christophe and Firmin Lambot stopped to flip their back wheels over to select the correct gear for the descent. Conveniently, there was a mountain spring by the side of the road where they all quenched their thirst, washed the mountain dust from their faces, refilled their bidons and set off. That's all except Honoré Barthélémy, who had punctured at the wrong moment, and couldn't find his pump. It had dropped off somewhere en route and he had to borrow or buy one. Eugéne Christophe must have been smiling inwardly to himself, as he was well in touch with his rivals, and he just needed to ensure he didn't bump into the Green-Toothed Witch, as he negotiated the sharp bends of the descent, to the control in Prades.

*

As we hurtled down the mountain, in our yellow missile, we ran parallel to the cycle route, and I could imagine the Old Gaul, slipping and sliding around the sharp bends, tightly gripping his brakes, avoiding any potholes, punctures and fatal crashes. On one particularly sharp bend with a steep drop down to the valley, a young man suddenly appeared in front of us and climbed over the crash barrier. It was a rock climber! I laughed and thought the sight of a rock climber, suddenly appearing at the side of the 1919 route, would have scared the shit out of the peloton. My companions on Le Petit Train Jaune, jumped up and down, pointing cameras and iPhones at each stupendous mountain view that revealed itself, as we exited numerous dark rocky tunnels, or crossed stunning suspension bridges, on the way down to the medieval town of Villefranche-de-Conflent. Everybody was having the time of their lives, except for one family 'Les Misfits'. Monsieur Misfit was a rather rotund gentleman, sporting a pork pie hat, which didn't fit his head, an Hawaiian shirt which didn't extend around his ample torso, a pair of shorts that shouldn't have been allowed out in public, all topped off with the worst fashion mistake in mankind, sandals and socks. Opposite him was his spoilt teenage daughter, who didn't want to acknowledge that she was part of this dysfunctional family, and stared at her iPhone for the whole journey, only occasionally lifting her head to look at the stunning scenery that was flashing by. In contrast to her father, she was trying to be a catwalk fashionista, wearing the hip brand labels of the day. She wore a Fred Perry polo top plus l'Olympique Marseille football joggers, topped and tailed with an American baseball cap and a pair of Le Coq Sportif trainers. Her state-of-the-art fluorescent iPhone was, of course, kept in her Gucci mini handbag, slung carelessly over her shoulder. Absolutely ridiculous! Monsieur Misfit was trying to point out the wonders that were passing her by, as unimpressed she tried to shelter from the strong sunlight, and murmured 'Ca tombe bien, je suis malade' – Good timing, I feel sick! His long-suffering wife, looking rakish in her flowing floral dress and straw panama hat, was trying to hold the family outing together and read stories to the younger female sibling, who was dressed from head to foot in pink. It was with a sense of relief that 'Les Misfits' disembarked, not only to myself, but to the rest of the fellow travellers in my compartment, as Monsieur Misfit's belly button was now on show, bursting out from his untucked shirt.

We'd arrived in the UNESCO World Heritage site of Villefranche-de-Conflent and there was just time to visit the narrow streets and ramparts of this fortified town. Built in 1374, Villefranche had its defences strengthened in 1707, to protect the inhabitants from invasion from the nearby Spaniards. I resisted the temptation to buy a miniature witch from one of the numerous craft shops. Legend has it that the toy sorceress would keep me happy on my route.

"In a remote past where magic and sorcery still prevailed, witches lived in the caves of Conflent where they would spend winter. As winter came to an end they would get on their brooms and come out of the caves to celebrate the arrival of spring with Villefranche's villagers. This brought the villagers happiness, cheerfulness and prosperity for the rest of the year. It is Catalan tradition to offer a close relative, or child, a witch as a sign of friendship. The witch is hung in the house, or in the child's bedroom, to keep bad spirits away and create space for happiness."

Maybe the Old Gaul, Eugéne Christophe had purchased such an enchantress to ward off the Green-Toothed Witch, as he was still in joint lead with Jean Alavoine as they reached the final control point in Prades at 1.37p.m., just a minute in front of Firmin

Lambot. The danger and risk of a disaster in the Pyrénées was over now, as the three riders (Lambot had caught up) headed into Perpignan, past the old prison of the Castillet, to the finish on the treelined 'Allées des Platanes'.

There was only going to be one winner of this stage. Gars Jean, won the sprint and pipped The Old Gaul and The Saddler by a length, ensuring his third stage victory of the Tour. Three wins out of seven stages. Not bad, eh? The band of the 63rd Infantry burst into life, and Eugéne Christophe allowed himself a wry smile, as he knew he had successfully protected his 28-minute lead at the head of the G.C. As the couriers escorted the riders to the 'sign in' at the splendid Café du Palmarium (the palm tree Café) he knew he'd gained 10 minutes on Honoré Barthélémy, and more importantly 25 minutes on Henri's favourite Emile Masson. With the strain and tension of the Pyrénées behind him, he could relax (?) and look forward to the next 370km stage to Marseille! He might even allow himself a glass of the local aperitif Quinquina, known throughout France as 'Taking a Trilles' (Prenéz un Trilles). Quinquina was created by none another than Albert Trilles who it turned out was in charge of organising the reception of today's stage.

CHEERS ALBERT!

Then and now: 'Les Allées des Platanes' – Stage 7 Finish, Perpignan

Stage 7 : Luchon – Perpignan (323km)

1. Jean Alavoine	in 13h 12m 43s
2. Eugéne Christophe	at a length
3. Firmin Lambot	at a length.
4. Honoré Barthélémy	in 13h 22m 56s
5. Emile Masson	in 13h 37m 18s
6. Léon Scieur	at a length
7. Paul Duboc	at a length.
8. Jules Nempon	at a length
9. Jules Masselis	in 14h 33m 45s
10. Jacques Coomans	in 14h 33m 46s
11. Félix Goethals	in 14h 48m 59s
12. Joseph Vandaele	in 15h 16m 47s
13. Luigi Lucotti	in 15h 39m 53s
14. Alfred Steux	in 15h 48m 25s
15. Alois Verstraeten	in 16h 35m 52s

General Classement (G.C.)

1. E. Christophe	(Old Gaul)	113h 00m 25s
2. F. Lambot	(The Saddler)	113h 28m 48s
3. J. Alavoine	(Gars Jean)	113h 47m 59s
4. E. Masson	(Unknown)	113h 54m 24s
5. L. Scieur	(Locomotive)	115h 56m 53s
6. H. Barthélémy	(Glass Eye)	116h 00m 34s
7. J. Masselis		117h 34m 56s
8. A. Steux	(The Kid)	120h 07m 37s
9. J. Coomans	(The Smoker)	120h 13m 08s
10. F. Gœthals	(Sock Seller)	120h 23m 37s
11. J. Vandaele	(Waterloo)	122h 23m 20s
12. L. Lucotti	(Italian Job)	123h 33m 07s
13. J. Nempon	(The Upstart)	125h 20m 43s
14. P. Duboc	(The Apple)	125h 45m 02s
15. A. Verstraeten	**(Licence B)**	**132h 35m 12s**

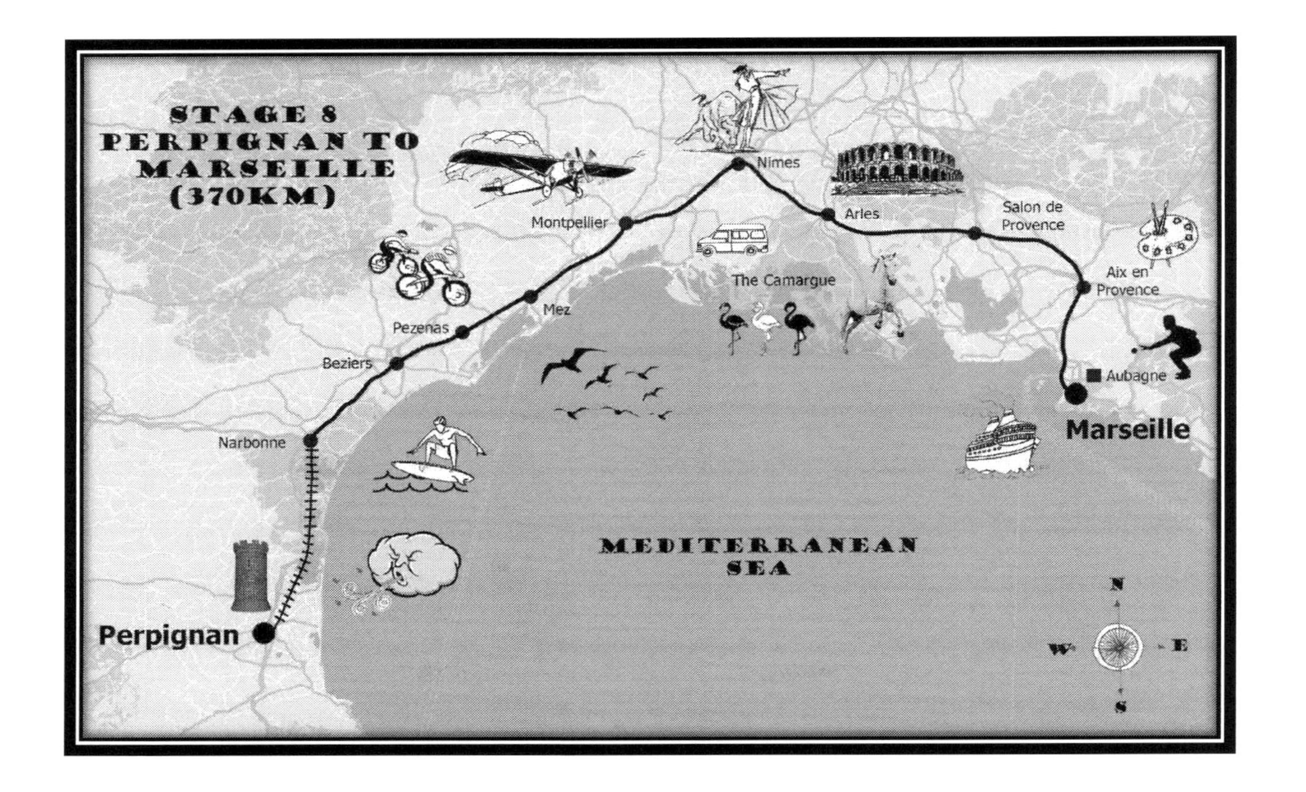
STAGE 8
PERPIGNAN TO
MARSEILLE
(370KM)
Nimes
Montpellier
Arles
Salon de Provence
Aix en Provence
The Camargue
Mez
Pezenas
Beziers
Aubagne
Marseille
Narbonne
MEDITERRANEAN SEA
N
W
E
S
Perpignan

Chapter 12 : 'Guilty or Not Guilty?'

Stage 8: Sunday 13th July 1919 (Perpignan - Marseille)
Saturday 13th July 2019 (Perpignan – Montpellier)

'READ ALL ABOUT IT, READ ALL ABOUT IT!!'
(The Verstraeten case)

In this morning's edition of L'Auto, the readers woke up to the following news,

'In Luchon, some people have discovered that Verstraeten, has caught the train between several points, whilst cycling Stage 2 in Normandy. Needless to say, this is news to us, and if we had known, or if we had the evidence, we would have immediately sent him back to Paris. We are checking the control sheets of the second stage, and when this verification is complete, we will question the offending rider!'

Alois Verstraeten, the Belgian Licence 'B' rider and current 'lanterne rouge', would have been unaware of these accusations, as he had signed the control sheets in the Café Palmarium in Perpignan, and set off with the other 14 riders at 2 a.m. before the newspaper hit the streets. There is of course nothing unusual in hearing accusations being made against a rider in the Tour de France. Ever since the first race set off from the café 'Au Reveil Matin' in 1903, riders have been finding ways to try and cheat the system, and bend the rules to their advantage.

In only the second edition of the Tour in 1904 the top four finishers of the race were disqualified. Maurice Garin, who was the winner of the inaugural Tour in 1903, was found guilty of putting his bike on a train, and alighting near to the finish line. Hippolyte Aucouturier, another top French rider, was spotted taking a tow from a car. Astoundingly, this was achieved by means of a length of string attached to a cork that he gripped between his teeth. He would have gotten away with it, but the car pulling him drove too fast, and Aucouturier reached the end of the stage just minutes after the race officials, who were also riding by car.

Different forms of cheating have existed throughout the life of the Tour de France. In 1947, Jean Robic won the first Tour to be held after the Second World War. Jean was a diminutive man measuring only 1.6m in height and weighing only 59 kilos. He holds the title to this day, but it was later found out that Robic's team had used an ingenious tactic, throughout his career, to ensure his 'petite' stature didn't serve as a disadvantage. Every time Robic reached the summit of a mountain his crew would hand him a water bottle. It was assumed he needed hydration following a difficult climb, but in reality, there was no water in the bottle. Typically, it would be filled with mercury or lead, designed to increase Robic's weight in the ensuing downhill section. Once he completed the section, he would jettison the bottle and continue to race. This tactic was adopted by other riders, and soon the practice of weighted bottles became commonplace in cycling.

I suppose the most obvious form of cheating is the use of performance enhancing drugs, or consuming alcohol, and this too was commonplace in the early days of the Tour. Riders such as Maurice Garin would openly drink litres of red wine or coffee mixed with champagne. Amazingly it took until the 1960s for alcohol to be banned in the race.

When Henri Pélissier won the Tour in 1923 he was quoted as saying '"You have no idea what the Tour is. It's purgatory. We suffer on the road. Do you want to see how we keep going?" From his bag he pulled out various items and explained. "There, that's cocaine for our eyes and chloroform for our gums. And pills? You want to see pills? In short, we run on dynamite."

Henri Desgrange would have been livid that there was another potential discretion that could cast a shadow over his 'La Vie au Plein Air' (Life in the Open Air). He'd nearly abandoned the idea of the Tour de France, after the misdemeanours of 1904, vowing that the race would not be staged again. Luckily for us, and the millions of avid fans that follow his Tour, he acquiesced.

Whilst there was a storm brewing in the press, there was also a real storm brewing out in the race, as the 1919 riders set off in the moonlight from Perpignan. Once they got out onto the salt plains of Old Catalonia, they were immediately confronted by a violent crosswind, blowing off the Mediterranean Sea. This restricted the riders to an average pace of only 20km an hour, which meant that dawn was just breaking when they reached Narbonne. A number of riders were suffering badly after their exploits in the previous two mountain stages. In fact, the Pyrénées had put paid to three 'pair-of-knees' and Jules Masselis, Alfred Steux and Emile Masson were all complaining of severe pains in their joints, as they pulled into the control.

Also, at Narbonne we found out more about the investigation into Alois Verstraeten. Whilst it seems that maybe he had not taken the train in the Le Havre-Cherbourg stage, the race Commissioner Monsieur Lucien Cazalis, believed that he was towed for more than two kilometres by a motorcyclist.

'The Child of Flanders will learn when he arrives in Montpellier that he must take the train back to Paris.'

*

At Narbonne we had reached the halfway stage of the Tour de France 1919, having completed 2,765km out of 5,560km and there were now only 14 riders (plus myself) left to face the second half of the Tour. I'd spent the previous night at a campsite in Nefiach around 22km east of Perpignan. The heat of the late afternoon sun was still intense when I'd arrived and checked-in. Then I remembered I was still only a few kilometres north of the Spanish border. Fortunately, my spot for the night was under the shade of some dense trees. The campsite is advertised as 'un camping familial' and it is exactly that and everybody seemed to know everybody else. Within minutes of arriving I was chatting with my next-door neighbour from Vannes, who coincidentally was interested in my van, and asked to look around inside. He was also interested in the Leicester City sticker in the side window. It seemed that the Foxes Premier League victory in 2015-16, against all the odds (5,000-1), had touched the hearts of football fans from all over Europe. I wandered down to the restaurant and found the place in party mood. Apparently, it was a 'pizza and cocktails' night and the party was already in full swing. Whilst the adults were consuming their first aperitifs of the evening, the children were attempting to rock-climb an artificial mountain, erected in front of the café. After various attempts, some more successful than others, the alcohol started to take affect and soon there were a few macho 'On y va's' as the dads started to compete to see who could get the highest. This was great entertainment, as I sat and watched and waited for my pizza 'Quatre Fromages' and a half bottle of the local Languedoc wine. As soon as my plate arrived a plague of flies and mozzies swarmed around me. The only way I could eat my meal, was to cover it with a serviette, and try and extract sections of the pizza, directly from the plate into my mouth. Meanwhile, the conquest of L'Everest was reaching new heights, or rather not reaching new heights, as the campsite cocktails were starting to kick in and cloud the judgement of even the most ardent mountaineering father. Soon there were a few semi-inebriated dads spinning around 'Mount Plastic' on their safety harnesses, like a swing-chair ride at the local fairground. I managed to get halfway through my bottle of wine before two flies managed to drown themselves, trying to swim two widths of my glass of chilled Corbières. Soon, it was time to drag myself away from 'Les Jeux Olympiques', as I had another early start in the morning.

The sun lifted its sparkling head, way out in the Mediterranean Sea, illuminating the hunched shoulders of the mountains of the Pyrénées-Orientales, now far off in the distance to the west. I cycled alongside the River Tet, travelling east towards the city of Perpignan, 10km from the coast. My aim was to find the starting point of Stage 8, in front of the majestic Café du Palmarium near the 'Allées des Platanes'. Initially I wasn't sure of the exact location as the only reference I could find stating 'Platanes' was the 'Pharmacie des Platanes' on Boulevard Wilson. There was a 'Brocante' (Vintage market) setting up across the road, and it soon became clear, as I walked down the avenue of trees, amongst the traders, that this was indeed the correct location of the finish line of Stage 7. In the centre of the alley is the splendid Fontaine de Perpignan, around which some acrobats were practising their routines, in readiness for the Bastille Day celebrations, due to begin in front of the former city gate 'Le Castillet' that evening. I asked the resting acrobats if they knew the location of the Café du Palmarium, and they told me to follow the nearby canal for a few hundred metres. I was amazed to find the building still existed but disappointed to find it now played host to the Perpignan Tourist Office, 'La Roma' pizzeria and the Hippopotamus steakhouse.

The majestic Café du Palmarium in Perpignan, the starting point of Stage 8. Given the day, maybe it should have been called Palm Sunday.

Today's plan was to follow the 1919 route by train from Perpignan to Montpellier. I realised, that for the first time in over two weeks, I would actually be travelling north. North towards the South of France, which felt a bit strange. When I studied the route map, I was fascinated to see that the SNCF train line actually passed through the centre of some of the 'etangs' (large coastal lakes) which had been converted into salt pans or salterns. In certain sections it looked as if the train was actually crossing the sea. I arrived at very modern-looking Perpignan station to be greeted by a tannoy announcing my train had been delayed by 20 minutes due to an 'incident étranger'. I sat down next to an elderly lady, who was trying to cope with her enormous suitcase. Whilst it was about the same size as her, it was at least double the weight of her tiny frame. As she tried to cope with the disobedient luggage, I stepped in an offered my assistance. It appeared she had been visiting her sister in Perpignan, and was now on her way back to Lisieux in Normandy. I was amazed to hear that this would involve a five-hour train journey into Paris, and after a two hour wait, another three-hour journey to her home town. When the train eventually arrived, I made sure I got her luggage into the compartment, somewhere near to her seat, and hoped and prayed she would find similar assistance 'en route'.

The train flew over the flat planes and vineyards north of Perpignan, and soon we passed the medieval Fort de Salses. Built on the former French-Spanish border in the 15th century, it protected the Catalans up until 1642, when they were eventually driven back over the mountains into Spain. Suddenly, the train seemed to be cutting waves through the water, as it crossed the middle of two large 'etangs', and we headed into Narbonne. There was obviously a crosswind blowing, as in 1919, and many of the locals were taking advantage of the conditions and windsurfing alongside the train. From my window seat I could see plenty of wading birds, such as herons, oystercatchers and egrets, feeding on the marshland shores.

Jean Alavoine and Paul Duboc lead the peloton over the river somewhere near Pézenas, just to the north of Beziers. Stage 8, 1919.

It was a delightful journey all the way into Montpellier, and it brought back memories of a family holiday, on the Cap d'Agde, during the Tour de France in 2011. Mark Cavendish already had three stage wins under his belt, and there was a chance for him to make it four, as the Tour embarked on Stage 15 from Limoux to Montpellier. Parking the car, down a dusty track in some vineyards, my wife and I tried to secure a vantage point on a roundabout, a few kilometres out from the finish line in Montpellier. As the pre-race motorcade of garish vehicles of every shape and size arrived, there was a massive scramble for the worthless freebies being thrown from the passing caravan. Grown men were having a tug of war over a free polka dot hat from Carrefour. A middle-aged man fell into a ditch trying to catch a naff rubber wristband from Cofodis, and a few young children were screaming and crying because they hadn't managed to catch a flying pack of Haribos. After all this drama, could the race be as exciting?

On the other side of the road a group of fans of the Schleck brothers, Frank and Andy, had gathered and set up their enormous Luxembourg flags. As the tension mounted and the race cars signalled the arrival of the peloton, the French crowd started cheering for their new hero in yellow, Thomas Voeckler. My wife, who is not particularly into cycling or the Tour de France, unexpectedly jumped up and patriotically screamed 'C-A-V-E-N-D-I-S-H' at the top of her voice, surprising most of the cycling fans around her. The Manx Missile must have heard this battle cry, and obviously used it as his inspiration to storm to his fourth stage win in Montpellier. That win ensured he retained the green jersey, something he would do all the way to his final stage victory (his third in a row) on the Champs Èlysées in Paris. This would be the one and only time Mark would wear the coveted green jersey on the podium, which was amazing for someone who now had 20 career stage victories under his belt.

Back to 2019 and it was time for me to pick up the 'Cavendish Cryer' from Montpellier airport, as my wife was joining me for a few days, at the midway point of my journey.

*

For the 1919 riders it was still only eight in the morning, and they had 204km to go to reach the finish in Marseille. 11 riders arrived at the first feeding station in Montpellier together, Alavoine, Duboc, Lambot, Christophe, Barthélémy, Vandaele, Scieur, Goethals, Coomans, Lucotti and Nempon. At 8.23 a.m. Steux signed in followed two minutes later by Henri Desgrange's favourite, Emile Masson (The Unknown), who arrived in agony and abandoned. The effect of his crash on Stage 7, and the fact that he'd had to cycle 20km with a bent front wheel, had put too much strain on his knees, and he couldn't continue. Finally, Masselis arrived at 8.40 a.m. and the peloton was complete, except for the disgraced Belgian Alois Verstraeten, who was told of his disqualification. However, instead of being ordered to take the train straight back to Paris, he was allowed to continue to ride to Marseille, where he would learn his fate in front of the official adjudicators on Bastille Day. Vive La Revolution!

Stage 8 – Monday 14th July 1919 (Day of Rest)
Sunday 14th July 2019 (Montpellier – Marseille)

It was an incredible sight. I focused my binoculars again. Flamingos are amazing birds. I studied a small family of them, tiptoeing through the shallow waters of the lake, like tufts of pink candy floss on stilts, occasionally dipping their heads into the saline water to feed on the algae. I focused my binoculars again. In the distance I could just make out a vast area of sandy beach about 1km long, on the opposite side of the lagoon. Looking again I realised it wasn't a sandy beach at all, but thousands upon thousands of pink flamingos, stretching out in a line as far as the eye could see.

My wife and I had pulled up to the Etang de Vacarres, one of the largest lagoons of the Camargue, near to our overnight campsite in Saintes-Maries-de-la-Mer. This is an area of intense beauty, filled with wonders that only nature can provide. The Camargue is home to the famous water horses that roam freely in the area. Traditionally, they are the workhorses of 'Les Gardians' (the cowboys) of the Camargue, and are known for their agility and strength. The romantic image of these legendary white horses, galloping freely through the salt waters of the 'etangs', is on the front page of every tourist leaflet. The foals are actually born with grey hair, but within three years this turns to a brilliant white, due to constant exposure to saltwater. The Camargue is also a region of bullfighting, and the locally bred black bull (biou), with its white lyre-shaped antlers, can be seen taking on the matadors and picadors, in the amphitheatres of Nimes and Arles, which happened to be our next two destinations.

After the quiet and solitude of the Camargue National Park, Arles was busy, very busy. After all this was the Quatorze Juillet (Bastille Day). We followed the 1919 route onto the Pont de Trinquetaille, which crosses the majestic river Rhone, leading into Arles itself, one of the provincial capitals of ancient Rome. We arrived on the Boulevard de Lices at 11 a.m., at a similar time to the 1919 riders. We sat under the trees in the dappled morning sunlight and ordered a 'petit dejeuner simple' at the Bar du Marche. As we ate breakfast, my thoughts turned to Paul Duboc (The Apple), who stopped somewhere here and consumed a fatal drink (although not poisonous this time). It may have been a small glass of his traditional Calvados, or maybe, being in Provence, a pastis with freshly chilled water. Whatever he drank, it was another drink in Paul's career, which was to have dire consequences.

No visit to Arles is complete without a visit to the UNESCO listed circus theatre and amphitheatre, which are both evidence of the Roman occupation in 123 B.C. Today they are completely surrounded by a multitude of terracotta Provençal houses and obligatory gift shops, which seem to imprison these ancient sites, ensuring will always be there to feed the local tourist industry. The tiny back streets and pavement cafés of Arles have been an inspiration to such artists as Vincent Van Gogh, who created 300 paintings and drawings of Arles and the surrounding Provence landscape, during his stay here in 1888.

The Roman amphitheatre at Arles. If you stop for a drink, make sure you pay for it!

As the 1919 riders left Arles, they passed the workshops of the P.L.M. (Paris-Lyon-Méditerranée) railway, and came to the Roman Aqueduct, that carries the magnificently named 'Canal de Craponne'. Soon they were in open countryside and crossing 'la plaine de la Crau', a desert like area, covered in rocks and pebbles, stretching down to the Mediterranean Sea. The heat of the sun was now intense and booted eagles could be seen circling in the sky, ready to feed on the bones of any stray rider. Don't puncture here! Fortunately, a strong Provençal wind was blowing at their backs and this carried them safely across the 40km of the plain in record time. The more experienced riders took advantage of the strong winds and averaging 35km an hour, they sailed into the final feeding station in Salon de Provence, 23 minutes ahead of schedule. The leading group of eight riders arrived at 12.37 p.m. and contained Luigi Lucotti, Jean Alavoine, Eugéne Christophe, Jules Nempon, Firmin Lambot, Paul Duboc, Léon Scieur and Félix Goethals. Almost an hour later Alfred Steux pulled in at 1.39 p.m. Then, after a further half an hour, Jules Masselis arrived suffering with his ankle, along with Alois Verstraeten. Salon de Provence is the resting place of the famous prophet Nostradamus, who is buried in the nearby Franciscan chapel. Many of his supporters agree that he predicted the Great Fire of London, the French Revolution, the rises of both Napoleon and Adolf Hitler, both World Wars, and the nuclear destruction of Hiroshima and Nagasaki. I wonder whether the injured Jules Masselis or the disgraced Alois Verstraeten went to visit his grave in the 'Collegiale Saint-Laurent' to see if he could predict whether they would make it to Stage 9.

*

It was lunchtime, and the 1919 riders had already feasted on their oysters, chicken cutlets, rice cakes, boiled eggs and tapioca, all washed down with red wine and a mixture of coffee and champagne. My wife and I were starting to feel hungry, so we stopped for our 'ravitaillement' at the next control point in 'Aix-en-Provence'. Of course, trying to find somewhere to park and eat on Bastille Day was not going to be easy. After a couple of circuits of Aix, we managed to find a space in the train station car park, not far from the town centre. Most of the restaurants were full to the brim and we were childishly amused to see that one restaurant called Fanny's was 'Complet'. We were also amused to see a sign proclaiming,

'NE VENDEZ RIEN SANS NOUS CONSULTER'

C.R.A.M.P. (Depuis 1985 – Diamantaire)

I bet a few of the 1919 riders had suffered a touch of cramp, and I thought about giving them the phone number to see if they could sort out their knee problems. However, on getting through to the customer service team at CRAMP, they may have been surprised to learn that they needed to buy or sell their family gold and jewellery.

We came across a convivial square called the 'Place des Augustins' where a number of quaint restaurants surrounded the

'Fontaine des Augustins', whose bubbling water jets were a welcome watery relief to the heat of the midday Provençal sun. We took shade in a tapas bar called 'Le Petit Bistrot' and ordered a delicious king prawn and garlic dish, which we washed down with two cold beers, as they didn't seem to serve any coffee and champagne cocktails.

Walking back up to the main square, with its imposing fountain 'La Fontaine de la place de la Rotonde', I tried to imagine the six leading riders signing in at 1.50 p.m. somewhere nearby. In 1919, this elegant square was called the 'Place des Allies' and we know that our peloton approached it from the Boulevard de la République, signed in at the control and headed out onto the Cours Mirabeau, both of which still exist today, either side of the square. Today, the square is home to a statue in honour of Aix's famous son, the Post-impressionist artist, Paul Cezanne. His portrayal of Aix-en-Provence and the light and warmth of the surrounding landscape, was perfectly captured in his paintings. Interestingly, the Bourgeoisie of Aix didn't appreciate his paintings at all, believing them to be ugly and they sent him messages to leave home, as he was dishonouring the town.

Then and now : 'La Fontaine de la place de la Rotonde' Aix-en-Provence.

The six riders in the leading peloton was now comprised of Jean Alavoine, Léon Scieur, Eugéne Christophe, Firmin Lambot, Paul Duboc and Félix Goethals. Next, it was the turn of Jules Nempon who arrived alone at 1.56 p.m., followed shortly afterwards by Joseph Vandaele and Honoré Barthélémy at 1.58 p.m. It was another twenty minutes before Jacques Coomans arrived in the square at 2.19 p.m. and nearly another further hour before Alfred

Steux pulled in at 3.08 p.m. At this point, Jules Masselis and Alois Verstraeten didn't warrant a mention.

It was now time to head south again towards the finish in Marseille. The route took the riders around the Massif de l'Ètoile, a mountain range to the north of the city, as they headed through the towns of La Bouilladisee, Roquevaire and Aubagne. This is the heart of Provence, and the area has been immortalised in the books of Marcel Pagnol, who was born in Aubagne in 1895. In particular, his books 'Jean de Florette' and 'Manon des Sources' went on to achieve international fame, and in 1986 they were made into two separate films starring Yves Montand, Gerard Depardieu, Daniel Auteil and Emmanuelle Béart. These were the first two books I had read in the French language in an effort to improve my vocabulary, when I had arrived in France. The only trouble was that a lot of the words were from the old Provençal language and hardly used today. When I practised my newly learned French vocabulary on my fellow co-workers they burst into laughter. It was as if I was speaking to them in the language of Shakespeare.

I had to stop and pay homage to the author of my chosen French dictionary, in the modern-day version of Aubagne, which given it was Bastille Day and a Sunday, was perhaps not the best time to visit. The town square was absolutely choc-a-bloc with cars and tourists, as the bistros prepared themselves for the evening's festivities. My rose-tinted image of old beret-wearing gentlemen, playing boules under the shade of the olive trees, whilst onlookers sipped a chilled pastis at a nearby bar-tabac, was quickly evaporating. In fact, they were drying up completely, just like the fresh water supply did from Jean-de-Florette's (Gerard Depardieu) hidden spring in Claude Berri's films of Marcel Pagnol's books.

*

Marseille, is France's largest sea port and the second largest French city after Paris, and given the large crowds at every 1919 stage finish so far, you would anticipate that the arrival in Marseille would attract an enormous amount of people. You would be right, the only problem was that the local municipality and authorities in Marseille had not restricted the crowds that were gathering at the finish line on the Avenue du Parc Borély, leading up to the Chateau. With this amount of people, they needed a larger police presence than had been seen in all the other stage finishes, to keep the crowd behind the barricades, and to keep the finish line clear. It was evident that this was not the case from the start, and when the six riders appeared, they were soon completely engulfed by thousands of spectators. Fortunately, there were no accidents. Henri Desgrange was not impressed. "I know the people have hot heads in Le Midi (South of France), but this should not be to the detriment of our sport."

The arrival into Marseille on the Avenue du Parc Borély was always going to be a bumpy affair.

Jean Alavoine again came out top in the sprint. It was his fourth stage victory of the Tour, and if had not been for his third place in Luchon, he would have achieved five consecutive stage wins. A record held to this day by François Faber, the Giant of Colombes, in 1909. Gars Jean was also unhappy with the lack of control at the stage finish, and got off his bike waving his fists at the crowds that had swarmed over the finish line.

"It is unfortunate, all the same, that we could have damaged our kidneys and well, next time I'll remember this arrival in Marseille, and think twice, before sprinting into Parc Borély. Well at least I won and I haven't broken anything which is the main thing. Mind you, this does not prevent it from having been hot, extremely hot!"

Marseille's finest take a chilled glass of pastis on the terrace of the Café du Sport on the Place Castellane.

The remaining riders proceeded to the Café du Sport to sign in and we learnt that, despite finishing in the leading group, Paul Duboc was given a thirty-minute penalty. Apparently, he'd taken that drink at the café in Arles without paying and so subsequently he had been penalised. This meant he now inherited the mantle of 'lanterne rouge' as he dropped to last position in the G.C. This coveted position became vacant because the decision to disqualify

Alois Verstraeten had been upheld. Originally, he was alleged to have caught a train during the second stage. The jury pronounced:

"His signature features on every control paper of this stage, including the secret control. In addition, the masseurs and mechanics, who were travelling in the only train that Verstraeten could have taken, hadn't seen him."

Alois Verstraeten, himself protested saying that the Buysse brothers, who had abandoned, saw him continue. Also, he can quote precise details of the route that he followed between the last control point and the finish in Cherbourg. His arrival at Cherbourg at 23h 20m 45s, coincided with the arrival of the train at 23h 20m and there was no evidence to suggest that this train was delayed by a few minutes. So, if the train arrived on time, how could Verstraeten, who does not speak French, have had the time to take his bike off the train and get from the station to the control in 45 seconds.

Whilst this seemed to be a malicious rumour, the fact that he had been caught holding onto the shoulder of a motorcycle rider for two kilometres, meant he was out of the race. So, with seven stages and just under half the race to go, we are now down to 13 riders. Ignoring the multitude of abandonments of the first stage, the average rate of attrition over the last seven stages is two per stage. If this continued, we should be down to 'minus one' rider by the time we get to Paris, so not far off Henri Desgrange's perfect tour!

Stage 8: Perpignan – Marseille (370km)

1. Jean Alavoine	in 13h 50m 32s
2. Luigi Lucotti	at a length
3. Léon Scieur	at a length
4. Firmin Lambot	at a length
5. Eugéne Christophe	at a length
6. Paul Duboc	at a length
7. Honoré Barthélémy	in 13h 58m 22s
8. Joseph Vandaele	at a length
9. Félix Goethals	in 14h 04m 05s
10. Jules Nempon	in 14h 11m 36s
11. Jacques Coomans	in 15h 03m 36s
12. Alfred Steux	in 15h 32m 32s
13. Jules. Masselis	in 16h 21m 57s

General Classement (G.C.)

1. E. Christophe	(The Old Gaul)	126h 50m 57s
2. F. Lambot	(The Saddler)	127h 19m 20s
3. J. Alavoine	(Gars Jean)	127h 38m 31s
4. L. Scieur	(The Locomotive)	129h 47m 25s
5. H. Barthélémy	(Glass Eye)	130h 31m 56s
6. J. Masselis		133h 56m 53s
7. F. Gœthals	(The Sock Seller)	134h 27m 42s
8. J. Coomans	(The Smoker)	135h 16m 44s
9. A. Steux	(The Kid)	135h 40m 09s
10. J. Vandaele	(Facing his Waterloo)	136h 21m 42s
11. L. Lucotti	(The Italian Job)	137h 23m 39s
12. J. Nempon	(The Upstart)	139h 37m 19s
13. P. Duboc	**(The Apple)**	**140h 05m 34s**

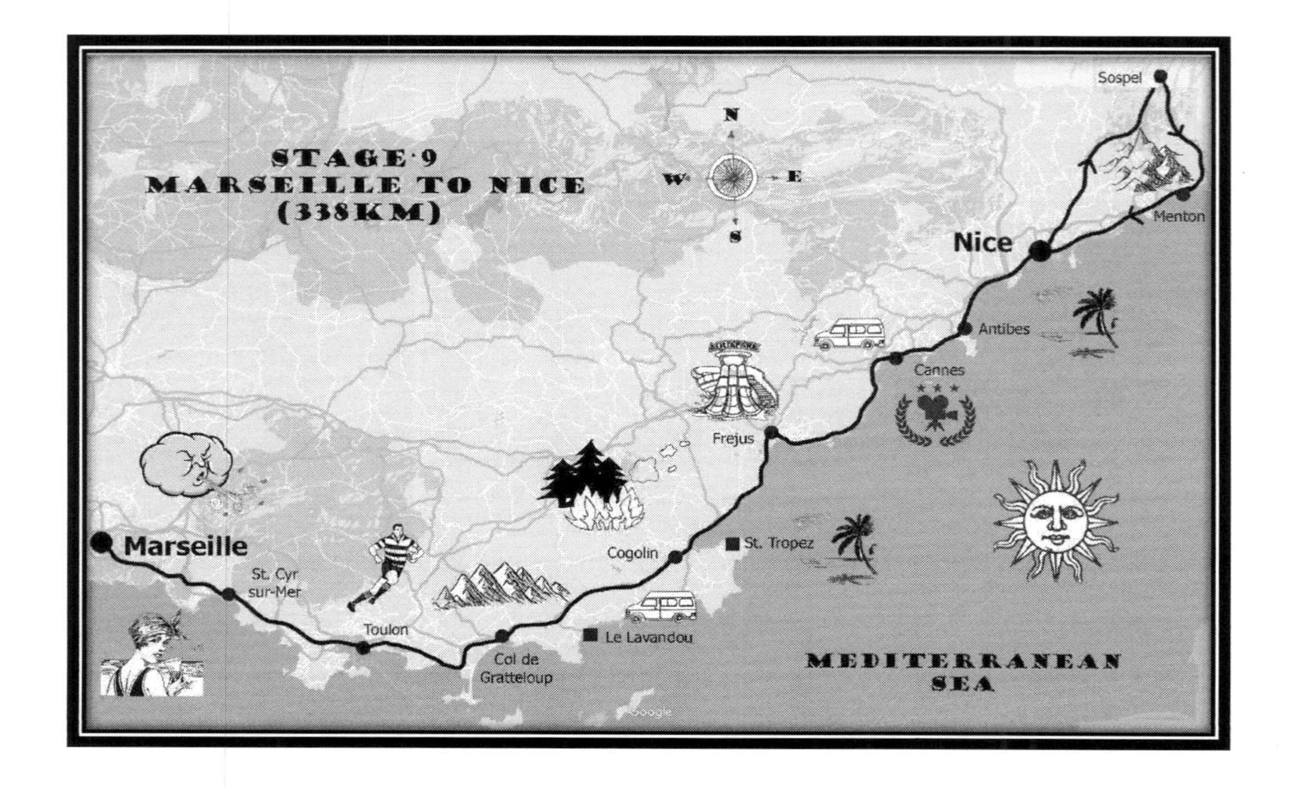
STAGE 9
MARSEILLE TO NICE
(338KM)
N
W
E
S
Sospel
Menton
Nice
Antibes
Cannes
Frejus
St. Tropez
Cogolin
Le Lavandou
Col de Gratteloup
Toulon
St. Cyr sur-Mer
Marseille
MEDITERRANEAN
SEA

Chapter 13 : 'The Riviera Incident'

Stage 9: Tuesday 15th July 1919 (Marseille - Nice)
Monday 15th July 2019 (Marseille – Le Lavandou)

"Bloody bedbugs, the room is full of bed bugs, and the noise, the bloody interminable noise!"

Last night, Henri Desgrange visited the remaining riders in their hotel rooms, as he did after each stage, to get some stories for the following day's edition of L'Auto. Most of the main hotels in Marseille were still being used as military hospitals, following the end of the Great War, and as a consequence the 13 remaining riders had to seek rest in some uncomfortable lodgings. To make matters worse, the Bastille Day celebrations had gone on long into the night, keeping most of them awake and disrupting their much-needed sleep. On top of this the two Belgians, Firmin Lambot and Jules Masselis, were sharing a room which had an infestation of bedbugs. Can you imagine having a sleepless night before a 338km mountain stage along the Côte d'Azur? Surprisingly, Firmin Lambot was still looking fresh, but Jules Masselis was suffering from a bad ankle, and murmured that he was unlikely to be able to take part in the following day's stage. As for the other riders, Jean Alavoine was looking through all his fan mail. There was no way he could reply to them all, but he did find time to write to the directors of the Paris Velodrome, who had put a proposition to him. The Old Gaul, Eugéne Christophe, shared a room with his fellow countryman, the young (Glass Eye) Honoré Barthélémy. Whilst the old master was feeling in good form, the youngster was suffering from his in-growing toenails. The rest of the group seemed fit and ready to go.

Mind you, with the field now effectively down to 12 riders at the halfway stage, Henri Desgrange was worried about the future of the Tour de France. He wrote that there were two future solutions to the current predicament. One was to continue as is, with around 70 riders, and risk a lack of participants at the finish in Paris. The second would be to flood the race with 200 riders to ensure around 50 made it to the Parc des Princes. Henri favoured the first option but thought that L'Auto should take care of all the riders' needs. i.e. massaging them, feeding them, ensuring they had good lodgings, refuelling them during the route and paying their prize-winning monies. (Prizes were currently awarded at each stage finish and quite often at control points along the route. The prizes were offered by local sports clubs, businesses or well-meaning benefactors, who would often give prizes for the first three riders to reach their town.) Of course, this was going to need a lot more money to finance the race, and whilst Henri was happy for his newspaper to fund some of this budget to ensure the future success of their race, he felt it was time for the French cycle manufacturers to put their hands in their pockets, and to properly fund professional cycling in France. After all, they benefited greatly from the publicity of stage wins and race winners who had completed the Tour de France on their trusty steeds. They didn't hesitate to splash their victors' names all over their adverts in Henri's newspapers, and perhaps now it was time for a bit of a payback. Henri even went as far as to suggest a financial plan, outlying how this could operate. He had calculated that, in his opinion, the manufacturers would save around 50 French Francs (FF) per rider by not having to administer them. So, in this instance, if they paid 25FF to subsidise the Tour de France and 25FF for each rider they chose to enter the race, then they could forget all about looking after the riders, their bikes and paying them a salary or win bonus.

Adverts from the cycling manufacturers in L'Auto during the 1919 Tour.

You could see the logic in his plan, and it highlighted Henri's business acumen, in getting the salary and prize money from the manufacturers up front, at the start of the race. Of course, not all the riders would be paid bonuses and therefore the excess funds could go towards the organisation of the race, all under his control.

*

The following day, as predicted, twelve riders signed in at the Café du Sport in Marseille at 1.20 a.m. From here they were led out to the usual start point at Le Redon, some seven kilometres outside the city, where Robert Desmarets gave them the signal at 2 a.m. to depart for Nice. This truly is a beautiful part of the world and it was shame that our 12 heroes were to complete the first section of the Côte d'Azur in complete darkness. This part of the route ran through Le Ciotat, Cassis, Saint-Cyr-sur-Mer, Bandol and Sanary-sur-Mer, a mixture of quaint fishing villages, whose pastel coloured houses reflect beautifully in the clear blue waters of the Mediterranean, and the expansive sun-drenched beaches invite you to dip your toes into the cool, refreshing water. There was one rider who was not reflecting on the coastal beauty he was missing, and that was Jacques Coomans. The Smoker had an accident with his bike somewhere between Saint-Cyr-sur-Mer and Bandol, and he lost valuable minutes trying to repair it. On top of this, having been dropped by the group, he now proceeded to lose his way in the dark, on the way across to Toulon. Upon arriving at the control, he was dismayed to discover he was now nearly an hour behind the others.

Advertising posters tempting you to the blue waters of the Côte d'Azur.

I'm afraid to say that my wife and I could not pass up the opportunity to rest a while on the coast. In deference to Jacques Coomans, we'd stopped at Saint-Cyr-sur-Mer for an hour, to contemplate his misfortune. The only trouble with the beauty of this part of the Côte d'Azur, is everybody knows about it, and the roads and car parks were packed full of holidaymakers. We were in luck and managed to find the last parking space, much to the disgruntlement of the car behind us, who stared at us as we unloaded the van and headed to the beach. It always amazes me how the most beautiful of places can be full of people who don't really want to be there. As we sat and looked out to sea, a French family set up in front of us. It seemed that this was the ideal holiday location for the father, probably escaping the stresses of a high-flying city job, whereas the rest of the family were obviously there under duress, and giving him their begrudging support. The youngest of the two teenage sons, resembled a pack mule, loaded with all the various beach sports gear you'd need for a week's vacation. His elder brother's holiday entertainment consisted of constantly teasing and annoying his younger sibling, pinching and punching him at every opportunity. The mother was dressed like one of the bright young things, straight out of a F. Scott Fitzgerald novel, with her paisley silk head bandana and flowing beach robes. Being an adjudicator in her offspring's petty disputes was not what she was born for. She should be sipping a Kir Royale, on a sun dressed terrace, somewhere in Saint Tropez or Cannes, listening to music from The Jazz Age.

All of a sudden, the clouds gathered and it was time to get off the beach and get back on the route. By the time we got to the naval port of Toulon, the first spots of rain started to appear on the windscreen, and the wind started to pick up. Coincidentally, in 1919 the renowned Provençal Mistral also started to blow. The Mistral is a strong cold north-westerly wind, that blows from southern France, up to the Gulf of Lion in the northern Mediterranean.

*

Henri Desgrange was full of praise for the organisation of the control in Toulon, whom he referred to as Le Petit Marseille, and he stated that one day it could become a 'ville-ètape', or at least a feeding station. Was this a warning shot across the bows, to the organisers in Marseille, and a threat that if they didn't put their house in order, they could lose the prestige of being a stage town? This was indeed the case and Henri Desgrange wrote profusely about this in a later edition of L'Auto. On the 17th July 1919, he stated that Marseille would no longer host Stage 8 of the Tour de France, due the shoddy reception they had received in the past. In previous years they had been forced to stage the sprint finish on a road that contained tram rails. Then, in a subsequent year, the officials had kept their arrival into Marseille secret, only to find that the following morning, some jokers had slashed the tyres of the L'Auto car with a knife, prior to the departure of Stage 9. Henri didn't think that the authorities in Marseille understood the importance of the sport of cycling to the nation, and especially the significance of the Tour de France. He quoted Toulon, as a great city, who would be delighted to host the Tour. As it happened in 1920, the honour was passed to Aix-en-Provence and Marseille lost out. But in 1921, it was Toulon's turn and the town became the 'ville-ètape' of choice between Perpignan and Nice, from 1921 to 1927, when Marseille was reintroduced. It was a lesson, well learnt by the Marseillaise, that you don't upset Mr Henri Desgrange.

In Toulon, as dawn was breaking, we learnt that Eugéne Christophe had punctured and Joseph Vandaele had suffered a nasty fall, both losing two minutes to the leading group. By the time they reached the first feeding station of Stage 9 in Hyères, the group were back together with Jacques Coomans, the only straggler, still an hour behind. The first 100km of this stage had largely been flat along the Côte d'Azur. Now it was time for the riders to head inland and cross the 'Le Massif des Maures', which is a wild range of wooded hills, shrouded by pine, chestnut and cork oak trees, lying inland between Hyères and Fréjus.

*

As a family, we had holidayed numerous times on the beautiful coastline, between Le Lavandou and Cavalaire-sur-Mer. Not only are the beaches stunning, but as you sit and read your latest page-turning novel, you can occasionally rest your eyes on the distant group of islands 'Îles d'Hyères', which stretch out along the blue horizon, like a golden necklace. Unfortunately, this is also an area of inland forest fires, and prior to one of our visits in 2003, a criminally induced fire had destroyed 20% of the flora and fauna in the region. During our stay we frequented the 'Maurin de Maures', an authentic Provençal style restaurant, with a great terrace overlooking the sea. It's one of those restaurants, which is empty one minute and completely packed a few minutes later, with diners chatting noisily, as they're served their favourite Provençal dishes. The bottles of local wine were served with a cardboard neck-piece, detailing the destruction caused by the recent forest fires, and asking for donations to assist in the reconstruction of the area. With each donation or with each large tip, the waiters passed the entrance to the kitchens and rang a large bell on the counter. 'MERCI BEAUCOUP!'

Stage 9 – Wednesday 16th July 1919 (Day of rest)
Tuesday 16th July 2019 (Le Lavandou - Nice)

For old times' sake, my wife and I rested the night in Le Lavandou, and took an evening stroll down to the bustling restaurants on the seafront. We were on a personal mission to find a hotel called the Beau Rivage, which a close family friend ran for many years in the eighties. A quick walk through the town and there it was, on the Boulevard du Front de Mer, looking a bit jaded as compared to my childhood memories.

The following day we headed along the coast (Corniche des Maures) and cut up the narrow winding road through the Massif, to get back onto the 1919 route. This was not the usual tourist route and the locals had little regard for a nervous English van driver edging up to the summit. There were numerous occasions when I had to swerve slightly when confronted with a Renault Clio haring down the mountainside. It wasn't long before we arrived on the road to Cogolin and the stretch of the French Riviera, made famous by film stars such as Bridgette Bardot, Jane Birkin and Serge Gainsbourg in the 1960s. Signposts pointed to Saint Tropez, Port Grimaud, Saint Maxime, all the way to the Roman Port of Frèjus, which is more famous nowadays for the gigantic fun park 'Aqualand' than it is for its ancient Roman aqueduct and amphitheatre.

*

It was still only 9 a.m. when the 1919 peloton reached Frèjus, the halfway point of Stage 9. The main group was still largely together, although they'd dropped the Italian Luigi Lucotti (by 3 minutes) and the injured Joseph Vandaele (by 6 minutes). It was time for the first big climbs of the day through the Massif d'Esterel between Frèjus and Cannes and Luigi Lucotti would be looking to catch up those lost 3 minutes, as the stage was heading towards Italy, and his compatriots would be flooding over the border to support him in Nice.

*

One of the most beautiful train journeys in France follows the route from Frèjus to Cannes and it's worth taking a trip, if you ever get the chance. The tiny trains of the SNCF hug the coastline throughout the route, crossing tiny viaducts and passing through long dark tunnels, only to emerge next to a secluded bay, the deep blue sea sparkling like diamonds in the midday sunlight. The bright red-rock mountain scenery behind you appears like a film set from a Clint Eastwood movie, and you half expect the 'Man with No Name' to appear on horseback, smoking a cigarillo and holding aloft a Fistful of Dollars. Actually, this once was bandit country and the Massif played host to the hideout of infamous 18th-century brigands, such as Gaspard de Besse, who has been described as a Provençal Robin Hood.

Watch out for masked bandits on your way through the Massif de l'Esterel

There was also a paragraph in L'Auto which was intriguingly headed 'A skirmish on the Esterel'. The riders were expected to arrive together at the control point in Antibes, and yet after passing over 'Mont Vinagre' (Mount Vinegar), the main group had dropped Eugéne Christophe and Jules Nempon. This was probably a collaborated attempt to attack the G.C. leader on the first mountain climb. Mind you, they only gained one minute on the Old Gaul and three minutes on Nempon, so it hadn't been that successful.

By the time they reached Nice it was 11.39 a.m. and Christophe and Nempon were back in the peloton so there was no real change to the G.C. as they proceeded down the Promenade des Anglais to the Place Massena. Luigi Lucotti was given a standing ovation by his Italian supporters as he arrived in the lead bunch. This was to be the riders' first feeding station in Nice, as the stage wasn't over yet. Sensing that this stage was too short at 243km, Henri Desgrange had devised the 'Sospel Loop', which would take the riders a further 95km through the mountains to the border with Italy, and return a second time to Nice. It was a punishing end to a punishing day in the heat, with the Mistral still blowing and covering the riders in thick red dust. Still it gave the Italian Luigi Lucotti the chance to show off to his fans, and it was he who led the peloton up the lacets (shoelaces) of Col de Braus (1002m) to considerable applause from his fellow countrymen. Would he be able to keep it up in the descent back down to Nice? Chi vincerà.

The Italian Luigi Lucotti finishes second on the Boulevard Risso in Nice.

The finish line in Nice was on the Boulevard Risso, a long straight stretch of road, leading into the Place Massena. This gave the riders ample room for a clean bunch sprint, as they raced to the finish line, which was covered in flags and banners. There was a tradition in Nice, that one of the old sportsmen, Monsieur Maccario, would hand a yellow flag of L'Auto to the winner of the stage. Unfortunately, Monsieur Maccario had been killed during the War in 1915, so instead the honour was passed to his son, who presented it to the eventual winner, the young Honoré Barthélémy, who arrived all alone, six minutes ahead of Luigi Lucotti. The Green-Toothed Witch had tapped Luigi on the shoulder and he punctured twice, on the way down the dirt tracks of the Sospel loop, finishing in second place. Eugéne Christophe had also punctured in La Turbie, 17km from the finish, and Jean Alavoine and Firmin Lambot, sensing an opportunity, took no pity and sped off. Things got worse for the Old Gaul, when he ran into a policeman, who was standing in his way, just after the finish line. Christophe went flying and injured his knee and hips. He was livid. This could cost him the Tour. The experienced rider, who was normally so calm in these situations, totally lost his cool and had to be restrained, whilst shaking a fist at the offending officer.

Mind you, Eugéne was still the race leader and as such shouldn't he be wearing the special jersey that had been written about in L'Auto's pages before Stage 7. On the 10th July 1919, they had announced

'A happy idea from our Editor-in-Chief! In order to enable sportsmen to recognise the leader of the Tour de France, at first glance, in the peloton, Henri Desgrange has decided that in the future, the rider who is in first place of the General Classement will wear a special jersey. This jersey has now been ordered. It is probable that as soon as we reach Marseille the leader of the Tour will be the holder.'

The Old Gaul had been the head of the G.C. as they left Marseille but there was no sign of this special jersey. Still Eugéne had his mind on other things. Firmin Lambot and Jean Alavoine had managed to put 4 minutes into his lead and Lambot, in particular, was starting to become a worry. There was some good news for Eugéne though, his wife had written to him, to let him know that their son, aged four, had won first prize in a local beauty competition. As Eugéne looked at his dusty and bloodied image in the mirror of his hotel bedroom that night, he couldn't make out where the beauty had come from.

*

For myself and my wife, there was another 'Riveria incident' near Nice. This was my wife's last day in France and we took a trip down memory lane, stopping at the beach in Théoule-sur-Mer, across from Cannes Bay. We'd stumbled upon this beach and its quaint harbour, when our son was young, and it is a perfect venue if you want to avoid the crowded beaches in Cannes, Juan les Pins and Nice. It's a delightful spot, where you can swim and bathe safely, and watch the coastal train winding its way from La Napoule, through Théoule, on its way to Marseille. After a hard day watching the world go by you can retire to the rear of the beach, and sit under the trees with a cold beer and a book, and watch the locals playing pétanque. After an enjoyable afternoon, we returned to our van to head to our campsite in Cagnes-sur-Mer near Nice. I opened the sliding door to the van and my wife blurted

"Where are our suitcases?"

"Oh my God, someone's smashed the windows!"

"Bloody Hell, they've taken everything!"

This was unbelievable. We had parked on the main road in front of the station at Théoule. This was the busy coastal road and cars were passing every second. Surely somebody would have seen them? We had to take stock and tried our best to clear up the broken glass. The driver's side window had been smashed as well as the window over the cooking unit. A quick recce, and yes everything had gone, including our valuables (phone, passport and driving licence) locked in the glove compartment. We managed to make the vehicle driveable, and headed to the nearest police station in La Napoule. After recording our losses and trying our best to remember what had been stolen, we were left with the stark reality of coming to terms with what this meant for my trip. My wife was due to fly from Nice the following morning and return to the UK. I had to see if I could get my van repaired locally and decide whether there was any chance that I could continue. Our evening was spent at the campsite trying to make the van secure for a night's sleep, whilst also making sure that we weren't attacked by mosquitos. Unfortunately, our camping spot was under some fruit trees and the squashed fallen fruit was attracting all the blood seeking insects in the vicinity.

Stage 9: Wednesday 17th July 2019 (Road to Nowhere)

1,145 kilometres !!! 10 hrs 59 mins - Autoroute de Soleil – Fastest route – tolls required

I'd tapped Calais into my Satnav, and this is what I was faced with. That morning I'd visited Carglass, a local garage, which carried out screen repairs. The news was that if they ordered the glass for the driver's side-window they might be able to fix it in a couple of days. However, the kitchen window, with its sliding panel would be at least a week, if not more. I was fast coming to the realisation that my trip was over for now. I was not going to be able to continue to follow in the footsteps of the 1919 riders, exactly one hundred years to the day, as I planned. I managed to find another local garage, which gave me the same news, but kindly covered my two broken windows, with a taut sticky plastic covering that would hopefully last me until I got home. And so, I planned my route. As it was already midday, I headed for an overnight stop near Lyon, and the following morning carried onto to a campsite north of Paris, as I had to travel into the city to the British Embassy, to pick up an emergency passport, which would allow me to travel back to the UK. My temporary plastic windows were fine, but extremely noisy, as they rattled in the wind as I drove up the Autoroute de Soleil. By the time I'd got to my first service station, the plastic window at my side was slowly starting to detach itself from the bodywork. Luckily, I had some black tape which I used for the handlebars on my bike, and I did a temporary repair. This became a pattern, as the further I drove, the more it came loose. I'd taken to listening to the radio, or audiobooks, at maximum volume, to drown the constant battering of my right ear lobe. It was like listening to a Motorhead album, at full blast, solidly for three days. By the time I reached Dover the window repair job was getting bigger and bigger and the weather forecast was getting worse and worse. The last thing I needed was for the incessant rain water to start entering the vehicle.

I made it home at around ten o'clock on the night of the third day, much to the relief of my wife Colleen and son, James.

Having lots of time to think on my journey home, I racked my brains as to how I might be able to continue my journey and complete the Tour. Like Eugéne Christophe I didn't want to abandon, I needed to do everything I could do to finish the race. Also, like Eugéne, I had a strong contact with the Riviera police, and also like Eugéne, I had lost my cool at my predicament.

Stage 9 : Marseille to Nice (338km)

1. Honoré Barthélémy	in 13h 39m 48s
2. Luigi Lucotti	in 13h 45m 57s
3. Alfred Steux	in 13h 53m 25s
4. Jean Alavoine	in 13h 56m 00s
5. Léon Scieur	at a length
6. Firmin Lambot	at a length
7. Eugéne Christophe	in 14h 00m 00s
8. Félix Goethals	in 14h 15m 40s
9. Joseph Vandaele	in 14h 28m 44s
10. Paul Duboc	in 14h 41m 46s
11. Jules Nempon	in 14h 57m 11s
12. Jacques Coomans	in 16h 43m 32s

General Classement (G.C.)

1. E. Christophe	(The Old Gaul)	140h 50m 57s
2. F. Lambot	(The Saddler)	141h 17m 20s
3. J. Alavoine	(Gars Jean)	141h 34m 31s
4. L. Scieur	(The Locomotive)	143h 43m 25s
5. H. Barthélémy	(Glass Eye)	144h 11m 00s
6. F. Gœthals	(The Sock Seller)	148h 43m 22s
7. A. Steux	(The Kid)	149h 29m 45s
8. J. Vandaele	(Waterloo)	150h 50m 26s
9. L. Lucotti	(The Italian Job)	151h 09m 36s
10. J. Coomans	(The Smoker)	152h 30m 16s
11. J. Nempon	(The Upstart)	154h 44m 30s
12. P. Duboc *	(The Apple)	154h 57m 20s

* includes 30-minute penalty on Stage 8

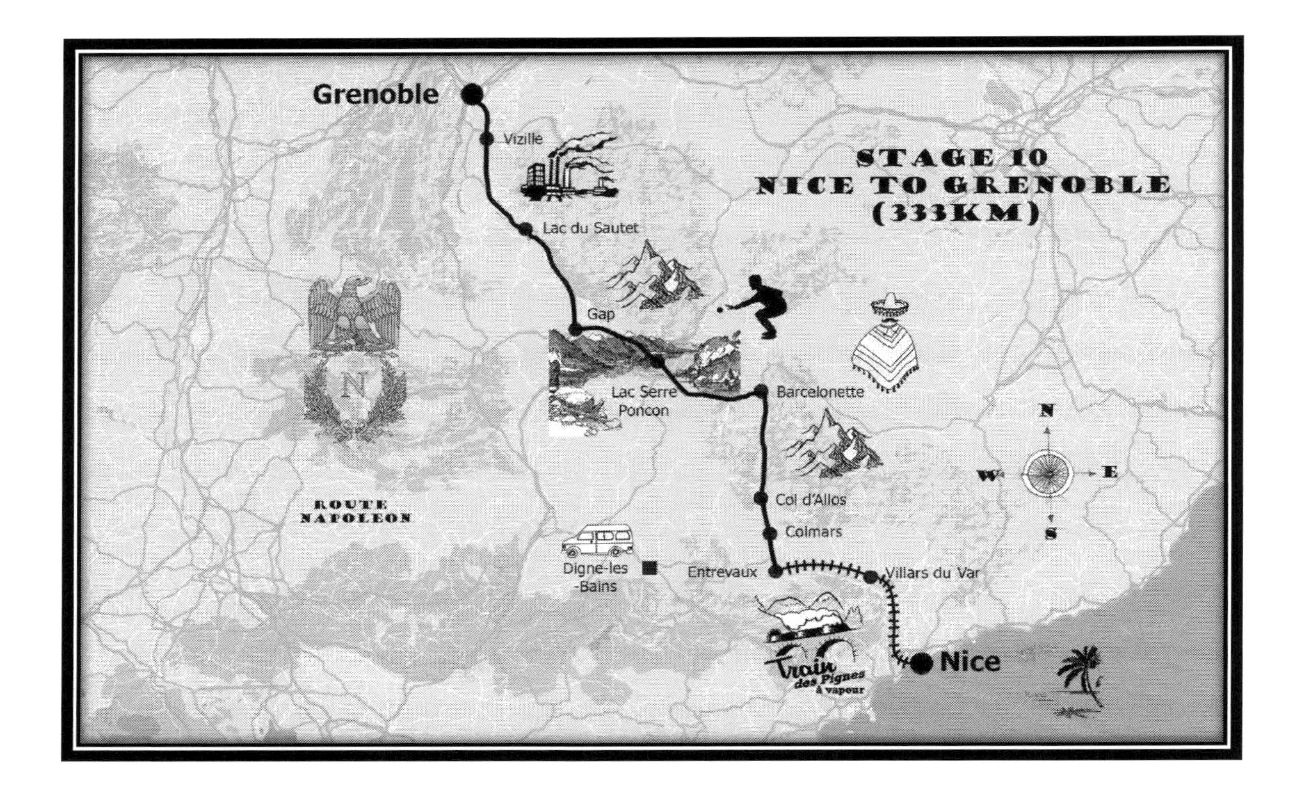
STAGE 10
NICE TO GRENOBLE
(333KM)
Grenoble
Vizille
Lac du Sautet
Gap
Lac Serre
Poncon
Barcelonette
Col d'Allos
Colmars
Entrevaux
Villars du Var
Nice
Digne-les
-Bains
ROUTE
NAPOLEON
N
W
E
S
Train
des Pignes
à vapeur

Chapter 14 : 'Victory on Napoleon Street'

Stage 10: Thursday 17th July 1919 (Nice-Grenoble) Tuesday 17th September 2019 (Nice- Digne-les-Bains)

'DINK-DINK-DINK-DINK-**DINK-DINK-DINK-DINK!'**
'DINK-DINK-DINK-DINK-**DINK-DINK-DINK-DINK!'**

It was 5.30 a.m. I had set my alarm early, as I was off to catch a train on another of France's stunning rail journeys, the 'Train des Pignes' through the Alps. I'd assumed 'Train des Pignes' meant 'train of the pine forest' but there seems to be some dispute as to its origins. One theory is that this was the name given to the type of train that was able to ascend and descend safely in the Mountains of the Alps which is a 'pinion train'; that is a mountain rack train or cog train. A second theory, which is quite quaint, is that the train's speed used to be slow enough for passengers to get off and pick up the pine cones along the track, because when the locomotive lacked coal, the drivers used the pine cones as fuel.

Whatever its origins, it was a train that I had waited a long time to travel on and again, what luck, it followed the 1919 Tour de France route exactly from Nice to Thorame-Haute, the first feeding station of Stage 10. However, I had to make sure that I caught the first train out of Digne-les-Bains at 7.15 a.m. as the 151km journey took three and a half hours each way. As there was around an hour's walk from the camp site to the station, I had to make sure I was up early to ensure I didn't miss it. I arrived at the station around 6.40 a.m., and given that it was now September, the station was in complete darkness, and there was nobody about. After ten minutes I started to get a bit nervous. Had I got the wrong train? Had something happened that I wasn't aware of? Finally, some car headlights approached the station and it looked as though it was the ticket master. He eventually opened his ticket booth at 7 a.m., and I purchased my return ticket to Nice. There were only two other people in the queue behind me, who it turned out were only travelling to Nice to pick up their car, which had broken down, whilst visiting their daughter.

I asked which platform the train was leaving from, which was a bit of a joke as there was only one! It soon turned out however, that we would be making the first part of the journey by coach. It transpired that there had been a rockfall somewhere on the line near Moriez, and we would now be catching the train from Saint-André-les-Alpes.

This suited me fine as this first section wasn't on the 1919 route, and Thorame-Haute was the first place I would reconnect with the riders after an absence of two months. After returning to the UK, I'd been over and over the disaster that occurred in the South of France, many times in my mind. I knew I had to continue and finish my journey. I could not let a few mindless idiots ruin my story and so I had decided to return in September and continue the route from Nice. I arrived in France on September 15th as this date coincided with the 103rd anniversary of my grandfather being wounded on the Somme, between Flers and Gueudecourt in 1916 after the battle of Delville Wood. As I hadn't had the time to properly visit the area whilst travelling through the Somme on Stage 1, I took this opportunity to follow in my grandfather's footsteps as I headed south to reconnect with the 1919 route.

I visited the train station at Ribemont-Bericourt, where Emmanuel had first disembarked on his way to the notorious battle at Delville Wood (known as Devil's Wood, because of the atrocious fighting), and wondered what was going on in his young mind.

I visited the River l'Authie, the tributary of the Somme, where my grandfather and his brigade had bathed, after a particularly hard day marching in extreme heat, in the Somme, and smiled at their joy.

I visited the National Memorial to the fallen South Africans who were slaughtered here in their thousands, and felt ill at their demise.

I wandered through Delville Wood, following the route of my grandfather's platoon, trying hard to imagine the carnage he would have witnessed, but happy that he made it through the wood and out to safety on the open fields beyond.

I got on my bike and rode in the tracks of the world's first tank to go into action in the history of warfare. Captain Harold

Mortimore set off in tank D1–Dolphin at 5.15 a.m. in the Battle of Flers-Courcelette on the 15TH September 1916.

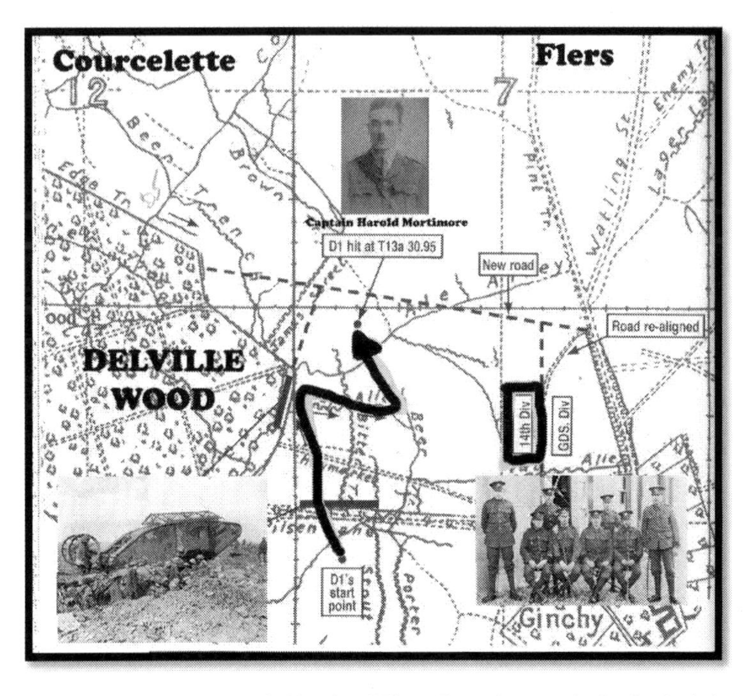

D1 Dolphin's route into the Battle of Flers-Courcelette, with the Oxford & Bucks Light Infantry, 42nd Brigade, 5th Battalion, 14th Division (right) – 15th September 1916.

I arrived in the tiny village of Flers, just as the church clock struck 4.30 p.m., the exact time my grandfather was wounded on 15th September 1916, whilst out reconnoitring in No Man's Land, with his second lieutenant, somewhere on the Bulls Road. I felt his pain.

I visited the grave of his best friend, who was not so fortunate, and died on the same day, aged 23. I shed a tear at both his and my grandfather's loss.

These were precious moments and I thought that maybe my return at this time was meant to be. It also meant that I arrived back on the 1919 route on the 17th September 2019, so exactly 100 years and two months from the original date.

My grandfather, Emmanuel Tarver. The church clock in Flers and No Man's Land, just to the north of the Bulls Head Road.

It felt good to be going back to the 1919 route once again, as I joined the other two passengers and boarded the coach. We were joined by the driver, a relief driver and one of their friends. It seemed a bit strange, nearly being outnumbered, by the railway staff. Still it all added to the excitement I suppose. We arrived at the 'Gare de Nice CP' at 10.30 a.m. and I headed down to the Promenade des Anglais which runs along the curved length of the seafront. I sat on a bench looking over the beach and watched the tourists, trying to make themselves comfortable on the grey-pebbled beach. I searched Google maps to locate the Boulevard Risso and the Café Riviera Glacier on the Place Massena, which was the finish point of Stage 9 and the start point of Stage 10.

Then and now: Café Riviera, Place Messina, Nice

I knew I was going to find them quickly as two seagulls shat on me from the wooden parapet above my seat. My luck was in and within five minutes' walk, I was sat in the Place Massena, imagining Honoré Barthélémy, flying down from the mountains, alongside the River Paillon, onto the final straight, the Boulevard Risso, and into the square, arriving six minutes before the others. This was despite the fact that he had bumped into a donkey, coming around one of the mountain bends, and the animal was so frightened, it stood there motionless. Honoré managed to catch hold of its bridle and held onto the poor animal, until its master came and rescued it.

He did all this and still had a six-minute lead. He proceeded to sign the control sheet at the Restaurant Riviera Glacier, where he was to collect his special prizes, a watch offered by the Municipality of Nice, a gold medal and 30 French Francs. Not bad for a days' work.

The following morning 11 riders gathered for the official start at the usual time of 2 a.m. The field was down to 11 as Félix Goethals (the Sock Seller) had to abandon on to his doctor's advice, due to the severe haemorrhoids that had been bothering him for some days now. This was a shame as Félix had ridden a brilliant Tour de France and had been sitting in sixth position in G.C.

*

I realised that, even with my early start this morning, I was still three hours behind these brave riders, and by the time I'd caught my train they'd already reached the fortified alpine village of Colmars and would be anticipating tackling the Col d'Allos, the first giant of the Alps. Henri Desgrange unusually complained that the Tour officials had been extremely cold, whilst sat in the official cars leaving Nice, heading up the valley of the River Var. It was not until midday when they arrived in Gap, that they warmed up.

I boarded the train for my return journey to Digne-les-Bains, knowing that I was now back on track with the 1919 riders, as they headed north for the first time in a long while, on a 1,812km journey, that would take them all the way to the coastal port of Dunkirk. This was a part of France I did not know very well and apart from visiting Alsace a couple of times, I had no knowledge of the eastern borders of France. The first 48km of the train journey out of Nice, follows the rock-strewn bed of the River Var, up to Villars-sur-Var, where the train starts to climb. Out of the train window, I could see pine forests and vineyards and overhead I could make out the road of the 1919 route. Soon the train arrived at Touet-sur-Var, a 12th century medieval village, which has been built along the side of a cliff. The ancient white stone houses, with their ochre coloured tile roofs, look like a brick necklace strung along a rocky outcrop, and topped with a 12th century Romanesque church.

Then, the train runs through a flat valley, to the station at Puget-Theniers. It is here that we get the first report on the remaining 11 riders, who all arrive together. This is not entirely unexpected as it is still 4.35 a.m. and the peloton always try to stick together whilst cycling in the dark.

Soon the train pulls into the old town of Entrevaux, with its rows of ancient houses, clinging onto the cliff top, like a skeletal hand, complete with outstretched bony fingers. The Citadel of Entrevaux, looks down on the village, from high up on a stony escarpment. It is well worth the climb, and the views back down the valley are out of this world.

The train continues along the valley floor, parallel to the 1919 route and the river, until it reaches Annot, where the road starts to climb again. Gently at first, but then steeper towards Fuguret and Meailles. I could still see the road, high above me, zig-zagging its way up to the first feeding station in Thorame-Haute. (1,150m above sea level). From here the train leaves the 1919 route and we headed back by coach to Digne-les-Bains.

Curiously, not much is reported about this section of the route in L'Auto. Maybe the officials had been so cold in their cars that morning that they raced ahead to Colmars, to get a hot breakfast and coffee, before the riders tackled the first Giant of the Alps, the 'Col d'Allos'.

Stage 10 – Friday 18th July 1919 (Rest Day) Wednesday 18th September 2019 (Digne-les-Bains – Grenoble)

WHOO OOH, WHOO OOH ! WHOO OOH, WHOO OOH !

This morning, it wasn't the sound of my phone alarm going off, it was the sound of an Eagle Owl, hooting in the dark, from a wood somewhere, faraway across the limestone mountain range. I was happy to be awake early; I had a long drive and a challenging cycle in front of me. I packed up my belongings, ensuring I didn't allow any of the hundreds of white moths, flitting around the lights of the shower block, the chance to enter into my van. It was a lovely drive back to the 1919 route as the sun rose slowly and lit up the 'Alps Maritimes' strewn out in front of me. This section of the stage follows the Route Napoleon, which the French Emperor took after his escape from exile on the Island of Elba. He arrived on the south coast of France at Golfe Juan, on the 1st March 1815, with 1,100 soldiers, and proceeded to march from here, through Digne-les-Bains and on to Grenoble. This 200-mile route has since become a tourist attraction, and all along its length are commemorative plaques and monuments, bearing the legendary French Imperial Eagle.

Camping in Digne-les-bains and the deceptive start to the Cold D'Allos.

I stopped for a quick breakfast snack, in front of the Chateau de Colmars-les-Alpes, ready to tackle drive up the Col d'Allos, knowing that the young climber, Honoré Barthélémy, had arrived at this exact same point at 7.04 a.m. with a five-minute lead over the peloton. Given the fact that he was still suffering from his ingrowing toenails , this was quite a FEAT indeed! He was benefitting from the lack of experienced riders that were left in the race, and the fact that Eugéne Christophe, Firmin Lambot and Jean Alavoine were fighting a G.C. battle against each other.

The following section of the route was probably one of the most challenging as it contained, not only the 1,000m ascent from Allos to the Col de Valgelaye (now called the Col d'Allos at 2,250m), but also the steep and narrow descent into Barcelonette and the wonderfully named 'Valley of the Mexicans'. As I set my Satnav ready for the climb, I couldn't help but take a screenshot of my impending route, which looked more like a modern linear-zigzag painting, than a road to be followed. It wasn't long before I had arrived in ski country, as numerous Swiss-type chalets started to appear, as I climbed the mountain. Even though there was no snow at this time of year, the bare mountain ski slopes with their thin wire chairlifts leading up to daunting summits, looked dark and uninviting. I passed through the ski resort La Foux d'Allos (The Madness of Allos) and nodded in agreement.

The imperious Col d'Allos. If you look closely you can see the road snaking across the mountains.

Even though the modern day Tour de France hadn't been over the Col d'Allos since 2015, evidence of its passing, was still clear to be seen. I stopped and took a photograph of a large scrawl across the narrow route, which simply read CONTADOR, in support of the talented Spaniard, who finished fifth that year, nine minutes 48 seconds behind the eventual winner Chris Froome. One of the downsides to hosting the greatest cycling event in the world is that the country roads, which wind through the most majestic scenery, tend to get horribly scrawled and painted on with all kinds of weird and wonderful words and images. Prior to the Tour, two Dutchmen travel around the whole of route, with a tin of white paint and a roller, and transform any scribbled penises, or political slogans into some other object before the TV cameras arrive. For example, a large piece of penis art could be transformed into a picture of an owl. This may be true , or imagined, or it could just be another 'cock and balls' story.

*

Luigi Lucotti may have been distracted by one of these images, as he crashed on the hairy descent down the mountain, although I doubt this was the fashion in 1919. Mind you, even in these early days of the Tour, the crowd weren't averse to a bit of sabotage or subterfuge on the roads. In 1904, some over exuberant fans had put tacks down on the road, to try and puncture the tyres of a perceived rival to their favourite rider. In one instance they'd even chopped a tree down to block the progress of the peloton. However, my view would be that it was the incredibly sharp bends, on the treacherous descent into Barcelonnette, that caused Luigi's crash. Luigi is a rider who, by his own admission, tends to be headstrong when taking on certain parts of the route, rather than conserving energy to complete the stage. Whatever had happened, it was a serious crash, and Luigi made a sign as if to say he was going to abandon. He must have been persuaded to continue, but by the time he rode into the wonderfully named 'Valley of the Mexicans' he had lost more than an hour to his rivals. Honoré Barthélémy had increased his lead to 10 minutes on Jean Alavoine and to 15 minutes on Eugéne Christophe and Firmin Lambot, who were still battling together, neck and neck.

*

I drove gingerly down the mountainside, making sure I was careful not to come close to any of the ascending cyclists. Apparently, the Col d'Allos is open to cyclists only, between 8 – 11 a.m. on Friday mornings. This was a Friday, and I was there around that time, but I was not aware of the restrictions, so I carried on oblivious. Luckily, there were only a couple of hardy souls working their way up the mountain. I arrived in Barcelonnette, and stopped for a look around this interesting town, to try and find out why a Spanish-sounding town had connections with Mexico.

I parked in a supermarket car park and nearly lost the handlebars of my bike as I'd forgotten it was on the rear carrier and I was 0.2 metres over the barrier height. Ouch. Still, all was ok, and I wandered around the narrow-cobbled streets of the town, dominated by the church and it's 14th century bell tower. It was market day, and a little old man sat on a stool and played his accordion, as the shoppers browsed the stalls, looking for a bargain. I soon came across a Mexican restaurant and a shop selling Mexican clothes, ornaments, tableware, Day of the Dead skeletons and ponchos. Apparently in the second half of the 19th century, a number of young men from Barcelonnette had left France for Mexico. They had made a fortune, trading in fabrics and subsequently founded one of the first department stores in Mexico City. Consequently, other local young men followed suit and left the town in droves, hoping to seek their fortunes. The 'Barcelonnettes', as they were called, were a tight knit community and successful businessmen, and by the end of the century they owned 110 stores throughout Mexico. Eventually, some of the most successful of these men retired and returned to their home town, building Mexican-style villas along the valley. Now I understood the connection.

The pass at Uvernet-Fours on the descent to the Mexican town of Barcelonette. Watch out Luigi, it's narrow and steep!

WOW, what a magical place! I had left Barcelonnette and headed along the Valley de l'Ubaye to the Lac de Serre-Poncon. My plan was to cycle the 1919 route along the east side of the lake to Savines-le-Lac. I parked the van in a lay-by and faced the midday sun, which was blasting out a heat of some 28 degrees. I checked I had enough water in my 'bidons' and set off on the windy road hugging the lake. I couldn't get over the startling deep-blue colour of this man-made reservoir.

I wish you could see this photo in colour. Imagine a blaze of red geraniums in front of the blue azur, cool mountain waters of Lac de Serre-Poncon.

Fed by the glacial water of the Hautes Alpes and the Alpes du Sud, the lake measures over 20km in length, and was built to control the severe floods, that had caused so much damage and loss of life in this region in the mid-19th century. If I had thought that this cycle was going to be flat, I was much mistaken, and I soon found myself struggling up the steep road into Le Sauze-du-Lac. The sun was beating down on the tarmac and the noise of the chirping cicadas was intense. At the summit I stopped and took a drink from the village water pump, and stared back at the incredible view that stretched out in front of me. Eventually I reached Savines-le-Lac and I walked down to the lakeside, delighted to find that an intense game of pétanque was in progress.

I sought shade under one of the nearby trees (that's not me in the photo) and watched the battle commence. These were no novices, and the accuracy with which they launched the metal boule from out of the back of their hand, to land nearest the smaller jack, had been honed over many summers. Sometimes an aggressive shot was required to knock the opposition away from the jack, and both the ladies and men did this, with equal amounts of power.

I watched for a while, and then had to drag myself back onto my trusty steed, I still had a 100km drive to Grenoble. After crossing the lake, I headed to the 1919 feeding station in the town of Gap. The only problem was I took a wrong turn and missed the town out completely, so you could say that I didn't 'Mind the Gap!'

Bien joué - ' well played'– an intense game of pétanque at Savines-le-Lac.

Honoré Barthélémy was gradually extending his lead, minute by minute, over the chasing bunch, and so long as he didn't have any accidents, it was looking like a second consecutive stage win for the young Parisian and his third stage win overall. He managed to keep his lead, as he headed over the Col Bayard into Grenoble, and the massive crowds cheered him on, as he headed to the finish line on the Cours Saint André in the 'Capital of the Alps'. The Cours Saint André was the perfect place for a stage finish. It was an eight-kilometre-long, perfectly straight avenue, bordered on both sides by beautiful trees and a small stream, that served as a natural defence against the large crowds that had gathered to witness the end of Stage 10.

Honoré Barthélémy arrived, all alone, to rapturous applause from the masses of people on the tribune, which had been especially built in front of the Brasserie Marronniers (chestnut trees bar). He had such a broad grin on his face, as he struggled through the crowd to get to Henri Desgrange, and excitedly he pronounced:

"The more I cycle the better I go. If I had known before that I had the legs in me to cycle for 200km, in front and all alone, then I would have done what is necessary to clear my mind. Perhaps it is not too late yet, and I will be able to gain some territory on those in front of me. Anyway, it's going very well, and I suffered less today than I usually do with my feet! And that's a good sign for the Galibier!".

Then and now: Cours Saint André, finish line of Stage 10. Where did all the trees go ?

Napoleon had arrived in Grenoble, over one hundred years before Honoré, to be exalted by his people, on his return to becoming the Emperor of France once again. He shouted to the massed crowds "Before I reached Grenoble, they thought me a soldier of fortune. When I got there, I became a Prince'.

Maybe, after his solo effort along the Route de Napoleon, we could now say the same about the young Honoré Barthélémy'.

Honoré had moved up from fifth to fourth place in the G.C. rankings with his stage victory, but was still three hours behind his roommate Eugéne Christophe in first place. The Old Gaul had punctured not far from the finish line, and ended up losing three minutes to Firmin Lambot, who was becoming more of a worry with his lead now cut to twenty-three minutes. Poor old Luigi Lucotti had made it to the finish line, after his horrendous fall on the descent from the Col d'Allos, but at what cost? He'd arrived, all alone, nearly six hours behind the leaders, and dropped into last position in the G.C., and at the same time became the new 'lanterne rouge'. This was such a shame after his Herculean efforts, on the way into Nice on the previous stage.

Eugéne probably didn't realise it at time, but his 23-minute lead on that day in Grenoble, was to become one of the most historic leads in the history of the Tour de France. On the rest day, he was visited in his hotel room by a journalist François Mercier, who presented him with a package containing five woollen yellow jerseys. One for each stage left in the Tour. He should be able to wear them all, if he could keep his current lead, all the way into Paris.

"I delivered this morning to the valiant Eugéne Christophe a great yellow jersey. You will already know that our Director has decided that the leading man of the general classification will wear a jersey in the colours of L'Auto. There will now be a passionate struggle for the possession of this jersey! I'm sure that Jean Alavoine, and especially Firmin Lambot, would like to wear it."

And so, one hundred years ago, the Maillot Jaune was born

Stage 10: Nice to Grenoble (333 km)

1. Honoré Barthélémy	in 13h 08m 10s
2. Jean Alavoine	in 13h 20m 29s
3. Firmin Lambot	in 13h 21m 08s
4. Eugéne Christophe	in 13h 24m 12s
5. Léon Scieur	in 13h 56m 15s
6. Paul Duboc	in 14h 00m 00s
7. Jacques Coomans	in 14h 25m 07s
8. Jules Nempon	at a length
9. Alfred Steux	in 15h 43m 33s
10. Joseph Vandaele	in 15h 49m 50s
11. Luigi Lucotti	in 18h 55m 00s

General Classement (G.C.)

1. E. Christophe	(The Old Gaul)	154h 15m 09s
2. F. Lambot	(The Saddler)	154h 38m 28s
3. J. Alavoine	(Gars Jean)	154h 55m 00s
4. H. Barthélémy	(Glass Eye)	157h 19m 54s
5. L. Scieur	(The Locomotive)	157h 39m 40s
6. A. Steux	(The Kid)	165h 13m 08s
7. J. Vandaele	(Waterloo)	166h 40m 16s
8. J. Coomans	(The Smoker)	166h 55m 23s
9. P. Duboc *	(The Apple)	168h 57m 20s
10. J. Nempon	(The Upstart)	169h 09m 37s
11. L. Lucotti	(The Italian Job)	170h 04m 36s

* includes 30-minute penalty on Stage 8

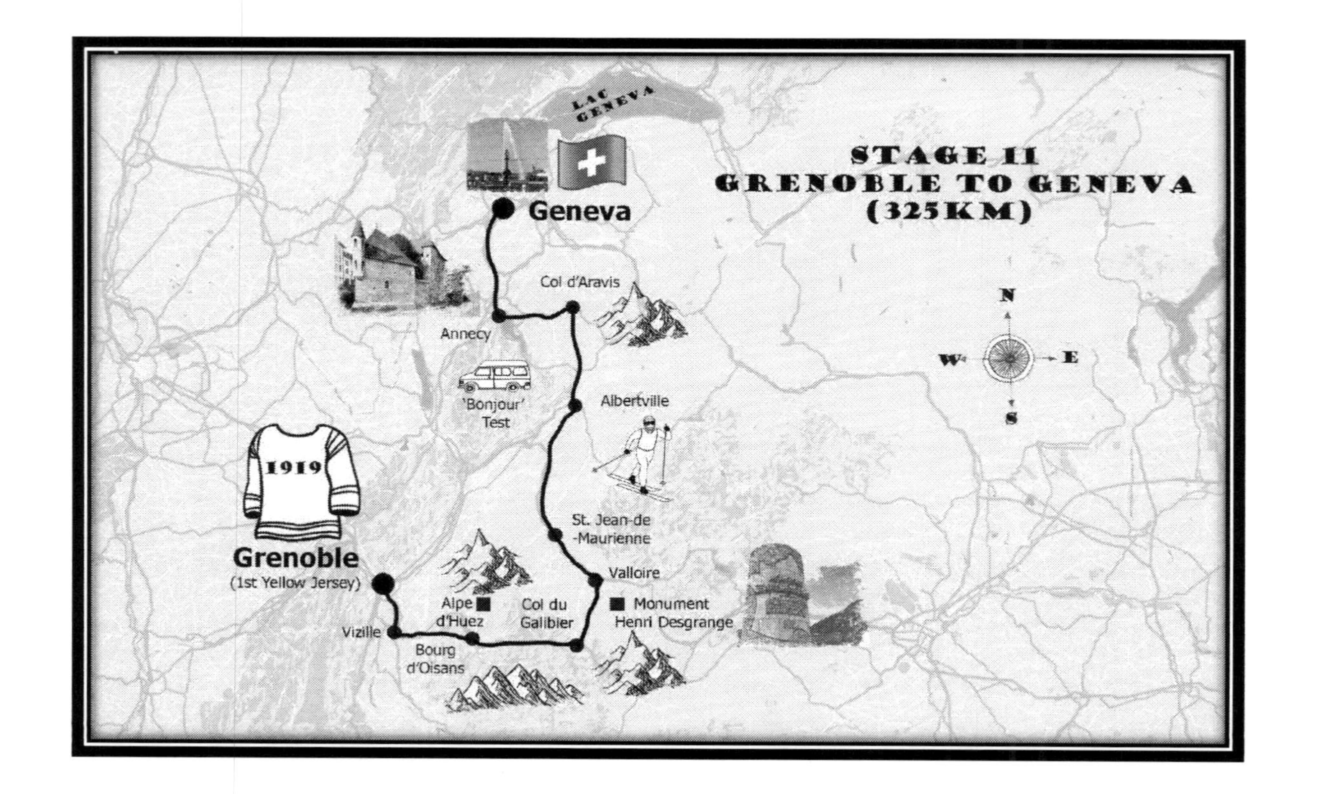

STAGE II
GRENOBLE TO GENEVA
(325KM)
N
W
E
S
LAC GENEVA
Geneva
Col d'Aravis
Annecy
'Bonjour' Test
Albertville
St. Jean-de -Maurienne
Valloire
Monument Henri Desgrange
Col du Galibier
Alpe d'Huez
Bourg d'Oisans
Vizille
1919
Grenoble
(1st Yellow Jersey)

Chapter 15 : 'Cri-Cri' the Canary

Stage 11: Saturday 19th July 1919 (Grenoble-Geneva)
Thursday 19th September 2019 (Grenoble – Lac d'Annecy)

"C'est vous – Eugéne Christophe!"

An old man whispered these words, over my shoulder, as I stared at the tiny plaque affixed to the side of the Caisse d'Epargne bank, on the Rue Beranger, just off the Boulevard Gambetta, in the centre of Grenoble.

"Dans mes rêves. (In my dreams)" was my reply.

I was pleased that he had recognised the old man, depicted on the back of the yellow T-shirt I'd had printed especially for the trip. So, this was it, this insignificant plaque, laid on the 19th July 2019, was to be the only lasting tribute in Grenoble, to one of the biggest events in the history of the Tour de France.

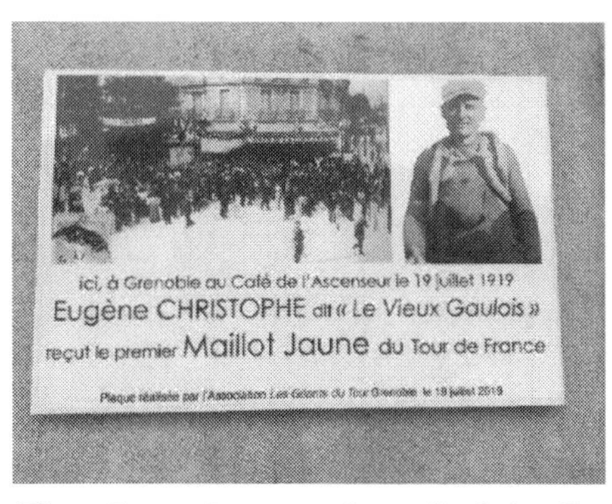

The solitary plaque on the wall of the Caisse d'Epargne, commemorating Eugéne Christophe receiving the yellow jersey on the 19th July 1919.

On the 25th October 2018, Christian Prudhomme, the Tour Director revealed the 2019 route of the Tour de France to the world press. I was convinced that on Friday 19th July 2019, the Tour would stop in Grenoble, to recognise and celebrate the 100th anniversary of the first yellow jersey ever to be awarded to Eugéne Christophe, outside the Café de l'Ascenseur. Imagine my surprise when I discovered that on this date, Stage 13 of the Tour, would be held nearly 700km away in Pau, on the other side of France. Not only that, it would be a time trial of 27.2km in length, as compared to the 1919 stage to Geneva of 325 km, which would tackle the giant Col du Galibier.

Then and now. The Café de l'Ascenseur in Grenoble. Birthplace of the iconic 'maillot jaune' 100 years old today.

The excellent cycling TV presenter Gary Imlach was also stunned and in his post-race summary that day he concluded. "It was July 19th 1919, that Eugéne Christophe was first awarded the yellow jersey at the Café de l'Ascenseur in Grenoble, before that day's stage to Geneva. So, he we are, neither at the café in question, nor even in Grenoble, which you might think a bit odd since a) it's the Tour's decision to turn this year's race into a three-week century celebration and b) they planned the route. However, I suppose the logistics of both starting in Brussels to honour Eddy Merckx, and finishing at the top of an Alp the final day before Paris, as the Tour likes to do these days, just made it an impossible date to keep. So, here we are instead in Pau, for a stage that doesn't even feature a yellow jersey. Julian Alaphilippe is in a skin suit today. It's the time trial."

I tried to put this non-event into some perspective. Yes, the Tour's organisers had created 21 special commemorative yellow jerseys to be presented at the end of each stage. Yes, the French President Emmanuel Macron had unveiled a plaque to commemorate the event in Pau. Yes, they'd made an anniversary yellow jersey cake, cut by the Tour legends, Eddy Merckx and Bernard Hinault; but was this enough? Maybe it was, after all, can you remember the celebrations in England for football's 100th F.A. Cup Final or cricket's 1,000th test match? No, nor can I !

*

It was midnight when Eugéne came out of the Café de l'Ascenseur bedecked in yellow. Henri Desgrange had watched him don the yellow jersey, without ceremony, at the counter in the corner of the café. Eugéne was a bit apprehensive and his mind was fixed on the stage ahead. He hardly noticed the jibes from the crowd.

"Oh, look, a pretty canary!"

"Hey Cri-Cri , what has mother Christophe done to you this morning? She's turned out her son in yellow!"

Apart from being called 'The Vieux Gaulois', Eugéne Christophe was also commonly known as 'Cri-Cri', which being the call of a small bird, lent itself quite neatly to him being called a canary. At the time the colour yellow would not have been the most popular of choices. It was normally linked to the weak and infirm, or it could designate a coward or a traitor. Yellow was also the colour of those excluded from society and was attributed to groups such as Jews, heretics and even lepers.

Mind you had his rivals even noticed? It was 1.30 a.m. by the time they'd all signed in at the Café de l'Ascenseur and headed out to the La Bajatière, on the Cours d'Eybens (not far from the rugby ground), in complete darkness for the official 2 a.m. start to Geneva. I would imagine that their thoughts were also concentrated on the fact that they had to tackle the giant Col du Galibier today. This would be the last real mountain stage before Paris, so maybe this was the stage for Firmin Lambot (The Saddler) and Jan Alavoine (Gars Jean) to try and attack Eugéne Christophe's lead.

*

The journey out of Grenoble is unremarkable and passes through a large chemical and hydro-electricity park, built to capture the natural resources supplied by the surrounding mountains. Large clouds of white smoke can be seen billowing across the tops of chemical plants, containing a maze of pipes, twisting and turning in all directions. The valley floor, out towards the town of Vizille, is laden with electricity pylons and power stations, supplying the whole of the alpine region with electricity. It would have been the same picture in 1919, as World War I had accelerated Grenoble's economic development. To sustain the war effort, new hydroelectric industries had developed along the various rivers of the region, and several existing companies moved into the armaments industry. Electro-chemical factories had also been established in the area surrounding Grenoble, initially to produce the diabolical chemical weapons needed to compete with the Germans. The 1919 riders had seen all of this the previous evening on their way down the Route Napoleon into Grenoble, but this morning, it was pitch black and it wasn't until they reached Bourg d'Oisans at the foot of Alpe d'Huez that dawn started to break. The peloton of 11 riders all arrived in a bunch together at 4.14 a.m., as was usual whilst cycling during the night. These first two to three hours of cycling in the dark, might as well of been neutral in the race. It did make you wonder about the validity of such early starts, introduced only to ensure Henri Desgrange could meet his publishing deadlines.

At Bourg d'Oisans, I had to veer off and have a quick look at the route to the notorious Alpe d'Huez. At the foot of the mountain I came across a little glass building, looking something like a bus stop. The glass has an imprinted image of a cyclist on it, resembling the infamous American, and seven-time winner of the Tour de France, Lance Armstrong. A survivor of testicular cancer, and a cycling hero to many, he was subsequently disgraced because of his involvement in a doping scandal and stripped of his seven titles. The Alpe d'Huez was not introduced to the race until 1952, but is seen as a challenge for any 'wannabe' wearers of the yellow jersey. On the surrounds of the glass image is the following statement written in French and English.

You are at the bottom of the legendary Alpe d'Huez road, made famous by the Tour de France cycle race. 21 loops. An average slope of 10% over an ascension of 14km. A record of 37 minutes! Tempted? Then take a ticket at the bottom and check your performance when you reach the top, on your bicycle of course.

The roundabout at Bourg d'Oisans and the challenge of Alpe dHuez.

As much as I was tempted, I hadn't got 37 minutes to get to the top, and I faced a long and daunting journey ahead, so I turned down their kind offer and turned around and headed back to the 1919 route. Bourg d'Oisans (Altitude 725m) was at the start of the 47km ascent to the top of the Col du Galibier (2,558m), a rise of 1,833 metres, passing the Col du Lautaret (Altitude 2,058m) on the way. Would Firmin Lambot and Jean Alavoine decide to attack Christophe somewhere on this climb?

12km out from Bourg d'Oisans, the road takes you alongside the turquoise clear waters of the alpine Lac du Chambon. At one point you actually cross the water on top of the hydro-electric dam, that was constructed in 1935. This would have been a much-changed scene in 1919, as there was only a dusty mountain track to take the riders over the edge of the lake and the River Romanche. I stopped in the ominously named town of 'La Grave' (1,450m), and I looked around to see if I could see any deceased riders buried at the side of the road. Thankfully I couldn't, but it was worth stopping to take a moment and stare across at the stunning view of the imperious 'Grand Pic', Mount Meije (3,893m). This was the last major peak in the French Alps to be climbed by mountaineers, and from the range of dark, snow-capped jagged peaks, stretching out in front of me, I could see why.

The dam on Lac du Chambon and the ominous Mount Meije at La Grave.

It was here Honoré Barthélémy struck out again. By the time the peloton reached the mountain road that overlooked the hamlet of Villar d'Arené, he had dropped Jacques Coomans and shaken off Luigi Lucotti, who had recovered from his accident on the previous stage. Would this be Honoré's fourth stage win? And where were Firmin Lambot and Jean Alavoine? Had they made their predicted attack on Eugéne Christophe yet? It was fast becoming a time of now or never.

At the Col du Lautaret (2,058m), Barthélémy had gained two minutes on Lucotti, five on Alavoine, Lambot, Christophe and Scieur, and he headed up to the snow-laden Col du Galibier all alone. There was still no attack by the second and third placed riders on Christophe, as they continued to play their game of 'cat and mouse' all the way up the mountain.

Honoré climbed the 5.3km of the terrible Col du Galibier in 38 minutes 59 seconds, with the sun shining brightly off the mountains. It was as if his feet were in harmony with the pedals of his bike, and no matter how steep the road, he produced the same raw power. Henri Desgrange called him the red squirrel, because of his red hair and his agility to jump from one mountain pass to another, like a squirrel jumping from branch to branch in a tree. He was increasing his advantage over his rivals, bit by bit, and by the time he had reached the tunnel of the Galibier, the lead had increased to nearly 8 minutes on Jacques Coomans and Léon Scieur and 11 minutes 30 seconds on Christophe and Lambot. The young Frenchman was surely one of the best climbers the Tour had ever seen!

Some local shepherds tending their flocks, stopped and saluted each rider as they arrived at the mouth of the newly built tunnel. Constructed in 1891, it was built for military purposes, and at 365m in length, there is one metre for each day of the year. We know that the 1919 riders passed through the tunnel as L'Auto quotes, that Coomans and Scieur were engulfed by the tunnel, and they published a photo of the exit, on the other side of the mountain (Côte de la Maurienne) in the following day's edition. At the south portal to the tunnel, there is a monument to Henri Desgrange, which was inaugurated when the Tour passed on 19 July 1949. Whenever the Tour crosses the Col du Galibier, a wreath is laid on the memorial. There is also a special prize, and the Souvenir Henri Desgrange, is awarded to the first rider across the summit of the highest mountain in each year's tour. The Col du Galibier was first used in the Tour de France in 1911; the first rider over the summit was Emile Georget, who, with Paul Duboc (The Apple) and Gustave Garrigou were the only riders not to walk.

*

In this year's race (2019) Stage 18 had passed the Henri Desgrange monument on its way over the summit to the finish in Valloire. The stage was won by the Columbian Nairo Quintana, in what was a solo sideshow compared to the real battle for the yellow jersey. On this day, Julian Alaphilippe had nearly lost his hold on the 100-year-old jersey. He had already collected 13 of the 14 special edition yellow jerseys, including the anniversary one on the 19th July 2019 in Pau. He was greedy for more, and whilst he had been distanced by the yellow jersey group, climbing up the Galibier, he had taken enormous risks on the descent into Valloire and somehow managed to collect his 14th yellow jersey. There were now only two stages left before the ceremonial final stage 21 into Paris. Could he be the first Frenchman to stand on top of the podium since Bernard Hinault in 1985, an incredible 34 years ago?

I could still see traces of the 2019 stage, as I parked in front of the Henri Desgrange monument, and admired the view back down the valley. I could see the tiny road I had driven up. It looked as though someone had dropped a ball of string, which had unravelled itself, rolling down the bare mountainside.

The Col du Galibier and the monument to Henri Desgrange.

I saw one gigantic 'G' THOMAS painted across the road, and a number of tributes paid to the Frenchman THIBAULT PINOT, who looked well placed to challenge his compatriot Julian Alaphilippe, for the yellow jersey, after his heroics in the Pyrénées. Mysteriously, there were no slogans in favour of Julian, the leader. As well as racing bikes, these roads are heaven for fans of the more heavily engineered variety. Small packs of black leather encased riders weave and lean their way up the mountain, with speed being their only motive. I had to strain to see if I could see them coming down the mountain roads, which zigzagged above me, as I knew they would probably be veering over to my side of the road, as I headed around the corner. There were teams of professional photographers capturing them on each bend, as they tried to scrape their knees on the Col du Galibier tarmac. I hoped my van wouldn't appear on one of their photo resale internet sites, rolling all the way back down to the Col du Lautaret.

It was time for me to head off and wind my way down the steep descent from the summit of the Galibier, down the Col du Télégraphe, and into the ski resort of Valloire. The Col and tunnel du Télégraphe were other mystical place names on the Tour de France route that I had been intrigued to visit. Was this a hole in the side of the mountain covered in radio masts and antennas? Nope, it was just an ordinary tunnel, although the Col itself was bedecked with a tribute to the Tour de France leader, complete with yellow jersey and made entirely out of straw.

The Swiss ski chalets of Valloire and a straw tribute to the yellow jersey.

Valloire itself, is a pretty modern ski resort, complete with many large Swiss-type wooden chalets with balconies exploding with the colour of the local mountain flowers. The town itself, is probably best known for the glass memorial to the great Italian climber, Marco Pantani, who won the Tour de France in 1998, but who unfortunately died of a drugs overdose, alone in a Rimini hotel room in 2004. The memorial is a simple glass sheet, with a cyclist engraved on it and the memento 'PANTANI FOREVER'. Known as Il Pirata (the pirate) because of his shaven head, bandana and shiny earrings, the aggressive Italian rider became a fans' favourite, and is held up as one of the race's all-time greats.

It was 8 a.m., when Honoré Barthélémy arrived at the first feeding station of the stage in Saint-Michel-de-Maurienne, at the foot of the Galibier. He had increased his lead to four minutes over Lucotti, seven minutes over Scieur and Coomans and ten minutes over the three leaders of the G.C. Jean Alavoine, Eugéne

Christophe and Firmin Lambot. As the riders tucked into the specially prepared meal of chicken legs, accompanied by 'Les Petites Savoyardes' (a local pasta made from flour and fresh eggs), I'm sure they would have taken their time to pay their respects to the victims of the rail disaster that had taken place here 18 months earlier in December 1917. A troop train carrying at least 1,000 French soldiers, on their way home from the Italian Front in World War I, derailed as it descended into the valley. It caused a catastrophic crash, and the subsequent fire ripped through the 19 wooden coaches, stoked by the grenades and ammunition on board, and 675 soldiers lost their lives. However, the riders would not have known the full extent of the tragedy as, France's and at the time, the world's biggest ever rail disaster, was kept a military secret, for a number of years, due the implication of some French officers, who had overloaded the carriages.

Train crash at Saint-Michel-de-Maurienne, December 1917

I parked in front of the SNCF Gare de Saint-Michel-Valloire, the scene of the accident, and sat and thought about the victims of this needless disaster. It is still one of the biggest world rail disasters of recent times, and has only been surpassed by the terrible tsunami rail disaster in Sri Lanka in 2004.

After the peace and tranquillity of the mountain pastures, the area around Saint-Michel-de-Maurienne, was an entirely different landscape for the 1919 riders to experience. In the early 20th century, many industries were established around the Maurienne valley. Most involved the control and use of the water thundering down the mountainside and included hydro-electricity plants, aluminium smelting plants and paper mills.

The second and final feeding station followed quite quickly, and having eaten at 8 a.m., the riders were forced to refuel again at 10.18 a.m. in Albertville. I guess this was as a result of the geography of the 11th stage, as the organisers would not have fancied serving up hot grub on snow-capped mountain passes and so the riders had one stop after the descent from the Col du Galibier and one stop before the ascent of the Col d'Aravis. It was here that Firmin Lambot made his move, speeding away from Christophe, and attacking with the Italian Luigi Lucotti at his side. By the time they reached the summit they had gained two minutes on the Old Gaul.

After the descent into Annecy, by the shores of the fluorescent-blue lake, the pair had increased their lead to four minutes, and all was looking well for the Belgian, but then the Green-Toothed Witch struck out at Lambot on the way into Geneva, and the resulting puncture allowed Christophe to catch up. Was this the moment in which the 13th Tour de France was decided? Lambot had taken his chance and failed.

*

It was time for me to stop and I pulled into my campsite on Lake Annecy, in Talloires and set up ready for tomorrow's early morning cycle. I headed to the local Bar-Pizza-Restaurant for my own 'ravitaillement'. The front of the bar was full of locals having an after-work drink or two. It was all extremely convivial, but I couldn't help wondering why they smoked so much? They were all still relatively young, but smoked liked chimneys and coughed like them too. It did seem incongruous, with all the fresh mountain air surrounding them, that they would want to suck copious amounts of nicotine into their lungs. I looked around the bar to see if I could spot Jacques Coomans (The Smoker) puffing away in the corner.

I finished my microwaved lasagne, and fully revitalised I headed back to the campsite pitch to discover I was surrounded by a group of teenage campers, all of whom were so excited to be outdoors for a night. The singing, dancing and euro pop music went on into the early hours of the morning, as 'les hormones' kicked in. As for myself, all was ok as luckily, I had packed 'les earplugs!'

Stage 11 – Sunday 20th July 1919 (Day of rest)
Friday 20th September 2019 (Lac d'Annecy - Geneva)

'Get out of the bloody way!!'

I'd set out early this morning for a 52km cycle around the beautiful Lac d'Annecy. The mountain scenery was absolutely breath-taking, as its reflection sparkled on the silvery-blue waters of the lake. The early morning mist hovered over the tiny fishing boats, that would soon be heading out to try and get the first catch of the day. The cycle path I followed, hugged the shoreline for a few kilometres, and headed across a small wooded area called the 'Reserve Naturelle, Marais du Bout du Lac'. Suddenly I was stopped in my tracks by the sight of a small family of wild boar, quietly eating on the grassy verge in front of me. I got my phone out quietly to try and take a photo without disturbing them. Suddenly two Americans pulled right in front of me and screeched to a halt.

"Well, would you look at that, sweetheart, wild boar!". By this time, the noise of their brakes had frightened the family and they started to dart for cover in the nearby woods. The American, obscuring my view and shot, started to unfasten his GoPro camera from his cycling helmet. I'd had enough of this. It was as if I didn't exist. I stormed in front of him, and at least got some sort of blurred image, before they disappeared into the woods completely.

By the time, I headed down the opposite shore of the lake, all sorts of keep fit enthusiasts were out, enjoying the early morning sunshine. There were some serious cyclists, joggers and brisk alpine walkers. I even saw one woman on a pair of dry-land training skis. I decided to do a 'Bonjour' test to see what reaction I got as I headed into Annecy. I reckoned, out of a hundred 'Bonjours' from me, I got four 'Bonjours' in return, one 'Good Morning' , one smile and a grunt. A six percent return was pretty poor, but I suppose a lot of them, were too busy trying to beat their own P.B.s, or checking their number of steps, to be bothered with a Brit grinning inanely and interrupting their serious pursuits.

Annecy, or the 'Venice of the Alps' is one of the quaintest old towns, you could ever hope to visit. Sitting, as it does, on three canals and the Thiou river, the old medieval town is a maze of narrow cobbled streets, leading through mysterious archways, and over the tiny bridges which breach the canals.

Early morning on Lac d'Annecy on my way to the beautiful lakeside town.

Today was market day and the streets were packed with tourists. A lot of them were Japanese who took pictures of everybody and everything, including me. A French market, is a heady mix of sights and smells, and the aroma of roast chickens, freshly baked bread, pungent goats' cheeses and cured meats, make an assault on your senses at each turn. Annecy has a special place in my heart, as it was the town where my wife and I spent our first wedding anniversary. I always recount the story of our celebratory meal to any French friends and it usually raises a smile. My wife and I were still learning the French language, and it was sometimes necessary to consult the French dictionary, when trying to decipher a restaurant menu. On this particular occasion, one of the 'entrées' was called 'Crottins Chauds'. I knew that the word 'chaud' meant 'hot' but had to look up the word 'Crottin'. I burst out into fits of laughter and my quizzical wife said "What does it mean? Shall we order it?" I replied that according to the dictionary we would be ordering a plate of hot shit with salad, so maybe it was best to be avoided! As it turns out, as well as being a swirl of chocolate or cheese, 'crottin' can also mean a swirl of dog shit. When the dishes arrived, we were relieved to see, it was actually goat's cheese on toast, on a bed of vinaigrette salad, covered in crushed walnuts. This is quite a common dish in the UK now, called Salade de Chèvre Chaud, but in those days, it was unheard of.

Leaving Annecy, I headed into my first new country of this trip, Switzerland. I pulled up at the Border Control and got my passport ready, but there was no one there to greet me. I felt a bit cheated as I sailed through and headed into Geneva.

*

As for the 1919 riders, the rules for passports were pretty strict and L'Auto devoted a few paragraphs to the expected requirements.

1. The exit from France is done at the Pont de la Caille (where Lambot had punctured). The riders, whose bikes have been checked and sealed by the French customs, have nothing to do and will be able to pass through customs without stopping. The official L'Auto cars and manufacturers will have to be issued with a pass or show it, if they already have one. Drivers will also have to affix a seal on their car. The 'passavant' carries the detailed description of the car and its accessories. The customs will take around a quarter of an hour. The Office of the Pont de la Caille will take care of these operations.

2. The entrance into Switzerland will be done at Perly, that is to say five kilometres before the finish. The riders will pass freely. The cars that follow the race should allow time for a halt, but shouldn't receive any visits from the customs.

Honoré Barthélémy had passed freely, and he was well on the way to his fourth stage win of this Tour, and also his third consecutive stage win. Glass Eye arrived at 2.46 p.m. and was cheered to the finish line on the Route de Grand Lancy, south of the city, by up to 30,000 spectators apparently shouting,'Vive La France, Vive Le Tour de France, Vive Barthélémy, Vive L'Auto !', which is a bit of a surprise considering the race was now in Switzerland. Ten minutes later, Luigi Lucotti arrived to an ovation. His marvellous achievement of second place moved him up to eight position in the G.C. passing the title of 'lanterne rouge' to the Licence B rider, Jules Nempon. The top three in G.C. (Alavoine, Christophe and Lambot) all came in together 5 minutes later along with Leon Scieur. There were just four stages to go now to Paris.

It was a three to four-kilometre walk, from the finish line to the Grand Café de la Couronne, where the riders were due to sign in. The riders had to walk through crowds, at least three-deep, and were followed by a cortège of around a hundred cyclists. When they got inside the café on the Rue du Rhone, near Lac Leman, they were greeted with quite a display. The owner had covered his café walls, with portraits of all the French generals and Allied generals, who had played a prominent part in winning the Great War. Maybe, he now needed to put a portrait up of one yellow canary, Mr. Eugéne Christophe. This man, this jersey and this day, would now be enshrined forever in the history of the Tour de France.

"Go on, tell him he looks like a canary!"

Eugéne Christophe looks unimpressed as he arrives in Grenoble sporting the first ever yellow jersey. To the left of him are Léon Scieur, Jean Alavoine and Firmin Lambot. (left to right) - (Saturday 19th July 1919)

The Grand Café de la Couronne, Geneva, where a distracted cyclist, watching the midday diners, is about to crash into a streetlamp.

Stage 11: Grenoble – Geneva (326km)

1. Honoré Barthélémy	in 12h 46m 41s
2. Luigi Lucotti	in 12h 56m 49s
3. Jean Alavoine	in 13h 01m 47s
4. Léon Scieur	at a length
5. Eugéne Christophe	at a length
6. Firmin Lambot	at a length
7. Jacques Coomans	in 13h 12m 42s
8. Paul Duboc	in 14h 06m 31s
9. Alfred Steux	in 16h 00m 20s
10. Jules Nempon	at a length
11. Joseph. Vandaele	in 16h 49m 15s

General Classement (G.C.)

1. E. Christophe	(The Old Gaul)	167h 16m 56s
2. F. Lambot	(The Saddler)	167h 40m 15s
3. J. Alavoine	(Gars Jean)	167h 56m 47s
4. H. Barthélémy	(Glass Eye)	170h 06m 35s
5. L. Scieur	(The Locomotive)	170h 41m 27s
6. J. Coomans	(The Smoker)	180h 08m 05s
7. A. Steux	(The Kid)	181h 13m 38s
8. L. Lucotti	(The Italian Job)	183h 01m 25s
9. P. Duboc *	(The Apple)	183h 03m 51s
10. J. Vandaele	(Waterloo)	183h 29m 31s
11. J. Nempon	(The Upstart)	185h 09m 57s

* includes 30-minute penalty on Stage 8

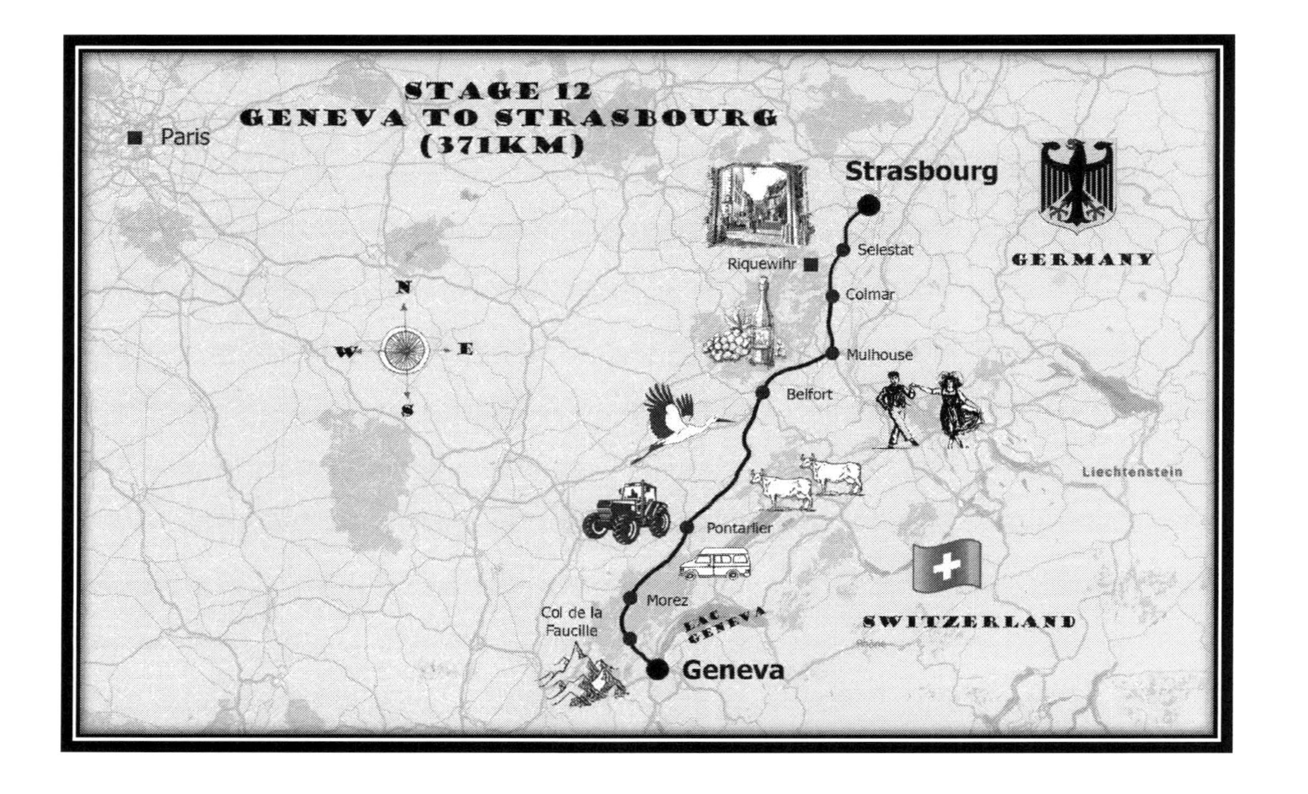
STAGE 12
GENEVA TO STRASBOURG
(371KM)
Paris
Strasbourg
Selestat
Riquewihr
Colmar
Mulhouse
Belfort
Pontarlier
Morez
Col de la Faucille
LAC GENEVA
Geneva
GERMANY
SWITZERLAND
Liechtenstein
N
W
E
S

Chapter 16 : 'The Return of France's lost sisters'

Stage 12: Monday 21st July 1919 (Geneva - Strasbourg)
Saturday 21st September 2019 (Geneva – Lac de Saint-Point)

'My little men, my dear little men, my little French men. Listen to me well. Throughout the last 14 years L'Auto has been published daily, and it has never given bad advice, eh? So, listen up. The Prussians are bastards. If I use the title 'Prussians', it is so as not to confuse them with Germans, because I believe that not all German brains have yet been moulded into that of a Prussian. You can see their dirty square heads, like stupid sheep, without thought, the heads of butchers. My little men, you have to fight these bastards. Believe me. It's not possible for a Frenchman to surrender to a German.

But watch out. When your rifle butt is on their chest, they'll ask for your forgiveness. Don't let yourself be taken in. Smash it down on them without pity and when you've smashed it well and you've crushed a good number, then we'll see. But in the five litres of blood that their carcasses hold, make four of them flow and you'll see that, when they're down to one litre per man, they'll understand that Alsace and Lorraine are French lands. We must be rid of these evil imbeciles who, for four years, prevented us from living, loving, breathing and being happy.'

These are the shocking words of Henri Desgrange, written in L'Auto in 1914, at the outbreak of the First World War. As we know, Henri was so shocked by his country's capitulation, in the Franco-Prussian war of 1871, that he felt he needed to help create a nation that would be fit and ready to face any future acts of aggression by the Germans. The challenging stages of his Tour de France would build lean, fit athletes, that would be physically ready to repel any future attempts of invasion. The Treaty of Frankfurt, signed after the Franco-Prussian war, had annexed the French territories of Alsace and Lorraine to Germany and given them a stronger military border across the River Rhine. The Treaty of Versailles, that was signed the evening the 1919 Tour de France had set off from Paris, now returned France's 'lost sisters' to French control. During the 47 years of German occupation of Alsace and

Lorraine, Henri Desgrange took great delight in ignoring these rewritten borders. In 1905, the Ballon d'Alsace mountain range was included in the Tour, not just for its climbing challenge, but also because it ran close to the border with the German Empire. He continued to challenge the Germans in 1906, 1907, 1908 and 1910, by sending the Tour into the "occupied" Moselle (Lorraine) region, albeit with their initial agreement. In 1911 and with tensions rising, Berlin refused Henri Desgrange entry into their country, and so Henri staged the race right along the Lorraine border, with a visit to the town of Longwy, a part of the Moselle region held by France.

Now, even before the ink had dried on the Treaty of Versailles, the Tour headed across the plains of Alsace, for the first time in its history, visiting the old French towns of Mulhouse, Colmar, and of course, the capital, Strasbourg. After the welcome sunshine of the previous week in the mountains, it was raining again, as the 11 riders signed in at the Grand Café de la Couronne, and headed out over the Pont du Mont Blanc, which crosses Lac Leman. It is doubtful that it would have been light enough for them to see one of Geneva's most famous landmarks, but they could probably hear it, as the Jet d'Eau (water fountain) fires the local mountain waters, 90 metres in the air, and then drops back majestically into the lake. The official 2 a.m. start was given by a correspondent of L'Auto, Monsieur Max Burgi (maybe Robert Desmarets, the official starter, had not made the short trip across the border into Switzerland) outside the 'Brasserie de Montbrillant' opposite Geneva's main train station 'La Gare de la Cornavin'.

*

It was a bright and sunny Saturday morning, when I drove past the Jet d'Eau, rising majestically and arching its spray into the bright blue sky. This immediately brought back memories of the opening sequence of the late 1960's TV series 'The Champions', which features the water fountain, in all its glory, dancing behind the three glamorous secret agents, who work for a law enforcement organisation linked to the United Nations. It's all based in Geneva. Catch it on 'YouTube' if you dare.

I located the Café du Montbrillant (or at least, the Brasserie of the Hôtel Montbrillant), and imagined Eugéne Christophe's thick new woollen yellow jersey, soaking up the early morning Swiss rain. He would, of course, have to wear it all day, even if it got heavier and heavier, as the rain seeped into the yarn. He would only have cycled 5km, when together with the 1919 peloton, he arrived at the French border at Le Grand Saconnex, and all 11 riders were checked through customs without delay.

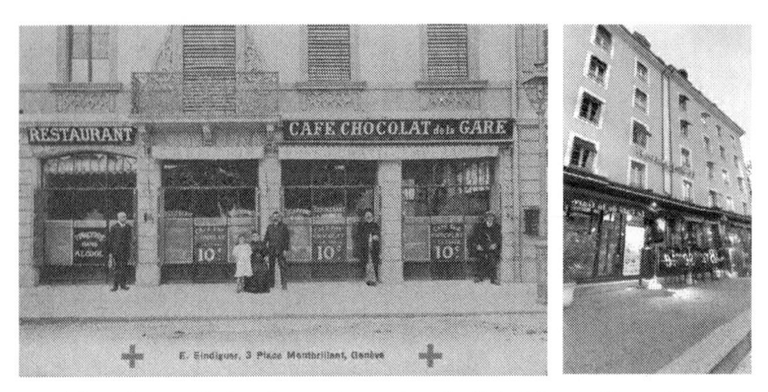

Time for a café chocolat at the station Café du Montbrillant, Geneva.

I hadn't even realised I'd crossed the border. The country road I took towards the town of Gex, had no border controls whatsoever, and I had passed back into France, without realising. Mind you, I soon knew where I was, as I drove down the high street of a little village called Grilly, and counted nine zebra crossings! Yes nine, the joint leader! I was definitely back in France.

*

If the organisers were hoping for an exciting day ahead, then the geography of Stage 12 didn't lend itself to a long-sustained attack on the yellow jersey. The toughest part of the stage was the first section, climbing up out of Geneva, up the Col de la Faucille (1,323m), and this was going to take place in rain and complete darkness. True to form, all 11 riders arrived together at dawn in Morez, on the other side of the mountain at 4.25 a.m. From here it was practically all downhill to the arrival in Strasbourg.

*

I edged up the Col de la Faucille, taking care to give the weekend cyclists and motorbike riders a wide berth. In contrast to 1919, it was a beautiful autumn day and time for my cycle around the Lac de Saint Point. Before I reached my campsite, I had the unusual experience of passing into Switzerland again, turning right and ending up back in France, all in the space of a few hundred metres. The border control at 'La Cure' is right on the Franco-Swiss border and I slowed down in front of three heavily armed policeman, chatting at the border control. As I reached for my passport, they looked at me quizzically, as if to say, don't interrupt our conversation, we're discussing tonight's football matches, drive on. After the descent, 8km at 8% gradient into Morez, I climbed up through dense pine forests to Chapelle-les-Bois. Here the scenery changed dramatically and suddenly I was driving through rolling bright green pastures, with cattle grazing gently under a bright blue sky complete with fluffy white clouds. (The 1919 riders were warned to take great care, through the villages here, due to the heaps of timber they would encounter on the roadside) I was welcomed by a giant statue made out of hay bales, looking rather like a rural Bertie Bassett (liquorice allsorts), and announcing 'Chapelle-les-Bois vous accueille , le 21.09.2019, Comice du Canton du Mouthe.'

Bertie Bassett welcomes me to the farming community of Chapelle-les-Bois.

It appears that today was the day for the local agriculture show, where farmers would be competing for best animal in show. Unfortunately, I didn't have time to visit the main event but I did stop to top up my supplies at the local supermarket. This was a beautiful area and although the rural villages looked slightly tired and well lived in, the overall feeling was one of warmth and friendship. This was only reaffirmed as I passed through the supermarket, and everybody had time to chat with me from the till girl to the baker, selling his baguettes and croissants at the entrance. Not for the first time on this trip, I wished I could have stayed a while longer. This seemed to be a place anybody could feel at home in. I'm sure they were all hard-working people, labouring diligently to bring the local produce in, but once work was over, it was time to enjoy life with old friends. As I passed a wonderfully named hotel and restaurant called the 'Auberge du Grand Git', I thought this is the place for me.

As I got on my bike and set off from my campsite, I could feel the warm September air on my back. I thought it was time to try my 'Bonjour' test again. The one that had failed somewhat miserably, whilst cycling around the lake in Annecy. Whilst the Lac de Saint-Point is not as grand a lake as Lac d'Annecy, what it lacks in sophistication, it makes up for with rural charm. There are far less cars and people here, and far more cows and sheep. Here it is the sound of clanging cow bells, which competes with the bird song on the green open hills that surround the lake. Not surprisingly, this region of the Haut-Doubs, is renowned for its Fromage de Mont d'Or, a soft cheese made from the local raw cow's milk, that tends to be served with a spoon. I completed a circuit of the lake, and headed up the wonderfully named River Doubs, to the town of Pontarlier, the next control point of the stage. My Bonjour count was going well. I got 10% of blank looks, 10% of grunts and 80% of smiling Bonjours.

The beautiful cycle along Lac de Saint-Point to the wedding in Pontarlier.

It was late afternoon when I arrived in Pontarlier, just in time to get the football results on my iPhone and discover that my team had won 2-1 at home, so I had a smile and a spring in my step. Pontarlier was busy. It turned out there were two weddings being held at the Mairie, on the 'Rue de la République' , as well as a fête in the town square. The well-dressed guests were smoking, drinking and chatting on the streets in the sunshine, and admiring a magnificent green and yellow John Deere tractor. It was festooned with bright yellow balloons, ready to whisk the bride and groom away to a life filled with future happiness and Montbeliarde cows.

*

It was a different picture in 1919, and it was only 7.05 a.m. when 7 out of the 11 riders (Alavoine, Barthélémy, Scieur, Lambot, Christophe, Lucotti and Nempon) arrived at the control in Pontarlier near the main square. Coomans and Duboc arrived five minutes later having punctured somewhere near the lake. (Or maybe Jacques Coomans – The Smoker, had persuaded Paul Duboc to stop for a smoke of the local tobacco!) All of them were complaining of the damp and the cold. There was a long wait for Vandaele and Steux, both of whom were suffering badly. Joseph Vandaele (facing his Waterloo) was still feeling the effects of his bad fall in Toulon on Stage 9, and Alfred Steux (The Kid) was suffering from the damage done to his knees after his crash and somersault on the Col du Galibier. The two close Belgian friends were, however, both determined to see this out until the end in Paris.

So was I, despite the intense afternoon heat. As I returned to my lakeside campsite, I passed a garage sign indicating the temperature had reached 32 degrees!

Stage 12 – Tuesday 22nd July 1919 (Rest Day)
Sunday 22nd September 2019 (Lac de Saint-Point- Strasbourg)

And so, the 1919 peloton headed towards the old border with Germany at Soppe-le-Bas. I supposed the riders would be wondering what sort of reception they would get from the newly liberated Alsatians. Apparently, the crowds on the border were moderate, but after signing the control sheet the five remaining

French riders, got together and sang 'Le Chant de Départ' (The Departure Song), partly in patriotic fervour, and partly to raise their spirits, as it was chucking it down! Not much had changed with regards to the G.C. up to this point. Coomans and Duboc had caught up with the main group after the first feeding station in Morteau, and all nine were together as they headed into Mulhouse for the second 'ravitaillement' of the stage. It was 1.13 p.m. when they tucked into their first Germanic influenced food stop. The injured Vandaele and Steux had to wait another hour and a half to taste these new delights as they pulled in at 2.42 p.m.

L'Auto reported that the Tour de France was an enormous success across the whole of Alsace, and whilst it was true that there were some large crowds in Mulhouse, Colmar and Strasbourg, it was also true that in rural Alsace, the Tour wasn't really followed. Even the coverage in the regional newspaper 'Derniers Nouvelles d'Alsace' was limited to a couple of mentions. However, the weekly illustrated sports magazine, 'Vie au Grand Air' (Outdoor Life), featured a full-length article on the Tour and included on its cover, the first image of a rider cycling through rural Alsace wearing a yellow jersey.

The first image of Eugéne Christophe, wearing the yellow jersey, riding through the newly reclaimed lands of Alsace & Lorraine.

Given the lack of exciting new stories coming out of Stage 12, the reporting in L'Auto turned to other cycling matters. After the scandals and blatant cheating, which had taken place in the 1904 Tour de France, the organisers had decided to change the rules to a system based on points. The cyclists would receive points, equal to their ranking in a stage, so the winner of the stage would receive 1 point and the rider coming in 87th place, 87 points. The cyclist with the fewest points was therefore the leader of the race. In 1912, it had changed back to a system, based purely on the amount of time taken on each stage. There were supporters and detractors of each system. A Mr. Gabort from Paris had sent a letter to L'Auto:

"You must feel, as many sportsmen do; the injustice of the classification by time."

Henri Desgrange did not hold back in his reply:

"Ah! no, my dear reader, let me tell you once and for all and then let it go no further. Have you already forgotten the period, where the vagaries of the system of ranking riders by points, made us change to ranking them by time? Can you not remember the ridiculous situation, where a rider who is beaten by four lengths, could end up being penalised by 20 points more than the winner, just because of the number of riders that could end up between the two of them? And do you not remember the other idiosyncrasy, where the last rider to finish in the first stage in Le Havre would receive 87 points, because there would be 87 riders arriving, whereas in the penultimate stage to Dunkerque, for that same last place you only get 18 points, because the peloton has reduced dramatically since Le Havre?

Then you say to me, 'Jean Alavoine is the best rider of the bunch, and he is only third in the Classement-General, although he has won four stages.'

So, what gives you the right to say that Alavoine is the best, having won four sprint stages versus Barthélémy, for example, who has won four stages in the mountains? Why do you think that the best man of the Tour de France should be a sprinter, and that Alavoine was right to sleep in a ditch, in the first stage and that Christophe was wrong to stay on his bike? The Tour de France cannot belong to the best sprinter or the best climber, nor to the rider who appeals to the public, nor to any specialist. It must be the prerogative of the rider who has shown the best performance overall. This, undoubtedly, is Christophe, because even if he regularly gets beaten by Alavoine at each stage finish by one or two lengths, he managed to defeat his rival by more than half an hour in that first stage from Paris to Le Havre! Also, don't take it as a reflection of his performance, the amount of points you think that Christophe would have at this stage versus Alavoine? I'll have you know that Christophe would have been smart enough to change his tactics if the ranking had been based on your calculations!"

It is worth noting that the points system lasted from 1904 to 1912, when it was realised that Eugéne Christophe had come second to Odile Defraye of Belgium, by only seven minutes over 5,319km. The points system showed that Defraye had only 49 points, whereas Christophe had amassed a massive 108 points. This appeared to be a crushing victory for Defraye, which it wasn't, and so Henri decided the Tour would return to a system based on the overall time taken in the race. This system has lasted through to the present day. However, in 1953 to celebrate the 50th birthday of the Tour de France, the points system was reintroduced, but this time as an additional classification. Because the leader in the general classification wears a yellow jersey, the leader in the points classification also received a special jersey, a green jersey. The colour green was chosen because the sponsor was a lawn mower producer 'La Belle Jardinière'. The awarding of this jersey also kept other riders interested in the race. It meant that the sprinters would keep going in the mountain stages as there could be points to be won when the race returned to the flat.

Another interesting aspect of the race's extension into Alsace, was the importance of being awarded the 'Ville d'Ètape' (Stage Town). The town of Belfort, near to the German border, had been the regular Ville d'Ètape from 1907 to the pre-war Tour of 1914. This honour had now, of course, passed to Strasbourg, the capital of Alsace, much to the disappointment of the Belfortains and one gentleman in particular. Henri takes up the story:

"Yesterday, I met a brave sportsman from Belfort, who wanted to convince me that we should continue to hold the stage finish in his town, as we had done before the war. I told him, with the stage now going through to Strasbourg, this is no longer possible, but he kept insisting. I asked him to give me some valid reasons why we should continue to use Belfort."

"The merchants of Belfort are extremely unhappy with your decision and you could do a stage from Belfort to Strasbourg!"

"What?", I cried, "that would be a stage of only 150 kilometres!"

"You could do a zigzag for this stage!"

"No," I said, "think of something else."

He immediately added "Instead of going to Geneva, come straight from Grenoble to Belfort!"

"Oh! No!" I objected, "that would make it a 600-kilometre stage!"

Then he immediately came up with a solution to this:

"You could forget the Col du Galibier, Les Arravis and La Faucille and come through Lons-Le-Saulnier."

"For this to happen it would require the sportsmen who follow the Tour de France, to consent to seeing the Tour take a different course. Our competition is not made for the commercial businessmen of Belfort, who have stayed in their homes for more than ten years, without ever showing any sign that they were particularly interested in the Tour. Nor is it made for the traders of any of the stage finish towns! The Tour de France, as its name indicates, needs to follow the periphery of our country and not be raced in zigzags. Our challenge is set and we must not abandon the cities of Bordeaux, Nantes, Toulouse, Lyon, or lose the climbs in the Pyrénées and the Alpes. We have done nothing different, except to only cross through Belfort. And what should Nancy say, given the fact that we are not visiting her at all this year? I think that sportsmen, who take a professional interest in the Tour de France, will be convinced of the good sense of our route, and we should ignore any requests for the race to finish in any particular city."

It is interesting to read Henri's words, exactly one hundred years later, as in the modern era, nearly 250 towns apply to become a ville-ètape each year. It can cost €45,000 to make an application to host the start of a stage, and up to €100,000 to host the more complex stage finish. If you want to host the Grand Départ of the Tour you have to dig deep into your pockets. For example. London paid €1.5M to the ASO (Amaury Sports Organisation), the organisers of the race, to have the Grand Départ, set off in the country's capital city in 2007. Monsieur 'Sportsman of Belfort' would have been happy in this change of thinking though, as his home town Belfort had coughed up the €45,000 to host the start of Stage 7 of this year's 2019 Tour. You see Henri, commercialism wins out in the end!

And as for no zigzags! Well, I'm sorry Henri, but you will be turning in your grave as the modern-day plans of the route look more like a game of 'snakes and ladders' than a Grand Boucle (Big Ring) around France. And as for the race following the periphery of the country, well, we'll talk more of that later.

*

Today, I was also being unfaithful to the 1919 route and its ide. Part of Stage 5 of the 2019 route, ran parallel to the 1919 route, between Colmar and Selestat (called Schlesta in 1919). It was a choice between cycling the correct route between the two, and risking the heavy traffic of the E25 Autobahn, or following the picturesque 'Route des Vins' through the chocolate box villages of Colmar, Eguisheim, Kayersberg, Riquewhir and Ribeauville. Inevitably I chose the latter, in reverse!

I was sweating a bit on my arrival into Ribeauville, as the website of my campsite showed it closed for lunch between 11.30 a.m. and 2 p.m., and I didn't want to lose valuable cycling time waiting to check in. As I pulled up at the campsite barrier at 11.35 a.m., I could thankfully see someone in reception. I waved hopefully and got a thumbs up, so I marched up the path to the front door with my papers. It was locked. I got a stern look from the chap inside, who was pointing at another door, on the other side of the room. So, I walked round and entered his office.

To make conversation I said "Thank goodness, you're still open, I'm so glad to have caught you."

He looked at me blankly and said. "Vee are open until 12 a.m. and the door for the reception is marked 'Reception' and vee have five signs pointing you here."

I don't want to be picky but why does your blooming website say you're closed at 11.30 a.m. then? Also, if you are outside the campsite, because the barrier is down, you can't zee the bloody door marked 'Reception' and the sign, pointing you here is behind you! Still, just being happy to have caught him, I didn't complain and headed to my allotted pitch. Here, I was greeted by a couple of white storks, strutting freely around the site, and pointing me to my camping slot. I unloaded and had a quick look around the campsite, which seemed to be full of groups of German tourists, who had invaded back over the border.

I didn't hang around the campsite long, and soon I was cycling through the main street of Ribeauville. It was lunchtime and the pavement cafés and restaurants, were full of people dining 'al fresco', and enjoying the midday autumn sunshine. I looked longingly at the large steins of ice-cold beer being served and consumed along with traditional dishes such as 'choucroute garnie' (sauerkraut and cured meats) followed by Munster cheese, and perhaps a Kugelhopf cake and cream. I was looking for some signs of the French influence in this region bearing in mind it had been part of France for one hundred years and I was struggling. Everything about this area seemed to be German. Towns with names such as Niederhergheim and Oberhergheim suggested membership of the Third Reich, rather than 'La Belle France'. Also, this region is famous for its predominantly white wines such as Riesling and Gewürztraminer, which again would be more likely to grace the table of an Obergruppenführer than a Capitaine in the French army.

I soon found myself out on the open road, engulfed by hundreds of acres of vineyards, stretching over the rolling hills as far as the eye could see. Over in the distance, I could see the Vosges mountains, strewn along the border and protected by the fairytale castle, the 'Chateau du Haut Koenigsbourg', that looked back down onto the valley below. I turned off to the sleepy village of Hunawihr, which proudly proclaimed itself to be a 'Village Cigogne d'Alsace, elsassiches storcka-dorf' - the home town of the white storks I'd seen earlier. It felt so peaceful as I trundled along the roads through the vineyards, towards the village centre. The tiny huddle of timber framed houses, seemed to have been built close together, to carry the church 'Saint-Jacques-le-Majeur' on their shoulders, as it looked down on its congregation below. I was in my element, the birds were singing, a white stork flew by, long and large in front of me, heading over the vines. I turned up a narrow track leading through the vineyards. There was a down-hill section, which then headed sharply upwards in the direction of the village of Riquewihr. I hit the incline quite fast to ensure I had enough speed to get to the summit and BANG!

'The Witch with the Green Teeth' had struck both myself and my bike for the first time on the trip, and I had broken my chain. I stopped on the dusty track, turned my bike over and tried to fix the broken link.

The quiet before the storm – the vineyards near Hunawihr, Alsace.

Not for the first time in my cycling life, did I think there were worst places in the world to break down. As I toiled away, a young teenager approached, whistling without a care in the world. He offered to give me some help. Apart from holding my bike, there was not much he could do, so I thanked him for his offer and he sauntered off up the hill. He'd told me he was the son of the priest of the local church. If I'd thought about it long enough, maybe I should have asked him to say a couple of prayers for me. After half-an-hour, I'd managed to fix my bike chain so I continued happily on my route. All was fine, until I emerged back onto the 'Route des Vins' at Schlossburg and BANG, my chain broke again. I soon realised that the gadget I had to fix my chain had bent ever so slightly, and there was no way I could get a strong enough connection to hold the chain link. So, what to do?

I was so near to the picturesque town of Riquewihr, so I had to continue on in the hope of finding a solution there. Riquewihr is one of those places, which you must visit if you are ever in Alsace. As you pass through the arched gateway, leading into the ancient town, you are greeted with a sight that hasn't changed since the 16th century. The Alsatian style half-timbered houses are painted in pastel shades, covering all the colours of the rainbow, and each window is adorned with boxes, packed with pretty summer flowers. Restaurants, bistros and shops are adorned with delicate wrought iron signs, with images depicting the food and trades that are offered within. Look closer and you will see inner courtyards embellished by old wells and fountains. Truly a delight.

The chocolate box town of Riquewihr, and 'Triomphe d'Alsace' grapes.

However, I was looking for somewhere to wash my oily black hands and get a cold drink. Fortunately, the local pompiers (firemen) were holding a fundraising event in the main courtyard of the town and selling chilled glasses of Riesling and ice-cold beer for three euros. I purchased the latter and sat down to listen to the German Oompah band that was entertaining the crowd, whilst trying furtively to clean my hands on the paper serviette which accompanied my beer. Riquewihr is the place to go if you wish to buy the finest Alsatian wines and cheeses, and a keyring with a white stork dangling on the end, but it isn't the place to go to get a chain fixed. So, reluctantly, I had to walk, and push my bike, six kilometres back through the vineyards to the campsite.

My planned cycle to Colmar was over. Fortunately, I'd visited the town previously and knew it to be another stunningly beautiful Alsatian town. The area known as 'Little Venice' is a photographer's dream, as the colourful 'Hansel and Gretel' timber framed houses reflect on the waters of the canal basin. Apparently, it was the inspiration for the fairy-tale of Beauty and the Beast, and I knew if

I had got there, covered in oil, I wouldn't have been offered the part of 'Beauty'.

*

There was no such problem for our 1919 riders, as a leading group of seven arrived in Colmar, with no incidents at 2.44 p.m. followed shortly by Nempon and Coomans. Vandaele and Steux were still miles (kms) behind and happy keeping each other company. It was the same situation as the riders headed into Strasbourg, with Jean Alavoine and Honoré Barthélémy both keen to get their fifth stage victory. The arrival was to be held on a flat 1km stretch of road, 20 metres wide, in front of the Mathis car factory. This should be ideal for 'Gars Jean' and a sprint finish.

Then and now -Factory Mathis - Avenue de Colmar, Strasbourg.

I was keen to find the location of the Mathis factory; the finish line of Stage 12. There are a few 'Rue Emile Mathis' around Strasbourg and they all turned out to be red herrings. I eventually located the address of the factory in an old Mathis car maintenance manual and set off to search for 200, Route de Colmar (now Avenue de Colmar), south of the city on the N83. When I got there, I tried to imagine the crowd sitting on the grandstand, that had been purposely built for them on this wide boulevard, for the stage finish. The crowd was swelled, by a huge blue-wave of hundreds of French soldiers in uniform, waiting to be de-mobbed after the liberation of Alsace. At 5 p.m. exactly the official cars arrived, followed eight minutes later by a group of seven riders. Who would win? It was going to be close. The riders sped for the line and in the scramble, it was the Italian Luigi Lucotti, who pipped Jean Alavoine to the line by a wheel, with the others centimetres behind. What an excellent finish! It was the Italian's first stage win, and thoroughly deserved, after his horrendous fall on the descent from the Col d'Allos, near Barcelonette. Honoré Barthélémy however, looked crestfallen, as he missed out on the opportunity of a fourth consecutive stage win by hundredths of a second.

Peace celebrations, Place Kleber, Strasbourg, 25th November 1918.

The crowd of blue soldiers swamped the riders, and ran a few hundred metres behind them, cheering as they headed up to the Grand Café de la République in the Place Kleber, in the centre of Strasbourg, to sign in.

The scenes replicated the events of eight months earlier, when the French general Henri Gouraud marched triumphantly into Place Kleber on the 25 November 1918, to confirm Alsace's liberation from the Germans. The crowds cheered France's victory, from under the balcony of the town hall, to the sound of the drums and bugles of the marching army.

However, now they had to celebrate the Italian Luigi Lucotti's win, as he denied the French crowd a victory, on their newly reclaimed lands in Alsace.

On the rest day, Henri Desgrange visited all 11 weary riders in their hotel rooms and distributed the entry tickets to the Parc des Princes. These were all received with great pleasure, as presumably Henri thought all 11 of them, with three stages to go, might actually make it to the finish.

STAGE 12: Geneva – Strasbourg (371km)

1. Luigi Lucotti	in 15h 08m 42s
2. Jean Alavoine	at a wheel
3. Léon Scieur	at a length
4. Firmin Lambot	at a wheel
5. Honoré Barthélémy	at a wheel
6. Paul Duboc	at a length
7. Eugéne Christophe	at a length
8. Jules Nempon	in 15h 12m 26s
9. Jacques Coomans	in 15h 48m 23s
10. Joseph Vandaele	in 17h 24m 21s
11 Alfred Steux	at a length

General Classement (G.C.)

1. E. Christophe	(The Old Gaul)	182h 25m 38s
2. F. Lambot	(The Saddler)	182h 48m 57s
3. J. Alavoine	(Gars Jean)	183h 05m 29s
4. H. Barthélémy	(Glass Eye)	185h 15m 17s
5. L. Scieur	(The Locomotive)	185h 50m 09s
6. J. Coomans	(The Smoker)	195h 56m 28s
7. L. Lucotti	(The Italian Job)	198h 10m 07s
8. P. Duboc *	(The Apple)	198h 12m 33s
9. A. Steux	(The Kid)	198h 37m 59s
10. J. Nempon	(The Upstart)	200h 22m 23s
11. J. Vandaele	**(Waterloo)**	**200h 53m 52s**

* includes 30-minute penalty on Stage 8

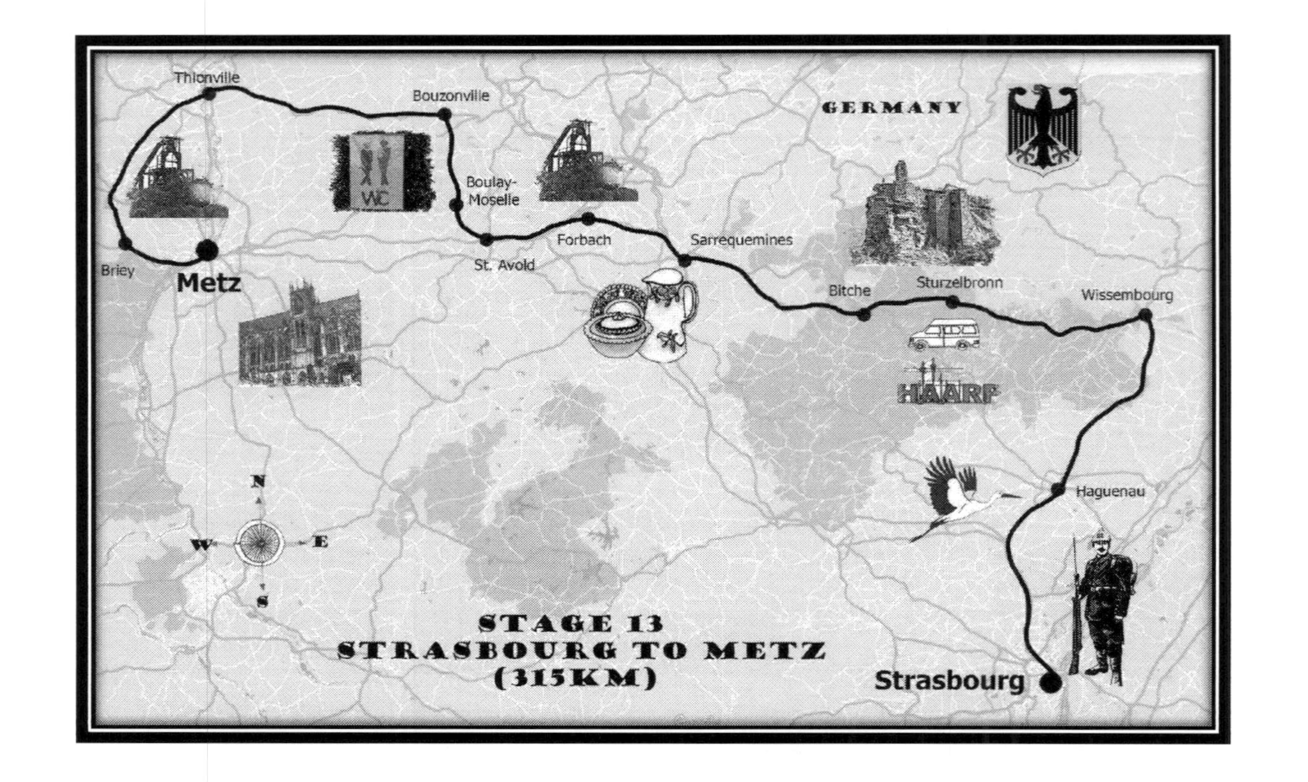

Thionville
Bouzonville
GERMANY
Boulay-
Moselle
Forbach
Sarrequemines
Briey
Metz
St. Avold
Bitche
Sturzelbronn
Wissembourg
HAARP
Haguenau
N
W
E
S
STAGE 13
STRASBOURG TO METZ
(315KM)
Strasbourg
WC

Chapter 17 : 'A Call of Nature'

Stage 13: Wednesday 23rd July 1919 (Strasbourg-Metz)
Monday 23rd September 2019 (Strasbourg - Sturzelbronn)

Today we are, at last, going to cycle to the far eastern parts of our country. Is it true? Are we dreaming? Strasbourg (Alsace) is only a few hundred metres from the River Rhine, and Metz (Lorraine) is where, just recently at Christmas, the effigy of the cursed Roman emperor (Charles V) appeared on the cathedral door. (*) Strasbourg! Metz! Magical names of places which have been returned to France. What joy for us! What emotions for those who fought for their freedom. What glory for our race to return after five years of interruption, and what an honour for us to cross the battlefields and avenge our dead. Wissembourg, and the heroic charge of our cavalry, Worth, Forbach and their horrible memories, Morsbach, Saint Avold and the cemetery immortalised by Neuville! This time our peaceful race will be like a triumphal parade. The triumph of French muscle, the strength of French willpower and the fury of the French against the barbarous Boche. What a glorious reality. Last night Strasbourg gave us a standing ovation. Tomorrow Metz will also give us their hearts on the same streets that were recently defiled by the Kaiser's henchmen, and where there now stands a monument to the Poilu!(**)

How happy Henri was to be returning to France's lost sisters. Stage 13 had been deliberately truncated in order to take in the two returned cities of Strasbourg and Metz, and as a consequence, it was the shortest stage of the Tour at 315km. (It was still 85km longer than Stage 7, the longest stage of the 2019 Tour, which was a mere 230km from Belfort to Chalon-sur-Saone).

The official start was put back to 4 a.m., and although the 11 remaining riders still had to sign in at the Café République in Place Kleber between 2 to 3.30 a.m. it did mean that for the first time they would have less time cycling in the dark. The official start line was a couple of kilometres north of the city centre in the suburb of Schlitigheim, and Robert Desmarets gave the starting orders on the unassuming street corner, between the Rue de Wissembourg and the Rue de Lauterbourg.

Henri had drawn his route as close to the border with Germany as possible, and within half an hour, the riders were cycling in the dark, through the forests of the Bas-Rihn. They passed through the village of Brumath, and crossed the wonderfully named River Zorn, which may have had a wizardly impact on the Harry Potter writer, J. K. Rowling as her great-great-grandmother, Salomé Schuch, had lived here.

The anonymous start to Stage 13 on the Rue de Wissembourg, Schlitigheim.

The 1919 riders came across immediate evidence of the war-torn border between France and Germany in the next town of Haguenau. During their occupation the Germans had built a military airport here to train their fighter and bomber pilots. Obviously, this became a strategic target for the French Artillery during the Great War, and they bombed it repeatedly in September 1918, in the lead up to the Armistice. It now lay in ruins, an unrecognisable field of rubble, just to the east of the route.

The riders were instructed to be careful on their way out of Hagenau, and to make sure they didn't take the immediate road to the left, which would take them on a long unnecessary detour. They needed to carry straight on and leave the town by the 'Porte de Wissembourg', following the military signs to Soultz and Wissembourg. It was then an 11km ride through the mystic ancient forest of Haguenau, the largest undivided forest in France. It was still dark and I could imagine the riders' sense of foreboding, as they cycled the rutted forest tracks, overshadowed by the ancient oaks and magnificent Scots Pine trees. In the middle ages this was known as the 'Holy Forest' and it attracted a large number of hermits who built shrines and places of worship here. There is one great oak, of which only the stump remains, which is the destination of a yearly pilgrimage on the last Sunday in July.

By the time the riders reached the new German border at Wissembourg, it was 6 a.m. and it was light. As usual the main group arrived together, although this time they had dropped Alfred Steux and Jules Nempon, who arrived 20 minutes later. Again, signs of war were aplenty. The battle of Wissembourg, the first of the Franco-Prussian war, was fought on the 4th August 1870. Napoleon III and General Le Boeuf, realising that the Crown Prince of Prussia's army was only 30km away, had retreated into defensive positions, leaving a small division to guard the town. The remaining soldiers fought admirably, assisted by the accuracy of their long-range guns (chassepots). Eventually they were overwhelmed by the Prussian and Bavarian artillery and their inevitable defeat allowed the Germans to enter Wissembourg and France for the first time.

L'Auto reported that the Tour was well received in Wissembourg and the riders were given a long and warm ovation. I'm sure that the arrival of the Tour was a welcome distraction to the events of the last few years. However, the people of the town must have had a sense of 'Here we go again' as they passed back under French rule. Wissembourg is one of those towns that straddle the border, defined by the River Lauter, which flows directly through it's centre. When in 1871, Alsace became German, the vineyards on the slopes to the north of the town were owned by German growers who live in the village of Schweigen, a stone's throw away. How do you redraw the borders on returning to French ownership? Not wanting to split the town in two, a decision was made to pass the frontier to the north of the town. As a result, the vines became French but as part of the deal, the crop would still remain under German ownership, and be transported into the village of Schweigen. This arrangement became particularly complicated at harvest time. First the growers in Schweigen needed a passport to cross the border to pick their grapes, and then the resultant harvest had to be checked by customs, before returning to Germany to be made into wine.

Having travelled north, since leaving Nice, it was now time for the 1919 Tour to turn westwards and head along the Western Front, and of course the Maginot line, which was built by the French after the end of the First World War, as a protection against future invasion. For our 11 intrepid riders they had to face the rather minor challenge of the Col du Pigeonnier (the Loft not the bird), which at 432m above sea level was more of an annoying blip than any serious test. At the top of the climb there was more evidence of the struggles that had occurred along this transient border. Away in the distance, they would have been able to see the domineering Chateau de Fleckenstein, a boat shaped ruin, stranded on top of a sandstone summit. There has been a castle, of some sorts here since the 12th century and many modifications had been made to it until it was destroyed by the French in the 17th century. The Germans then tried to rebuild it in 1870, when they regained control of Alsace, but now after the signing of the Treaty of Versailles it was back in French hands. Of course, these days it is a tourist attraction and you can climb the turrets of the ruined castle, roam the grounds pretending to be a knight or a princess, or simply buy yourself some medieval toys from the gift shop. The views over the treetops of the surrounding forests are impressive, and somewhere down amongst the Forest of Steinbach, our 11 riders were heading for the first and only feeding station of this stage, at Sarreguemines.

*

As for myself, I had spent the day getting my bike fixed in Strasbourg. This gave me time to explore the city and find the key locations of the finish of Stage 12 near the old Mathis car factory and the starting point of Stage 13 in Schlitigheim, but try as I might I could not find the Café de la République in the Place Kleber. Not to be outdone I had a light lunch in the Café Kleber, overlooking the square, hoping I was somewhere near to the 1919 location.

Café Kleber and Place Kleber in Strasbourg and the 'sign in' for Stage 13.

The upside of waiting to get my bike chain fixed was that it gave me a little time to stock up with some excellent Alsace wines. In particular some bottles of the fine sparkling white wine 'Cremant d'Alsace'. There are many versions of Cremant (Cream) available in different regions of France, but I can recommend those of Alsace, and once you've tasted it, you won't go back to Prosecco.

After recovering my bike, I followed the 1919 route to my campsite at Sturzelbronn, at the edge of the Forest of Steinbach on the border of Alsace and Lorraine. I was the last to check in that night and I struck up a conversation with the lady on reception. It appeared that her father had been a German prisoner during World War 2, and he offered to work in the coal mines of the region, as it was one of the few jobs that was paid. It was here that he lodged at the home of the receptionist's mother and subsequently they married. I suppose this was a story that could be told hundreds of times by people living on a border between two countries and the families would have roots and strong ties to both. However, her next story was not so common. We had been talking about the good weather that I had encountered during my trip following the 1919 route of France.

"Have you ever heard of an organisation called HAARP?"

"No," I honestly replied.

"Well, look it up on the internet. It is a station in Alaska from where the major countries can control the weather."

I felt a bit uneasy.

"Look at the major sporting events in the last few years." she continued, "Is it a coincidence that the Olympic games in Beijing in China or the football World Cup in Russia, both of which could have been ruined by smog blowing out from the cities, had magnificent weather and clear blue skies all the way through each tournament?"

I had no reply, but I knew that the weather had been excellent in both Moscow and Saint Petersburg, during my trip to the World Cup in Russia in 2018. Surely this couldn't be true, and if it was, obviously the British didn't have a seat at the control table. As soon as I could get some Wi-Fi, I googled HAARP (High Frequency Active Auroral Research Program) and it appears that there was a station in Alaska and one in Russia but scientists categorically denied the conspiracy theories stating "there's absolutely nothing we can do to disturb the Earth's weather systems." I must admit it did seem to be a strange conversation to be having with a receptionist on a small campsite, near a village of 190 inhabitants, in a thick forest in the middle of nowhere. Anyway, the following morning it was misty and raining, so obviously the campsite did not have a direct line through to the HAARP control centre!

Stage 13: Thursday 24th July 1919 (Day of Rest)
Tuesday 24th September 2019 (Sturzelbronn - Metz)

Only a couple of kilometres out of Sturzelbronn, you are once again reminded that you are travelling along a strategic border between France and Germany. Suddenly, large steel mesh fences appeared, emblazoned with signs stating 'Terrain Militaire, Defense D'entrer', 'Militar Gelande, Eintritt Verboten', 'Military Land, Entrance Forbidden' and 'Attention Passage de Troupes'. I was now driving through the French Military zone near the historic town of Bitche. Nowadays, the camp is the home of the French 57th Artillery Regiment, and it is used to train soldiers in the art of urban combat. As you approach the town of Bitche itself, you are overwhelmed by the imposing citadel that sits on an elongated hilltop overlooking the town. Rebuilt in the 17th century after the Thirty Years War, it was thought to be one of the most impenetrable fortresses in France, and its crowning glory was in 1870, in the Franco-Prussian war when it resisted the attacks and bombardments of 7,000 soldiers of the Prussian army. Today, the citadel sits like a crouched prehistoric beast, ready to pounce on any potential invader.

*

We were now in the French department of Lorraine and as the 1919 riders approached the first and only feeding station at Sarreguemines, they noticed a dramatic increase in the crowds following the race. In 1906 Henri Desgrange had dared to include the German occupied city of Metz into the route of the Tour. It was approved by the German authorities and in subsequent years he got bolder and made Metz a ville d'ètape during the Tours of 1907 through to 1910. However, the Germans eventually got fed up with the pro-French celebrations and banned the Tour from passing through Metz, up until the outbreak of First World War. So, it was with great delight, that the cycling fans and authorities of Metz and the whole department of Lorraine, welcomed back the Tour for the first time on French soil. In Sarreguemines, it was 9.35 a.m. when nine riders arrived, all still together, led by Firmin Lambot and Jacques Coomans. The long forest roads had taken their toll on Alfred Steux and Jules Nempon, who arrived half an hour behind the main group. They were all given a raucous welcome by the large crowd, which contained many ceramic potters, who worked in the local mills and workshops. Sarreguemines pottery was renowned, and in the 1800's Napoleon I was one of the factories best customers. The new designs they had created led to orders to supply tiles for the building of the Paris Metro in the early 1900s. The business had continued throughout the war periods, but latterly demand declined, and the mills were closed in January 2007.

The eery coal mines of the Saar-Wandt basin, close to Forbach.

The 1919 Tour now headed out across the Moselle region, an area rich in coal and iron ore, and the pit wheels and smelting plants could be seen all along the route towards Forbach, Saint Avold and Boulay-Moselle. It was some ten kilometres before Boulay-Moselle, that Eugéne Christophe felt a call of nature, or as Henri Desgrange delicately reported ' Christophe dismounted from his bike for small reasons of which I do not want to give you any further detail.'

I too, stopped here, not for a call of a nature, but to take a photo of the village sign at the entrance of 'Boucheporn' (mouth porn?). Perhaps not the best place to stop for a wee? It was here, whilst Eugéne was relieving himself, that the peloton and especially Lambot decided to attack the Old Gaul. The only one who held back was Eugéne's friend and fellow countryman, 'Gars Jean' Alavoine. However, Cri-Cri was enraged by the attack and he set off after the pack. By the time they got to the control in Boulay, everybody expected him to be at least three minutes behind the main group, but no such thing. Eugéne swung into the control at full speed and lost only 32 seconds to his adversaries.

*

Of course, these days there is a protocol to answering a 'call of nature' whilst cycling the Tour. The peloton may organise itself by arranging a 'nature break', during which the riders will collectively pee, at the side of the road. Normally the wearer of the yellow jersey will decide when this will be. Any cyclist that keeps moving during this break is bound by an unwritten law not to attack. Of course, like all unwritten rules, sometimes this can be conveniently overlooked. For example, on Stage 16 of the Giro d'Italia 2017 Tom Dumoulin was attacked, when he stopped for a little bit more than a wee. If the need to pee is only really affecting one rider, it's common practice for the cross-legged individual to make their way to the front of the peloton, before stopping off and giving themselves the longest possible window to empty their bladder. Should the rider take their time and be passed by the peloton, they can use the team cars to draught their way back to the bunch.

Other options are obviously to pee whilst cycling, and to rely on a team mate to give you a hand (?) to keep your bike steady. Also, the general public can be a tad offended if they see a member of the peloton pulling his other member out of his cycling shorts and crop spraying the road, and in a lot of races this can incur the rider a fine. The most discrete option is simply to pee freely into your shorts. Mark Cavendish confirmed that choosing this option can be particularly effective in cold conditions; "In races that are soaking wet and freezing cold, I like to piss myself. It warms me up for a split second. You get warm and you don't have to fuss around," he added.

Good for Mark!!

A scheduled stop for the 'Pee-low -ton'

All this toilet talk was having an effect on my bladder, so I too decided to stop in Boulay, and mark this moment. I visited the Café de la Halle on the Rue Saint-Avold, sat outside and ordered a 'petit dejeuner simple'. Despite the reasonably early hour, the group across from me were already partaking in something a little stronger and their order was vin rosè, crème de menthe and a glass of white wine (Gewurtztraminer €2). By the time I'd finished my coffee and croissant, the waitress, knowing their tastes, had already been out and refilled their glasses. I was tempted to stay longer, not for more alcohol but to taste the famous 'Macarons de Boulay'. These local delicacies have been made in the town since 1854 and the original family shop is still there, selling the tiny almond delights, in their traditional red boxes.

*

Boulay is only 27km from Metz, but Henri Desgrange couldn't have a stage that was only 228km long, (coincidentally the same length as the longest stage of the 2019 Tour) and the 1919 route now headed north towards the control point at Thionville, circling the city of Metz and adding an extra 87km to the stage.

Honoré Barthélémy won the sprint into the town by five lengths from Paul Duboc. It was 1.50 p.m. They were followed by the remaining seven riders in the peloton with Firmin Lambot and the wearer of the yellow jersey only 200m behind. The attack had failed. The enormous crowd had a long wait before Steux and Nempon arrived an hour and a half later. Both looked completely exhausted.

At Thionville, the riders had crossed the mighty River Moselle, and were now headed out on the open road to the iron-ore mining towns of Hayange and Briey. Here there were a couple of steep inclines one after the other, and Luigi Lucotti made his move. Without attracting attention, he changed his gears. The others quickly followed suit but were caught out by his early manoeuvre. There was still 34km to go. Could this be the decisive move that would win the Italian the stage? Barthélémy gave chase and the two battled it out, in the increasingly strong winds which blew on the final climb up to Saint Privat la Montagne. Who was going to win? It was going to be close now. Even Henri Desgrange was getting excited, comparing the battle between the two of them, to a pair of whirling dervishes flying at each other, full of religious fever.

The crowd in Metz awaited the victor on l'Esplanade, a large open area, off the Boulevard Poincare, and in front of the recently erected statue to 'Le Poilu' (**). The two riders arrived together, and at first it was announced that Barthélémy had won. This was later changed and Lucotti was confirmed as the winner of Stage 13 by half a wheel, and for the second time, the French were denied victory by the Italian, in their newly reclaimed city. Eugéne Christophe finished in fourth place, but more importantly five minutes ahead of Firmin Lambot. His lead in the G.C. was now 28 minutes on the Belgian. Surely the victory and yellow jersey was his now. What could go wrong? The riders headed up to the Café Francais et des Halles in the Place Saint Louis in the centre of Metz to sign the control sheet.

Meanwhile Henri Desgrange was most impressed with the organisation of the PTT (Postes, Télégraphes et Téléphones – now

France Telecom) of Metz, who had set up a telephone and telegram point, just 20m away from the finish line. Barthélémy and Lucotti had crossed the finish line at 3.55 p.m. and by 3.57 p.m., only two minutes later, the result was received by the L'Auto office in Paris. This was a record for a transmission which would be difficult to beat.

Le Poilu statue on l'Esplanade in Metz and the bus stop at Poincare.

I had fully intended to go for a cycle along the Moselle river between Thionville and Metz but there was now a raging storm blowing down the valley. Also, when I arrived at my campsite on the banks of the River Moselle in Metz, I saw a woman frantically waving at someone from the nearby car park. As I got closer, she appeared to be waving in my direction. I thought it was strange, so I looked directly behind me, to see if she was waving to a friend in the distance. No, it was definitely me, so I dashed through the parked cars towards her. There, lying on the floor in front of her, was a middle-aged lady who had slipped on some wet leaves and fallen awkwardly. She was in some considerable pain, and any attempt to try and lift her up to her feet, resulted in screams of agony. It was obvious that she had somehow damaged her knee and right shoulder. Amazingly it transpired that she was a nurse who was about to go on her shift at the nearby Hospital 'Belle-Isle'. I offered the waving lady my phone, and she phoned through to her colleagues at the hospital, to inform them of the accident. Her second call was to the fallen lady's husband, but he couldn't be reached, so it was time to phone the 'Vehicle de Secours et d'Assistance aux Victimes'. I covered the injured lady in my jacket to try and keep her warm and stoically tried to hold an umbrella over her to protect her from the violent wind and rain. Eventually, we could hear the distant sirens approaching and four paramedics chair-lifted her onto a trolley and into the ambulance. I now realised that I didn't have enough time for my planned cycle, and so, I decided to head off on foot, to find the key locations of Stage 13. Some reviews on TripAdvisor told me that ,whilst Metz was a city of great historic interest, they found it slightly austere in appearance. I thought exactly the opposite and even on a dark and dreary day I found the honey coloured (Pierre de Jaumont) buildings to be quite beautiful and the old traditional shops quaint. It didn't take me long to find the statue of 'Le Poilu' on the Esplanade just off Poincare, and I could imagine the crowds of soldiers and infantryman, in the blue French uniform, cheering enthusiastically as Barthélémy and Lucotti raced to the line.

The peloton appears through the dust clouds as they arrive in Metz.

It was a short walk, through the narrow cobblestone alleyways of the old town, to find the Café Français and des Halles at 34 place Saint-Louis. I searched expectantly amongst the ancient archways, trying to find this elegant café, the final signature point of Stage 13. Eventually I managed to work out where No. 34 was and I waited for the smell of aromatic coffee and freshly baked croissants to waft across my nasal openings. Imagine how disappointed I was to find that it is now a Damart clothes shop. I'm not sure whether the winner of the stage, Luigi Lucotti would have been up for buying a pair of Thermolactyl sports pants, even if they were 60% off.

Place Saint Louis, Metz and Damart , the signing in point for Stage 13.

(*) This relates to the story of the 1552-53 Siege of Metz and the war between France's Henry II and the Holy Roman Empire. During the festive period of this time, locals decided to burn an effigy of the Holy Roman Emperor, Charles V, and drag it through the city streets of Metz. This created a grotesque character, called Le Père Fouettard, who armed with a whip and bound in chains, punished any children who had been naughty. Now it was a part of French tradition that at Christmas time Le Père Fouettard would go around with St. Nicholas, deciding which children would get presents and which wouldn't.

(**) The Poilu (literal translation is a hairy soldier) statue was erected in January 1919, in honour of the ordinary French soldier in World War I. The name is still widely used as a term of endearment for the French infantryman and it reflects their rustic and agricultural background. The Poilu typically had beards and bushy moustaches and were known for their love of pinard, the ration of cheap wine they received on the frontline.

Stage 13: Strasbourg – Metz (315km)

1. Luigi Lucotti	in 11h 55m 13s
2. Honoré Barthélémy	at a length
3. Léon Scieur	in 11h 57m 17s
4. Eugéne Christophe	in 11h 58m 02s
5. Jacques Coomans	at a length
6. Firmin Lambot	in 12h 02m 48s
7. Joseph Vandaele	at a length
8. Jean Alavoine	in 12h 07m 40s
9. Paul Duboc	at a length
10. Alfred Steux	in 14h 12m 55s
11. Jules Nempon	at a length

General Classement (G.C.)

1. E. Christophe	(The Old Gaul)	194h 23m 40s
2. F. Lambot	(The Saddler)	194h 51m 45s
3. J. Alavoine	(Gars Jean)	195h 13m 09s
4. H. Barthélémy	(Glass Eye)	197h 10m 30s
5. L. Scieur	(The Locomotive)	197h 47m 26s
6. J. Coomans	(The Smoker)	207h 54m 30s
7. L. Lucotti	(The Italian Job)	210h 05m 20s
8. P. Duboc *	(The Apple)	210h 20m 13s
9. A. Steux	(The Kid)	212h 50m 54s
10. J. Vandaele	(Waterloo)	212h 56m 40s
11. J. Nempon	(The Upstart)	214h 35m 18s

* includes 30-minute penalty on Stage 8

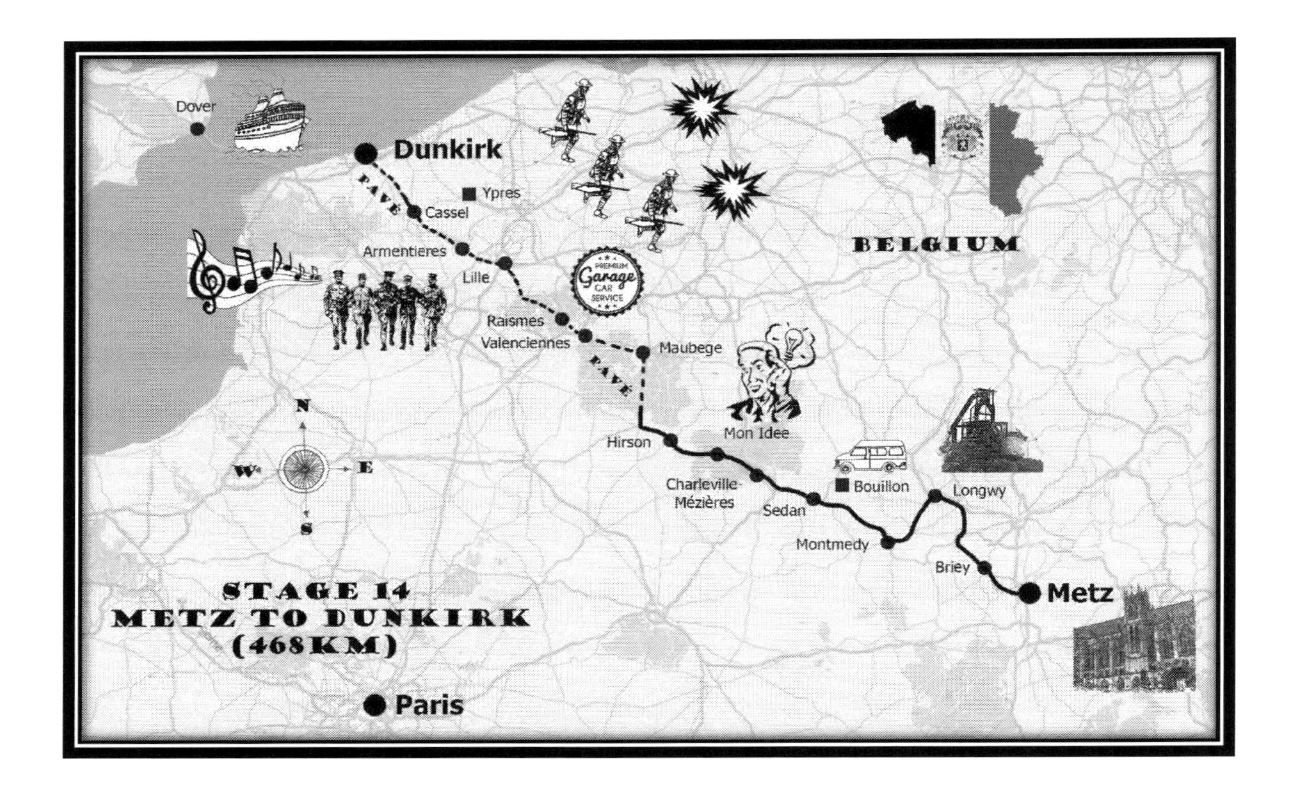
Dover
Dunkirk
PAVÉ
Ypres
Cassel
Armentieres
Lille
PREMIUM
Garage
CAR SERVICE
Raismes
Valenciennes
Maubege
PAVÉ
BELGIUM
Hirson
Mon Idee
Charleville-
Mézières
Sedan
Bouillon
Longwy
Montmedy
Briey
Metz
N
W
E
S
STAGE 14
METZ TO DUNKIRK
(468KM)
Paris

Chapter 18 – 'The Hunger Stage'

Stage 14: Friday 25th July 1919 (Metz - Dunkirk)
Wednesday 25-29th September 2019 (Metz - Bouillon)

Stage 14, the penultimate stage of the Tour, was set at 468km and was only just second in length to the tortuous 482km of Stage 5 (Sables d'Olonne – Bayonne). This was the first time that the Tour would go directly from Metz to the North Sea coastal port of Dunkirk. In previous editions (1907 to 1910) the Tour had started in Metz but stopped short of the coast in the town of Roubaix, acknowledging the famous race of Paris–Roubaix, called the 'Hell of the North', because of the multitude of cobblestone roads. Paris–Roubaix is still one of the oldest one-day cycling events in the world, with the first race having been held in 1896.

The riders had baptised Henri's new stage from Metz to Dunkirk, 'L'ètape de la faim' (The Hunger Stage), which was somewhat surprising, as Henri had included four food stops for 'ravitaillement' at Longwy, Charleville, Maubeuge and Lille. Maybe Henri had learnt some lessons from the interminable Stage 5, which had included only two feed stations, and had resulted in long delays to the timetable.

Henri noted, with two stages left to go to Paris, that Firmin Lambot had lost three kilogrammes in weight, since starting out in Paris. Jean Alavoine was also in a worse condition as he had lost over four kilos. However, the 'Old Gaul' and tactician, Eugéne Christophe was exactly the same weight as when he was weighed in at the Parc des Princes. This put him in a much better position to tackle the last two stages of the Tour, and hold onto his lead.

Weight control has become a science in the Tour these days and modern-day riders have a dietary program that not only exists for the Tour de France, but for all days throughout the racing calendar. Dieticians can control at what point a cyclist needs to build up calories prior to a Grand Tour, and also what his daily diet needs to be during the race so he can tackle different stages. For example, in a relatively easy flat stage a rider may burn up to 5,000 calories, whereas in a difficult mountain stage it could be up to 8,000. A typical daily program for one rider could be

09:00 Breakfast: A bowl of oatmeal with nuts, a large omelette, three cheese and ham sandwiches, 100g of pasta, one cup of yoghurt, 500ml fruit smoothie, one glass of apple juice, one coffee.

Those are not the options available. All of those items make up a breakfast for one Tour de France cyclist.

10:30 Pre-race snack : Apple, banana, handful of nuts, two energy bars, lots of water, one coffee. The point of breakfast, and this snack, is to try and ingest as many calories as possible before the race, to reduce the need for any calorific intake when out on the bike.

12:00 Race nutrition on the bike : Two croissants with jam or ham, seven energy bars, two isotonic gels, two cans of coke, six bidons of electrolyte drinks. Energy bars are efficient at replenishing energy, but nutritionists usually include some real food such as croissants for texture, so that cyclists have an easier time taking all of those calories in.

17:00 After-race recovery : A piece of chicken, 200g of rice, 500ml fruit and a vegetable smoothie plus two cups of coffee. A nutrient dense meal, with a good source of protein, after the race is important to help cyclists regenerate effectively.

20:00 Dinner : A large beef steak, 150g of pasta, one cup of yoghurt, 500ml vegetable juice plus two cups of coffee. Yes, they do drink a lot of coffee (without champagne) as it can improve performance and is not considered a banned substance.

23:00 Evening snack : A cup of yoghurt with cereals, a handful of nuts and a piece of fruit. Athletes' bodies continue to burn calories for hours after a Tour de France stage. That's why it's important to keep refuelling, even if it's late in the evening.

Whether Firmin Lambot was conscious of this weight loss and the fact that he was running out of opportunities to attack Christophe, I don't know, but the prudent Belgian stocked up with plenty of food in Metz. Instead of his usual ten sandwiches of butter, ham and gruyere cheese, he packed 15 into the pockets of his jersey and his satchel. He did the same with the amount of fruit tarts and rice cakes and added ten bananas, a large quantity of figs and some bars of chocolate!

Jean Alavoine joked with him:

'I hope you haven't drunk any milk' he laughed 'By the time you've crossed all the pavé (cobblestoned) roads, it will have all been shaken into butter in your stomach!'

Mind you, it wasn't all fun and games. Given the distance they had to travel, the official start time had been brought forward to 10 p.m. on the evening of the rest day, to ensure the riders would get to Dunkirk in time for L'Auto's deadlines to be met at 4 p.m. the following day. 3,000 spectators gathered at the Café Français et des Halles for the start, and the musical band called 'Lorraine Sportif' played a special concert to see them on their way. The riders were faced with a minimum of 18 hours in the saddle and for some it could be up to 20. On top of this, on the first section of the stage, the riders had to retrace their steps over the last 30km of Stage 13 back to Briey, and then face eight hours of cycling in complete darkness and incessant rain.

It was therefore no surprise when they arrived, all together, at the first feeding station in the iron mining town of Longwy at 1.18 a.m. It was the same again, at the second feed stop in Charleville at 6.48 a.m., where they crossed the River Meuse at day break. There was not much to report. Paul Duboc had punctured at the control point in Sedan, in front of the café at the train station, but he soon repaired it and had caught up with the main group. Even though it was now light, they were still altogether at the halfway point of the stage at Hirson, on the border with Belgium after 247km and 11 hours in the saddle. Firmin Lambot must have felt at home as he was only 60km away from his birth place, Florennes in Belgium, just over the border.

*

Whilst there was not much to report in the Tour, there was plenty for me to report. After exactly 5,000km following the route, my camper-van broke down not far from Florennes. My engine had been taking on water quite regularly over the route, something I put down to the exceptionally high temperatures I had encountered, and also the fact that I'd driven over 12 mountain ranges. At the mining town of Longwy, the temperature warning light came on again and I stopped to top up with coolant. This time the coolant bottle completely emptied itself and I ended up putting quite a bit of liquid into the bottle to get it to the correct level. I set the Satnav for Charleville and continued on my route. All went well for 60km and then, in the middle of nowhere, the engine died and white smoke started to blow out of the exhaust pipe. I had no option but to pull over onto the grass verge and come to a halt before I did any more damage. I could see a tiny green-toothed witch, cackling noisily at me, from the side of the road. I knew I should have bought one of those miniature witches, for good luck, back on Stage 7 in Villefranche-de-Conflent.

"Oh no, it wasn't going to be a case of so near, so far was it ?"

I had no option but to call my breakdown insurer, but those dreaded words appeared in the top left corner of my phone.........No Service.

"Shit, what was I going to do?"

"Don't panic", I thought to myself and I ventured out into the pouring rain to try and get a signal. Eventually I got through.

"Where are you?" asked the controller.

I'd seen a signpost a few kilometres back, and I knew I was on the N88, so I confidently informed them of my location.

"Somewhere near Florenville."

"Are you in France or Belgium?"

That was a good one! I assumed I was in France as I was following the 1919 route. When I looked at my map, I realised I had strayed slightly and discovered that I was actually right on the border between Belgium and France.

"Well, I'm in both countries actually."

"What? We have to know exactly which country you are in so we can contact the right recovery company."

Further investigation showed that I was actually 300m from the French border, and I was in fact in Belgium. After a three hour wait, I was towed to a garage in Bouillon, Belgium, where I was given the bad news that water had got into the engine, and it was going to be a 'gros travail' (a big job). They would have to order a new part for the engine from the dealer which would take a couple of days to arrive. I had no option but to hire a car and head to a local hotel.

After a day of walking around and around the pretty but extremely damp town of Bouillon on the River Semois, I decided I might as well use my time profitably and use the hire car to continue on the 1919 route to the halfway point of the stage at Hirson (where Paul Duboc had punctured). This took me through the historic town of Sedan, which had witnessed the devastating Battle of Sedan, fought during the Franco-Prussian War in September 1870. It resulted in the capture of Emperor Napoleon III, over 100,000 French troops and effectively decided the war in favour of Prussia and its allies. On being completely surrounded by the Prussian army, General Auguste-Alexandré Ducrot succinctly stated,

"We are in the chamber pot and about to be shat upon."

The town of Charleville-Mézières was quite a delight, with its charming honey and red brick coloured buildings, beautiful parks and ornate fountains. The Capital of the Ardennes could quite rightly be called the Paris of the North, and was one of those many places in which, I would have loved to have lingered a bit longer. My next destination was a tiny hamlet on the road to Hirson called 'Mon Idée' (My idea). It was here that Firmin Lambot mounted an attack on Eugéne Christophe and maybe it was the name of the village that inspired him. It could also have been the fact that, for the first time on the stage it was now light, and being in the region of his birthplace, he felt particularly inspired.

I returned to the garage, only to hear the news that my van would not be repaired quickly. Despite their best efforts it could be another week before I was back on the road. Quel Désastre!

Stage 14 – Saturday 26th July 1919 (Day of Rest) Wednesday 11th October 2019 (Bouillon - Dunkirk)

The sky is gloomy and washed out. Huge dirty grey clouds linger on the horizon. It's as if Nature itself seems to be in mourning! At the outskirts of the town of Valenciennes, Eugéne Christophe is on foot on the sidewalk, surrounded by five or six emotionless kids who want to hug him. He pushes his bike in front of him, his saddle pointed to the ground. He has a broken fork again! It seems like a mighty lyre, whose strings are broken, is singing of his final misery. And like a handsome warrior, who is defeated by fate, he looks straight into the eyes of his destiny. A destiny, which has just beaten him, after a month of effort, when he was just on the point of reaching his goal and winning a small fortune, and now he loses the pride of being put on the winners list of the Tour de France.

Henri Desgrange could have written those words for me. I'm not sure if nature was mourning my disaster, but the only positive I could get from my own personal situation, was that my vehicle breakdown had occurred at the same time as one of the key events of the 1919 Tour.

Firmin Lambot had attacked just before Hirson, and shortly after leaving the town, the riders hit the 100km pavé section of the route in the tiny village of Etroeungt. Was this a tactic? It was well known that the terrible cobblestone section required additional effort and strength to hold the bike down, as the wheels bounced around on the uneven surface. This section would sort the men out from the boys. By the time the Tour reached the third feeding point of Maubeuge, Firmin Lambot had gained two minutes on Eugéne Christophe, Luigi Lucotti, Léon Scieur, Joseph Vandaele and Paul Duboc. The other five riders were tiring and falling behind. At the town of Bavay, an important junction in Roman times, as it was at the confluence of seven roads, the gap rose to four minutes, and Christophe could start to sense the danger of Lambot's attack. When they reached Valenciennes, the gap was still the same but Paul Duboc had punctured, Lucotti had to get off his bike and fix his chain and Jean Alavoine, who was tiring more than the others, had fallen 19 minutes behind. Maybe Firmin Lambot's decision to stock up with so much food and energy wasn't to be laughed at after all, 'Gars Jean'.

In Valenciennes, the ugly aftermath of the war could be witnessed again. Just eight months earlier the British and Canadians had defeated the Germans on the 2nd November 1918, in one of the last battles of the Hundred Day Offensive. The Battle of Valenciennes was one of the last in a series of successful battles, which led to the Armistice being signed, just nine days later.

The day before the race, on the 24th July 1919, Henri Desgrange had written dramatically about Stage 14, calling it 'Le Dernier Coup Dur' – (The Last Hard Blow)

This can be a terrible route, and it has been proved numerous times, that with the cobblestones of the north, it can be murderous for even the best of our champions. Remember dear friends and readers, the Tour de France of 1913! There was one man, who everyone admired and who we followed, not only in our thoughts, but also with all our hearts. It was Lucien Petit-Breton, our late champion, struggling as the sole survivor of his team, against all the others, but he was not yet beaten. Mind you, he had not counted on the cobblestones of the fourteenth stage. He hadn't even got to Valenciennes when they came into play. He hit a gutter, and the frame of his bike gave way, and the unfortunate Lucien, just 450 kilometres from the capital, saw the collapse of all his hopes.

Question: Who can say whether this misfortune will happen today to one of our valiant survivors?

Answer: Fortunately, no!

The fateful level crossing - Route de St. Amand, Raismes, (Valenciennes)

Was Henri a visionary? Could he have foretold what misfortune would befall France's new favourite fellow 'Cri-Cri', the canary dressed in yellow. Five kilometres outside of Valenciennes, the Old Gaul was heading for the coal mining town of Raismes, just as the church clock was signalling lunchtime for the miners. The crowds were sparse, as most of the young men of the region had been killed in the trenches of the First World War, and the mines were being run by imported foreigners who weren't particularly cycling fans. Eugéne was headed for the Place de Raismes and the Rue de Vicoigne, which led to a tiny hamlet of the same name just outside the town. (This road has now been renamed the 'Rue Jean Jaures' in honour of the French socialist leader who was assassinated in 1914 because of his antimilitarist efforts to halt the war.) Eugéne came up to a level crossing (passage à niveau) where the gate was partially blocking the road. The gate keeper was in the process of closing the barrier behind him. There were two ways which 'Cri-Cri' could go. He headed for a narrow gap in front of him, to avoid his front wheel slipping into the tram-rails. To each side of him were the strewn bricks of the ruined houses that had been bombed during the war. The builders who were reconstructing the houses hardly looked up to see him flying across the cobbles, and falling on the railway tracks.

What they did hear though was like the cry of a beast!

"Noooooooooooooooo!"

Eugéne had managed to zigzag for a bit and managed to avoid the bike falling on top of him. He stood there, hands on hips, looking in disbelief at the wreckage in front of him.

"Nooooooooo, my fork, my fork has broken yet again!"

Eugéne picked up his bike. He was distraught and looked to the heavens in desolation. He'd fallen victim to another witch, 'La Chorchelle d'Arenburg' (the long length of cobbled road in the Forest de Raismes), which is now a protected area of pavé, and since 1968 has become an iconic section of the Paris-Roubaix race.

Eugéne hardly noticed a young child, who tugged at his sleeve, and spoke in a strange French accent of the north.

"Sir, I can see you are trouble. I don't know you, you're not from these parts."

"Hey, little one, I can't understand what you are saying. Repairs, I must make repairs to my bike, and quickly."

"I can't understand your words either. You can't be left beaten. Follow me to the mender."

"Is it far?"

The little one didn't reply but touched his cap and waited for the man in the strange yellow jersey to follow him. Cri-Cri followed, pushing his bike in reverse, with the saddle pointing to the ground, to make sure the damage didn't get any worse. Soon they came to the train station at Raismes and opposite, at Number 4, Rue du Marais, there was an imposing building. The upper windows were covered with lace curtains, and below was a door and a large double window, over which hung the signs 'ESTAMINET' (a small café selling alcoholic drinks) and then just what Eugéne was looking for PERSIAUX-CHARDON MECANICIEN, a garage. It was lunchtime, and there were a number of miners drinking outside the café, and children running around excitedly to see if anyone would put a penny in the lemonade fountain. They all looked in amazement at this creature that approached them, dressed in short pants, and wearing a woollen yellow jumper covered in mud. With his air pilot goggles, he resembled a drowned scuba diver.

Cri-Cri spoke to the owner Léonard Persiaux, and followed him into his sombre workshop. Inside five workers, looked up at him in amazement, without stopping work on their machines. Eugéne realised that this was a workshop making all types of metal items for the nearby railway. The owner led him to a rear courtyard where there was a forge and said:

"Here, I can fix your bike for you."

"I'm sorry, you can't, the rules don't allow it."

"What rules?"

Henri Desgrange and the official cars had been behind Christophe when the accident happened. Both he, Monsieur M. Michel, the commissaire and Alphonse Baugé had followed him into the workshop. Eugéne pointed to Michel and replied:

"The rules of this Cerebus (the multi-headed dog of Hell), the commissaire of the Tour de France will strip me of my yellow jersey if I break the rules of the race."

"My goodness, but what can I do for you?"

"Nothing, I'm afraid, but if you could supply me some materials to make my repairs, I would be most grateful. I notice you have some bikes in your shop window. Do you know what size the forks are?"

"I will go and measure them. Meanwhile I suggest you light the furnace in readiness."

Cri-Cri suddenly felt a ray of hope. Maybe all was not lost. Could he save his yellow jersey? All the materials that he needed were here. Thank goodness for that little boy. Eugéne got to work and used all his experience, having been a metal worker from the age of thirteen. By the time he had fixed his forks he had lost one hour and ten minutes. He was now back on the road, albeit three quarters of an hour behind Lambot. His good friend Jean Alavoine had not long passed through Raismes, and if he could catch him up, he was sure that 'Gars Jean' would give him some support to make up some of the lost time. Whilst assisting another rider was against the rules, Henri Desgrange and the race officials had sped off towards Lille, to catch up with the leader Firmin Lambot, and so Cri-Cri was left to his own devices. Surely, he couldn't make up the lost time? To catch back over an hour over the last two stages was impossible, wasn't it?

*

I had at last returned to France, and picked up my camper-van and I was happy to be back on the road again. There was only one place I could pick up the 1919 route and that was to cycle the roads from the outskirts of Valenciennes through Raismes and on to the 'Forêt Domaniale de Raismes-Saint-Amand-Wallers. Was I tempting fate by following in Eugéne's disastrous footsteps? Hopefully not. Nowadays the pavé roads and tramways leading out from the Valenciennes suburbs into Raismes are all smooth tar-macadam, and it was not until I reached the fateful railway level crossing in Raismes, did I experience any undulations in the roads. Luckily, the rail barriers were up and I bounced over safely. It was only a short ride to the place where Eugéne had managed to fix his bike.

Then and now: Number 24, Rue de Jean Jaures, Raismes –and the garage to the right where Eugéne Christophe repaired his forks.

There was no Number 4, Rue du Marais, so I looked down the Rue de Cesar Persiaux which seemed to be the best bet and found the Garage de la Gare, but this was situated at Number 2A. a relatively modern building, so maybe the old workshops had been demolished. I cycled up to the train station and back, but couldn't find any building that resembled the one I was looking for. I took some photos and headed back for the main road through the town. When I got there, I saw a white building across the road with the words, 'L'ATELIER MECANIQUE' in 1920's font, inscribed on the door. I took a photo and carried on my cycle through the forest to 'Saint-Amand-les-Eaux'. Later, when looking back at the old sepia photo of the 'Persiaux-Chardon' establishment, I noticed the

Number 24 (not No. 4 as I had read) above the door. The white building was also Number 24 and it had three upper windows, shrouded by lace, just as in the old photograph. This was it! I stared at the photo in amazement. The mystery was solved. Number 24, Rue de Jean Jaures was the exact location of the workshop, and I imagined Eugéne Christophe following Monsieur Cesar Persiaux, through the shuttered door to the right, carrying his bike upside down. There were no signs here to mark the event. There was no statue or plaque, as in Saint Marie-de-Campan, to commemorate Eugéne Christophe's exploits. Surely this was just as an important event in the history of the Tour de France?

*

Meanwhile, Firmin Lambot was still out in front, all on his own. Having negotiated the long pavé section successfully, he too now had to be careful of tram tracks. Just outside Amand-les-Eaux at Lecelles, the 1919 route followed the tramway all the way to Lille. It was impossible to go wrong and when he arrived at the fourth and final feeding station, he was greeted by a standing ovation, solely in his honour. This was a new experience for the Belgian rider, and he calmly signed in and replenished his immense stocks of food. By now, he would have heard of The Old Gaul's misfortune in Raismes, and would have been excited in the knowledge that he might win the Tour de France for the first time in his career. However, first he had to negotiate a tricky section of the route, which travelled along the worst section of the Western Front from Lille to Dunkirk. If he was under any false illusions that the task ahead would be easy, he would soon come across more undeniable evidence that the war-torn route ahead, would be full of pitfalls and danger.

As he arrived in Lille, which had just been released from four years of German occupation, he cycled past the decimated ruins of the '18 Ponts' munition depot. On 11 January 1916, at 3.30 a.m., Lille had been rocked by a violent explosion, that could be heard as far away as Holland. A bright yellow flash lit up the sky and the depot exploded. The German Army had been using the old fortified depot, comprising of 18 arches (the source of its French name), to store large quantities of explosives and munitions. Undoubtedly it was accidental, but the explosion left a crater 150m wide and 30m deep. 21 factories and 738 houses were brought down in the

Moulins district of the city. 104 civilians and 30 Germans died, and nearly 400 people were wounded.

It was 3.34 p.m. when Firmin Lambot signed in at the control, headed up the Boulevard de la Liberté and crossed the bridge in front of the pentagonal shaped 'Citadelle de Lille' . Built in the 17th century and dubbed the 'Queen of the Citadels' , this impressive military fortification is nowadays the location of Lille zoo. Behind Firmin, two more Belgians arrived in the shape of Léon Scieur and Joseph Vandaele at 3.41 p.m. Next, it was the turn of the Italian Luigi Lucotti who signed in at 4.07 p.m. The first French riders to arrive were Paul Duboc and Jean Alavoine who came in together at 4.25 p.m.; followed by Alfred Steux, at 4.44 p.m., Jules Nempon at 5.10 p.m. and Honoré Barthélémy and Jacques Coomans together at 5.12 p.m., Amazingly, seven minutes later, the crowd could see the broad shape of a yellow jersey heading towards them. It was Eugéne Christophe, the Old Gaul. He had somehow managed to catch up with the others as he signed in at 5.19 p.m. The 11 riders all looked exhausted. They had now cycled a staggering 380km in pouring rain, and still had 88km to go. They were already two and a half hours behind Henri Desgrange's ambitious timetable, which had estimated that the riders would arrive in Lille at 12.55 p.m. Henri obviously didn't build into his calculations such minor factors as the atrocious weather, cycling 100km on cobblestone roads and the fact that the 11 remaining riders had now cycled exactly 5,000km!

16km after leaving Lille, the 1919 group passed through the town of Armentières. The town motto is 'Pauvre mais fière (Poor but Proud), which I think gives an insight into this town, once known as the 'City of Fabric', because of the large amount of industrial spinning and weaving that went on. As the eleven riders passed through the control, I wondered if they were singing, as I did, the wartime marching song 'Mademoiselle from Armentières'

Mademoiselle from Armentières, Parlez-vous
Mademoiselle from Armentières, she hasn't been kissed for 40 years, Hinky-dinky `parlez-vous

Oh, Mademoiselle from Armentières, Parlez-vous
She got the palm and the croix de guerre, For washing soldiers' underwear, Hinky-dinky parlez-vous

Oh, Mademoiselle from Armentières, Parlez-vous
You didn't have to know her long, to know the reason men go wrong, Hinky-dinky parlez-vous

Oh, Mademoiselle from Armentières, Parlez-vous
She's the hardest working girl in town, but she makes her living upside down, Hinky-dinky parlez-vous

Oh, Mademoiselle from Armentières, Parlez-vous
The cooties rambled through her hair; She whispered sweetly "C'est la guerre", Hinky-dinky parlez-vous

Oh, Mademoiselle from Armentières, Parlez-vous
She'll do it for wine she'll do it for rum, and sometimes for chocolate or chewing gum, Hinky-dinky parlez-vous

Oh, Mademoiselle from Armentières, Parlez-vous
You might forget the gas and shell, but you'll never forget the Mademoiselle, Hinky-dinky parlez-vous

Oh, Mademoiselle from Armentières, Parlez-vous
Where are the girls who used to swarm, About me in my uniform? Hinky-dinky parlez-vous

The lines, singing about the gas and the shell, were particularly prevalent for Armentières, as the Germans had used mustard gas to capture the town to force the British retreat in April 1918. The contamination was so great, the Germans could not enter the town for two weeks, after the British evacuation.

As soon as Firmin had signed the control, he headed out of town on the Rue de Dunkerque, cycling along the border of his homeland Belgium. At this point, he was entering what was known as the 'Zone Rouge' of the Western Front, so named because it had been totally destroyed during the conflict. This would be his toughest test and he had to hope there wasn't a 'Witch with green teeth', hiding in wait for him, somewhere along a bomb-shelled road.

The first evidence he would have seen of the complete decimation of the area was at Bailleul. It had only been one year since the town was liberated from occupation by the Germans on the 31st July 1918. Prior to that the town had been shelled nearly every day by the British and, later, the French. More than 100,000 shells landed on the town, destroying 98% of its buildings. This was the closest you could get to a ghost town and was as bad as anything he had witnessed on the Somme. (Stage 1) To describe the scene in Henri's own unforgiving words,

We went through what can only be described as a lunar landscape. It should be shown to all the children in France, in all corners of our country, so that it stays in their memory and therefore the memory of their children, the horrors committed by the enemy, and the hatred that we owe them until we die.

Locals taking part in the annual 'Guess the number of bricks' competition, Ballieul, northern France.

At the control point in the town of Hazebrouck, less damage had been sustained. Apart from being on the confluence of seven major roads, Hazebrouck was also a major railroad junction between the northern sea ports of Calais and Dunkirk and the Western Front. Consequently, the Allies adopted it as a supply base, and given its strategic importance, protected it from any attempted German attacks. Lambot arrived there at 5.23 p.m. with 43km to go to Dunkirk. Surely Christophe couldn't catch him now. There was really only one major challenge left to face and that was the particularly severe cobblestone sections from the town of Cassel to Dunkirk. He was sped on his way by a troop of Belgian soldiers in Cassel, cheering their countryman, from the back of their armoured lorry.

*

One of the other upsides (?) of my breakdown in Belgium was, on returning to pick up my camper-van, I had time to stop and Tour the First World War battlefields around Ypres and Passchendaele. It was here in Cassel, that once again, I came across the footsteps of my grandfather Emmanuel Tarver. He'd arrived here as a 21-year-old on May 22nd 1915, as part of Lord Kitchener's new army. I stood on the platform at the Cassel train station (which is actually 2.5km away from Cassel at Bavinchove) and tried to imagine what was going through his young mind.

Emmanuel Tarver, aged 21, heading for the Fields of Flanders May 1915.

Here was a young man, who had probably never left a ten-mile radius of his tiny village in south Warwickshire who was about to embark on one of the darkest periods of his life. As he stepped off the train, he probably felt a certain sense of excitement of going into battle, for his King and Country, for the first time. He was surrounded by the new friends he had made, during his nine months of intensive training, in the purpose-built camps of south-east England. Now, the Western Front was only 30km away, and once the exciting chatter of the troops had died down, and they offloaded their rifles and kitbags, it was certain they could hear the incessant pounding of the guns, just over the horizon. They marched (footslogged) to Cassel and 66 men fell out en-route through exhaustion, partly due the heat of the midday sun, and partly due to marching on the horrendous cobblestones in hob nailed boots.

It was now my turn to ride on the dreaded cobblestones of the north and follow my grandfather's footsteps to his first sighting of action on the Western Front near Ypres. Most of the cobblestones in this area have been covered in tarmac now, but there is still a short section leading through the town of Cassel itself.

The cobblestones of Cassel. The starting point for both my grandfather and I to head for the Western Front.

The only way I can describe riding on pavé roads, is that it is like cycling on a cambered cattle grid containing as many potholes, as the Russian 'Road of Bones'. By the time I got to the end of this short section, I felt as though I had lost two vertebrae and my shoulders were now joined to my ears. Cycling on pavé is a bit like banging your head against a brick wall. It feels good when you stop. Luckily for me, it was a grey but dry day, which was in contrast to the incessant rain that had fallen in 1919. Cobblestones and rain are not a great combination and can be fatal to cyclists. Just ask Chris Froome who crashed twice on Stage 5 of the Tour in 2014 between Arras and Roubaix. The weather had been so bad that day that the officials decided to remove two pavé sections from the route. This didn't help Chris Froome to repeat his yellow jersey win of 2013 though, and unfortunately, he had to abandon with a suspected broken wrist.

*

Any minor discomforts I experienced, paled into insignificance when compared to what my grandfather went through with his regiment, the Oxfordshire and Buckinghamshire Light Infantry. They were to be in Flanders for nine months, with little or no respite. Upon arrival at the Front they had been issued with gas marks to combat the Germans' deadly new weapon of mustard gas, introduced four weeks earlier. I saw the battlefields where my grandfather first experienced combat in the Battle of Bellewaarde Farm on 16th June 1915. After nine months of training, the Battalion was initially excited to have their first taste of action, but in the end, they were left frustrated, as they were unable to push forward to engage with the enemy. Several platoons got stuck in the forward trenches, due to the number of dead and wounded soldiers and captured German POW's. As a consequence, my grandfather's regiment had to lie out in No-Man's Land, under the constant barrage of German bombs, unable to press forward to engage the enemy. On July 30th 1915, the Germans introduced another deadly form of weapon to the war, the flamethrower. The following day my grandfather's Brigade witnessed it first-hand.

The enemy used liquid fire yesterday against the 41st Brigade, and drove them back. The liquid is brought up to their trenches in cylinders, and with compression of about 5 atmospheres is sprayed forward, lighting spontaneously. It requires no fire to start it, and the maximum distance to which it can be thrown is about 40 yards.

Blimey, can you imagine the horror of being attacked by gas and flamethrowers. Mind you some of the officers saw the devastation in a different light.

It was a good experience for us all the gun and rifle fire, the blazing town of Ypres, the shell-shattered houses, and the stench of corpses.

Their next 'good experience' was again at Bellewaarde Farm on 25th September 1915 in an assault, which was to be a diversionary tactic and sacrifice for Colonel Haig's major offensive at the Battle of Loos, which was intended to break German lines. My grandfather was a batman 'a man servant' and on this day he saved the life of his 2nd lieutenant, Wilfred Theodore Beckingham, who was severely wounded in the neck in a crater near Bellewaarde Farm, losing a lot of blood. According to Beckingham's letters to my great grandmother, the young Emmanuel never hesitated. There was a shout 'We'd better get out the German bombers are coming.' My grandfather was slightly wounded himself but got Beckingham, who was weak and scarcely able to move, out into another trench. WTB was then put on a train to a military hospital in Le Touquet and transported back to a hospital in England, where it was discovered he had shrapnel in his spine. It is interesting to note the mindset of the soldiers in these early days of conflict, and Beckingham's comment was 'What tremendous escapes we had !!'

That day the Battalion's losses were 13 officers (out of 15) and 463 (out of 767) other ranks.

'We may think that we have lost but in reality, we have taken part in a great victory and in the biggest battle in the history of the World'

Little did they know!

It was time to get back onto the 1919 route and at Wormhout, 19km south of Dunkirk, I espied a sign to Esquelbec. This was to be the Oxford & Bucks and my grandfather's last day on the fields of Flanders for a while. In December 1915 the Battalion had been told that, on being relieved in the trenches, they were to refit, and go to Egypt.

When the relief came off, we saluted the Menin Gate as we passed, and wished it good luck, hoping at the same time to see it never again.

However, nothing happened until 11th February 1916, when they moved into billets in some farm buildings at Wormhout. Their Colonel reported:

We now received orders to entrain at Esquelbec for some unknown destination, and on the 20th February 1916, we marched to that place and duly took the train. When we knew for certain that we were really out of the salient, we heaved one, huge sigh of relief. Here the 14th Division had been for nine months without a rest. Our Brigade had had six weeks' rest—of a sort. The times had been hard, and had cost us dear, for the Battalion had lost 35 officers and over 1,000 other ranks— most of the flower of the Battalion when it first came out. Everybody was rather tired of Flanders. We had no idea whither we were going until we found ourselves passing through Amiens. A few miles farther on we stopped and ran back into a siding at Longueau.

They'd arrived on the Somme (see Chapter 5, Stage 1)

*

The 1919 riders were back on the cobblestones, after a brief relief of 6km of tarmac between Le Pleck and Wormhout. It had stopped raining but the dangerous cobblestones were still glinting back at them in anger, as the riders bounced into Dunkirk.

Organising a normal race finish into Dunkirk is not as easy as people might think. If it is not the Capital of Flanders, it is the Capital of Cobblestones, which run through all the streets, boulevards and avenues of the town. The organisers of the stage finish had found a few hundred metres of tarmac, running along the Canal de Bourbourg at the 'Porte de Bourbourg', as you enter the town. Unfortunately, due to a lack of maintenance, this section had been completely destroyed by the heavy English lorries that had continually crossed it, on the way to the front line. However, the officials of Dunkirk, had got together some engineers, who specialised in bridges and pavements, and using pebbles and rollers, they created a finish line as smooth as a billiard table.

Because L'Auto had forecast the first riders would be arriving into Dunkirk at 4 p.m., the crowds started filling the tribunes from 2 p.m. onwards. There were people everywhere, civilians in their dark city clothes and soldiers in the light blue uniforms of the French Army. It was estimated that there were 20,000 people, lining the route, that ran parallel to the canal. People were also sitting on their 'peniches' (large French canal boats), and on top of the fortifications surrounding the Quai de Saint Omer, ensuring they got the best view possible of the finish. They had a long wait before the first of the riders arrived at 7.04 p.m. It was Firmin Lambot. The Belgian had successfully negotiated the cobblestoned 'Ètape de la faim', and maybe it was those extra five bananas that had got him through it. What was sure, was that The Saddler from Antwerp, had got his first stage win on the penultimate stage of the Tour. Not only that, but once the 11 riders had fought their way through the crowds and signed in at the Café des Arcades on La Place Jean Béart, he discovered he was at the head of the G.C. Nearly every table inside the café had been taken up by his fellow countrymen, who had the time to fill their flutes of champagne, to drink to Lambot's success.

Firmin would now be the proud wearer of Henri Desgrange's new thick woollen yellow jersey for the final stage into the Parc des Princes in Paris. In the end, poor old Eugéne Christophe finished nearly two and half hours behind Firmin Lambot. Rather than making up any of his lost time after Raismes, he'd really struggled over the pavé sections leading up to Dunkirk. It was not surprising as he probably didn't have the confidence in his repaired bike to tackle the long stretches of cobblestones at speed, and on top of this he was still suffering from the severe bruising on his knee from his fall in Nice. And if that wasn't enough, a wound on his leg had reopened and was bleeding. It looked as though it was all over for the 'Old Gaul'. He'd now slipped to third position in the G.C behind his old friend 'Gars Jean'

"I have no luck," he said later, "Twice this has happened to me, and surely I deserve better than that. I was holding victory in my hands and my little fortune was surely secure. Fate, however wanted it to be different -too bad!"

That evening, the riders ate well at the official buffet in the Hôtel des Arcades. The menu consisted of the following dishes: Hors d'oeuvres, turbot in Hollandaise sauce with potatoes - English style, fillet of beef Richelieu, green peas, Entremets (small dishes served between courses), cheeses and desserts.

Poor old Eugéne missed out on all of this. When he arrived at the finish line with Jacques Coomans, it was dark and there was no one there apart from a small crowd who had followed them into Dunkirk. André Bazin, the timekeeper, had already left for the Café des Arcades. The two cyclists stayed on their bikes and headed straight to the control and signed in at 9.30 p.m. They went immediately to the hotel reception where Eugéne Christophe asked, not for his own room number, but that of Firmin Lambot. He somehow found the strength to climb the stairs, walk along the long corridor and knock on the door of the room number he had been given. He found the Belgian, already lying on the bed in his pyjamas. Without a word , he undid the three buttons on the shoulder of the yellow jersey, took off his cap and pulled it over his head. He handed the jersey, covered in mud and blood, over to the Belgian, and turned to go. He hardly heard The Saddler's words.

"Merci Cri-Cri. Je n'oublerai jamais." (Thanks Cri-Cri, I will never forget).

Hôtel des Arcades, Dunkirk. Eugéne Christophe hands the yellow jersey to Firmin Lambot.

Stage 14: Metz – Dunkirk (462km)

1. Firmin Lambot	in 21h 04m 27s
2. Léon Scieur	in 21h 11m 10s
3. Joseph Vandaele	in 21h 21m 35s
4. Luigi Lucotti	in 22h 02m 13s
5. Jean Alavoine	in 22h 36m 06s
6. Pail Duboc	at a length
7. Honoré Barthélémy	in 23h 10m13s
8. Jules Nempon	at a length
9. Alfred Steux	at a length
10. Eugéne Christophe	in 23h 41m 55s
11. Jacques Coomans	at a length

General Classement (G.C.)

1. F. Lambot	(The Saddler)	215h 56m 12s
2. J. Alavoine	(Gars Jean)	217h 49m 15s
3. E. Christophe	(The Old Gaul)	218h 05m 35s
4. L. Scieur	(The Locomotive)	218h 58m 36s
5. H. Barthélémy	(Glass Eye)	220h 20m 43s
6. J. Coomans	(The Smoker)	231h 36m 25s
7. L. Lucotti	(The Italian Job)	232h 07m 33s
8. P. Duboc *	(The Apple)	232h 56m 19s
9. A. Steux	(The Kid)	234h 18m 15s
10. J. Vandaele	(Facing his Waterloo)	236h 01m 07s
11. J. Nempon	(The Upstart)	237h 45m 31s

* includes 30-minute penalty on Stage 8

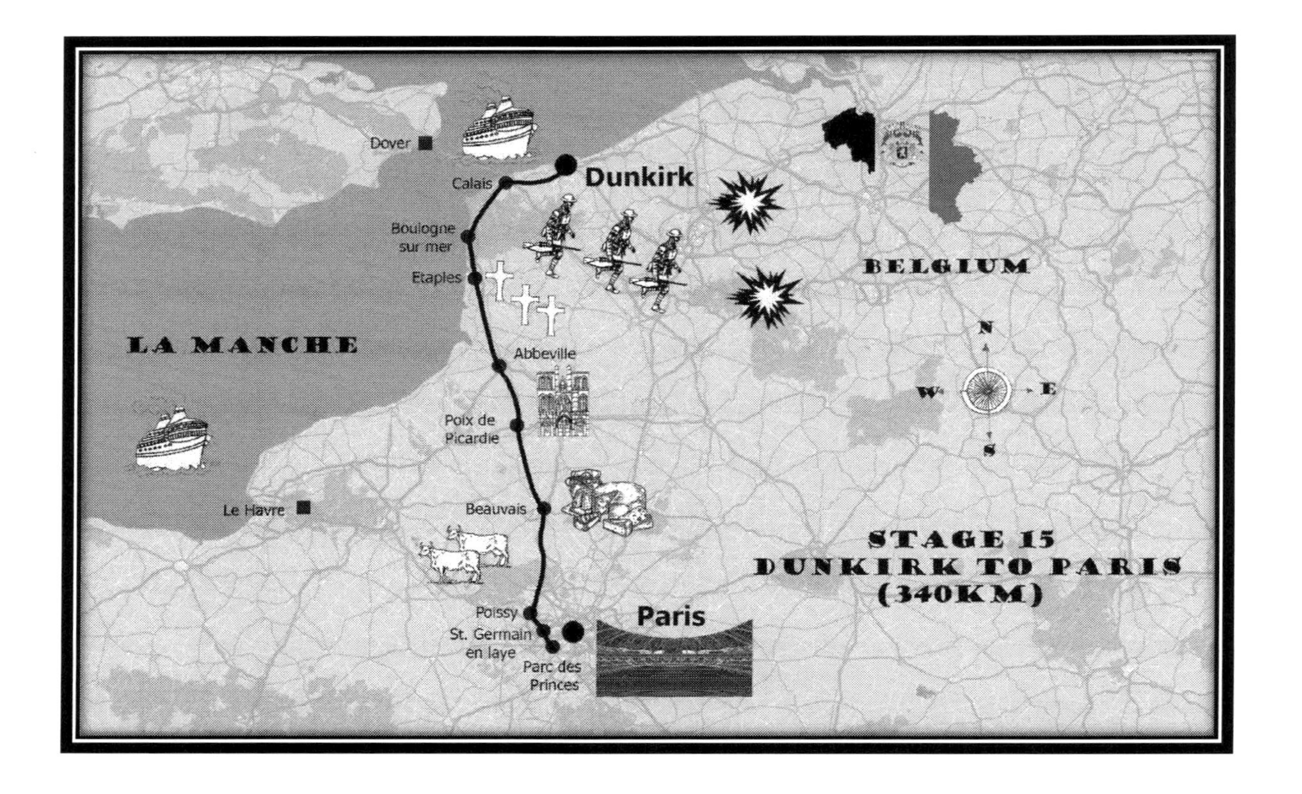
STAGE 15
DUNKIRK TO PARIS
(340KM)
BELGIUM
LA MANCHE
Dover
Dunkirk
Calais
Boulogne
sur mer
Etaples
Abbeville
Poix de
Picardie
Beauvais
Le Havre
Poissy
St. Germain
en laye
Parc des
Princes
Paris
N
W
E
S

Chapter 19 – 'Party in the Parc'

Stage 15: Sunday 27th July 1919 (Dunkirk - Paris)
Thursday 12th October 2019 (Dunkirk - Abbeville)

The Upstart, Jules Nempon couldn't sleep. Despite the long stage of the previous day, he was full of excitement. He'd made it. 5,220km all the way around France to the north coast. He was on home territory now, having been born only 10km outside the town of Dunkirk. In just a couple of hours, Julot would be cycling through his current home town of Calais, and hopefully some of his friends and family would come out to greet him. He was the only Licence 'B' left in the race and the exposure he would get from this, and the prizes he had won whilst en route, would put his business 'Nempon Cycles' on the map. Inevitably, he was the first rider to head downstairs from his hotel room into the café to sign the control sheet for the last stage. Despite the fact that it was just before 1 a.m., there was an enormous crowd waiting for him both inside the café and outside in the Place Jean Béart. He hadn't been expecting this and he would never forget the rapturous reception he was given in Dunkirk. By 1.30 a.m. all 11 riders had signed in and they were led out to the same point on the Canal de Bourbourg, where they'd arrived the previous night. At 2 a.m. the signal was given and this was it, the last stage into Paris.

Firmin Lambot had slept comfortably. He had a lead of 1 hour 43 minutes over his nearest rival Jean Alavoine, and all he had to do was to make sure he made it safely over the 340km into the Parc des Princes. It was not the time to be taking risks and The Saddler, renowned for his cool, calm and organised personality, was not going to make any mistakes. He was now the first Belgian to wear the yellow jersey, and by the end of the day, he also wanted to be the first Belgian to win the Tour de France wearing the 'maillot jaune'.

Whilst Jean Alavoine realised that, unless Firmin Lambot crashed, second place was the best he could hope for, he also wanted to finish on a high. His younger brother Henri, also a cyclist, had died three years ago, on the 19th July 1916, from the wounds he received in aerial combat, whilst fighting in Pau. Gars Jean wanted to do something in his memory.

As for Eugéne Christophe, he hadn't been able to sleep. He went to his room and lay on the bed without getting under the covers. It was as if his cycling clothes had become his second skin. In the morning, the floor boy offered to run him a bath, but he grunted 'Non'. He still couldn't believe his fate and hoped beyond all hopes that it was just a nightmare. He paid the boy 10 centimes for a copy of that day's L'Auto, and there printed on the yellow pages, was a photo of himself and Lambot, side by side, with the headline 'Lambot en tête' (Lambot in the lead). It was all true; he had lost the Tour de France.

It was still dark when the 11 riders arrived together in front of the Co-operative café in Calais at 4.22 a.m. Mind you, what greeted them was a sight to behold. The Mayor of Calais had instructed lighting to be placed on all the streets of the route through the town and the local shopkeepers had lit up their shop windows. It was reported that at least 10,000 spectators witnessed the local boy 'Julot' sign in. The peloton understood the significance of this for the gritty amateur rider and allowed him to receive the plaudits from the appreciative crowd.

*

As I continued along the coast, dawn broke on a potentially beautiful day. After the industrial areas surrounding the ports of Dunkirk and Calais, the views from the rolling hills around the town of Sangatte (and no, I couldn't see any of the refugee camps) back across to England and the white cliffs of Dover are quite stunning. In the distance I could see the cross-channel car ferries, merrily taking their expectant cargo to new adventures on each continent. The views in 1919 would have been completely different as there was only one cross-channel steam turbine vessel, 'The Queen', in existence which could carry up to 1,250 foot-passengers, between Britain and France. During the first World War, 'The Queen' had been used for troop transport and subsequently it was intercepted by a flotilla of raiding German destroyers in 1916 and, after her crew had been taken off board, unceremoniously sunk.

Whilst the sun was shining on myself and the 1919 peloton that morning, there were dark clouds ahead again for Eugéne

Christophe. He punctured in the tiny coastal town of Audreselles, and by the time the peloton reached Boulogne-sur-Mer at 6.26 a.m., he had lost another 12 minutes. This was not his time!

Quai Gambetta, Boulogne-sur-Mer. My grandfather takes his first footsteps on French soil.

In Boulogne, I followed the 1919 route down to the Quai Gambetta and the Port de Plaisance and came across my young grandfather again. It was here, in these docks, that his Battalion arrived on the HMS Invicta on the 20th May 1915. They had sailed from Southampton at 4.20 p.m. accompanied by a destroyer and reached Boulogne at 7.38 p.m. Again, I stood on the dockside and tried to imagine the young Emmanuel, arriving on foreign shores for the first time. It would have been a crowded and noisy scene as the ships offloaded 32 officers, 924 other ranks, 14 riding horses, 64 draught and pack horses, 25 military vehicles and 9 bicycles. After they disembarked, it was an hour's uphill march to their camp at Ostrokoye, where they arrived shortly after midnight. The following day they remained in their camp and at 3 p.m. the well-known Shakespearean actress, singer and suffragette, Miss Lena Ashwell gave them a rousing concert in the Y.M.C.A. tent.

The following day they were up at the crack of dawn and on parade at 2.15 a.m. They marched in the dark to Pont-de-Briques Station to catch the 3.35 a.m. train to Bavinchove, near Cassel, where they arrived on the Western Front at 10.30 a m. (Stage 14).

It was time for me to get on my bike and cycle this section of the route down to the seaside resort of Le Touquet. This would be the last coastal section of the 1919 Tour as it headed inland and southwards to Paris. On my route I had a couple of visits to make. The first was the Forest of Hardelot, a renowned hunting area for deer, wild boar, hares, rabbits, partridge, snipe and pheasant. It was here at the town of Neufchatel-Hardelot that Paul Duboc (The Apple) suffered a broken pedal. Alfred Steux (The Kid), and the poor Eugéne Christophe, had also suffered a number of punctures en-route and by the time they reached Ètaples they were falling further behind. The main peloton of eight riders arrived at 7.50 a.m. followed a quarter of an hour later by Cri-Cri at 8.05 a.m. and surprisingly only 5 minutes later Paul Duboc arrived, having managed to fix his broken pedal (8.10 a.m.). There was no mention at all of Alfred Steux.

My next port of call on the 1919 route was to pay homage to my grandfather in the tiny village of Camiers. Having seen where he took his first steps on French soil in Boulogne, I was now entering the village where he took his last steps. 20km south of Boulogne is the tiny village of Camiers, which was the base for a military hospital run by the US Army. Having been shipped back to England from Rouen after being wounded on the Somme in September 1916 (See Chapter 5), he had proposed and married his childhood sweetheart, Fanny Etta in her hometown of Bardney in Lincolnshire. They were married in February 1917 and by the May of that year he was back out on the Western Front. Having spent nine months in Ypres, and the same time on the Somme, he now found himself back on the Menin Road, just outside Ypres, and in the trenches in front of Polygon Wood. An advance of only 5km in two and a half years! He was later to fight in the first battle of Passchendaele which was to start on 12th October 1917. After a dry spell in September 1917, the rains had returned with a vengeance at the beginning of

October. Many of the field artillery guns that were needed for the attack remained bogged down and when their new placements proved impossible to reach, they were fired inaccurately and slowly sank into the mud. Under these auspicious circumstances the Oxford and Buckinghamshire Regiment 14th (Light) Division, 42nd Brigade, 5th Battalion moved forward on the 16th October. They left a place called Copse Wood and pushed forward through Clapham Junction to Inverness Copse. They were about 6km from Passchendaele when Emmanuel was shot in his right leg and received a shrapnel wound to his lower torso. He was immediately taken to a Casualty Clearing station and once patched up he was put on an ambulance train to Dannes-Camiers. So here I was, exactly 102 years later, sad that he was suffering from serious wounds for the second time in 12 months, but happy that the war was over for him, and he was one of the few that had survived. One of his young friends was not so lucky. Thomas Francis Halford Fremantle, had been shot at the Battle of Bellewaarde Farm on the 25th September 1915, which was the same day that my grandfather had rescued his 2nd lieutenant Wilfred Beckingham. Wilfred had written to my grandfather from his hospital bed in England and told him he had seen Thomas in the military hospital in Le Touquet, but unfortunately, he had died from his wounds, just three weeks later. The 18-year-old Thomas is buried at the Ètaples Military Cemetery which was the next town on the 1919 route, so I couldn't pass by without paying my respects. It was a gloriously sunny day as I entered the gates and walked along to the Cross of Sacrifice, overlooking the cemetery. Nothing really prepares you for the sight that unfolds in front of your eyes, as you pass through onto the extensive Stone of Remembrance, guarded by two imposing mausoleums on either side. Sitting, as it does on an elevated sand hill, the stark white graves of over 11,500 men and women fan out in front of you. This is the largest Common Wealth Graves Commission cemetery in France and over 10,000 of the graves contain the bodies of soldiers lost in the First World War. Luckily, I had noted the location of Thomas' gravestone and soon I stood before this brave teenager and reflected on the 14 words that had been carved onto his grave.

VALIANT FOR TRUTH
MY COURAGE I SHALL GIVE TO HIM
THAT SHALL SUCEED ME

The gravestone of my grandfather's young friend, the 18-year-old Thomas Fremantle. Military Cemetery Ètaples

I was now back in my camper-van and following the 1919 route southwards to head for the Somme once again. I had a wry smile to myself as I passed through the tiny village of Nempont-Saint-Firmin. Surely, they weren't guessing the final outcome of the 1919 Tour and were canonising Jules Nempon (the leading Licence B rider) and Firmin Lambot, (the leading Licence A rider).

At 9.52 a.m. both of them were in the group of nine riders that arrived at first feeding station and the midpoint of the stage at Abbeville. Eugéne Christophe and Paul Duboc were now nearly half an hour behind. It seemed a lifetime ago, but it was only just over four weeks, since the Tour had passed through here on Stage 1 on the 29th June 1919 and Louis Heusghem had arrived first, winning the prize of 25FF.

Stage 15 – Sunday 27th July 1919 (Dunkirk - Paris)

Friday 12th October 2019 (Abbeville – Paris)

My original plan had been to arrive in Paris the weekend of Saturday 27th July 2019 and head down to the finish line at the Parc des Princes, and then the following day head over to the Champs-

Èlysées and the Arc de Triomphe to watch the climax of the 2019 Tour. Those plans obviously went up in smoke, so I watched the finish on TV.

What a Tour it had been. It had looked for a long while that Jean Alaphilippe was going to end France's 34 year long wait for a Tour de France victory, as he defied the odds to retain the yellow jersey through from Stage 10 to Stage 18, the first stage in the Alps. However, Stage 19 from Saint Jean de Maurienne to Tignes, was to be as dramatic a stage, as had ever been witnessed in Tour de France history. The two breakaway riders, the Coulmbian Egan Bernal and Britain's Adam Yates were about to make the final ascent from the Val-d'Isère up to the finish line in Tignes. Suddenly a drama unfolded on our TV screens. A helicopter flew over a pass in the valley and filmed a mudslide flowing slowly and ominously across the road the riders were heading for. The news travelled fast and the race Directors acted immediately, catching the two riders up in the official car and pulling them over to inform them that the race had to be neutralised. Times for the general classification were taken at the summit of the Iseran, and as a result, Bernal, who had been in second place overall, moved ahead of Alaphilippe and took the yellow jersey. The following day snow and hailstones curtailed the penultimate stage from Albertville to Thorens, shortening it from 131 km to 60 km. Egan Bernal and his team mate, the pre-Tour favourite and 2018 winner Geraint Thomas took advantage and dropped Alaphilippe. It was all over for the Frenchman and the yellow jersey fell back into the hands of the young Columbian and 'Team Ineos'. The final processional stage into Paris had proved uneventful and the 22-year-old became the first Columbian to win the Tour de France.

*

And so, after my two encounters with 'La Sorcière aux dentes verts', my sole destination was to now follow the 1919 route in through the west side of Paris. The 1919 riders passed into Normandy and crossed the Pays de Caux (Chalk country) and the Pays de Bray (Mud country). This was a region that was ideal for the raising of dairy cattle, milk and cheese production. However, soft undulating countryside wasn't ideal for any attacks, and so the leading eight riders rolled into the last feeding station at Beauvais together at 1.33 p.m. Maybe they feasted on the local heart-shaped soft cheeses, such as Neufchatel and Fin-de-siécle, and drank the local milk. Alfred Steux appeared again and apparently; he was only six minutes behind the leading group. Duboc and Christophe rolled in together last, a further ten minutes behind Steux.

It was not until the tiny town of Henonville, before the National Park of Vexin Français, that five of the leading riders saw their opportunity to break away. After a sharp incline, it was all downhill to the suburbs of Paris. It was time for the sprinters to attack and Jean Alavoine, Honoré Barthélémy, Jacques Coomans, Luigi Lucotti and Léon Scieur sped off towards to the last control point at Poissy on the city's edge. They were all keen to get the stage win in front of the expectant crowds at the Parc des Princes. As for Firmin Lambot, in the yellow jersey, he sat back with Jules Nempon and Joseph Vandaele, not wanting to take any risks against securing his first Tour victory. There were just 81km to go.

All five leading riders crossed the bridge of the River Seine and arrived at the control point in Poissy at 3.56 p.m., so nearly four o'clock in the afternoon. The large crowds, lining the central streets of the town had been waiting patiently since half past one for their arrival. L'Auto had forecast that the arrival would be somewhere around 1.35 p.m., so the peloton was nearly two and half hours behind schedule. Again, Henri Desgrange had completely underestimated the effect the gruelling stage between Metz and Dunkirk had on the riders. The 120km of pavé had taken everything out of the riders. Jules Nempon was the next to arrive all alone at 4.01 p.m. He had broken away and gained five minutes on Firmin Lambot. The wearer of the yellow jersey was cycling cautiously behind with his compatriot Joseph Vandaele for company. Joseph was obviously there as a moral and phycological back up. Twenty minutes later Alfred Steux arrived followed at 4.30 p.m. by the French duo of Paul Duboc and the downtrodden Eugéne Christophe.

*

I arrived in Poissy, at a similar time, around 4 p.m. and crossed the bridge over the River Seine and imagined how the scene must have changed from 1919. Firstly, the bridge the 1919 riders had crossed had gone. It was completely destroyed by the British Army when Poissy was liberated from German occupation in August 1944. As I crossed, I could see the four remaining pillars of the old bridge to my left. To my right was the enormous 240,000 m2 Peugeot-Citroen car plant, which had been built along the banks of the River Seine in the late 1930's due to the excellent river and train connections into Paris and to the sea port of Le Havre. I found a suitable place to park, north of Saint Germain-en-Laye, to cycle the last section into Paris. I had come full circle. Setting off in Versailles after the Treaty had been signed on the 28th June 1919, I was now in the town where the Treaty of Saint-Germain-en-Laye (which brought to an end the hostilities with Austria and led to the dissolution of the Austrian-Hungarian Empire) was signed in its magnificent royal palace on the 10th September 1919, just six weeks after the Tour had passed through. As well as its historic links with the year of the 1919 Tour, Saint-Germain-en-Laye has strong sporting links with the Parc des Princes. In 1970, the local football team merged with a team in Paris to form the now famous club of Paris Saint Germain, or PSG as it is commonly known. PSG still play their home matches in the Parc des Princes, but have their training ground at the Saint Germain-en-Laye ground at Camp des Loges. When the 1919 Tour passed outside, it was still a military training camp, and French soldiers were in the process of being demobbed.

After a descent to the banks of the River Seine, there follows a steep climb up to Marly-le-Roi, where it was time to cross paths with Louis XIV again. Whilst waiting for his Grand Palace to be built in Versailles, he had another chateau constructed in Marly, just to the north of his intended home. This was to be used as a retreat to escape the rigours of court life in Versailles, and given the extensive surrounding forests of Marly and Saint Germain, it was to be used a lodge where he could house the Royal Hunt. At the front of the Chateau he built the 'Grand Abreuvoir à Chevaux', a massive horse trough, which could water all the King's horses after the hunt. After the French Revolution in 1799, the chateau fell into the hands of an industrialist, who built a cotton mill in the chateau and when that failed it was demolished in 1806. The following year Napoleon Bonaparte bought the estate and converted it into a park which still exists today.

All that remained in 1919 and today is the park and the magnificent water trough. The 1919 route instructions in L'Auto indicated that, after Saint Germain-en-Laye, the riders should turn off the route de Paris, which led along the banks of the river Seine and turn right and attack the pavé road to L'Abreuvoir de Marly. Here, they had to circle the horse trough to the left and climb the side of 'Coeur-Volant' (Flying Heart) and through the Royal gates to Rocquencourt. Here I found myself at the back of the Palace of Versailles gardens, where I had strolled on the day the Treaty was signed. Next, the instruction was to turn sharply left by a belfry in the garden of a private house and head out to Vaucresson.

The 'Grand Abreuvoir à Chevaux', (horse trough), at Marly-le-Roi.

I found a strange clock tower on the wall of a private house and wondered whether this was the aforementioned belfry. I took the D907 to Vaucresson and headed under the 'Autroute de Normandie'. The roads were getting busy now. It was Friday afternoon and the rush hour traffic was starting to exit the city. Still, there was only 9km to go to the Parc des Princes and by the time I got to Pont-de-Saint-Cloud, I was back on the road that I had travelled all those months ago, when I followed the supporters of the French women's football team up to the stadium.

For the five leading riders of the Tour, the situation was getting tense now. Already people were lining the streets to cheer them on as they headed up the 'Route de la Reine' towards the Parc. (Henri Desgrange estimated that 300,000 people had watched the Tour arrive in Paris from Poissy through to the Parc des Princes).

They could hear the noise of the expectant crowd as they approached their special entrance, which led them onto the race track. The crowd had been waiting since 2.15 p.m. and had read their programmes (costing 25 centimes) from back to front.

The entrance to the Parc des Princes Velodrome, Paris.

They had been entertained by several bike races around the Parc des Princes track including 'Le Grand Prix du Tour de France' featuring famous cyclists such as the 'Young Magician' Francis Pélissier, André Huret and the colourful character Ali Neffati, a Tunisian cyclist, who had been the first African to compete in the Tour de France, wearing a Fez. There was also a tandem race called 'Le Prix des Géants de la Route' and it would have been quite a spectacle to have seen 60 of these giants flying around the track. Other distractions included entertainment by the band of the 101st Infantry who played the following repertoire.

1. The Star of New York, A march (Paradis)
2. Le Petit Duc, A fantasy (Lecocq).
3. Joyeuse Espagne, A Waltz (Allier).
4. Les Saltimbanques (Ganne).
5. Marche Lorraine (Ganne).

It was 5 p.m. when the bugle sounded and the official cars led the five leading riders into the stadium. The 'Brasier' of L'Auto arrived first with its yellow flags flying resplendently on all four corners of the car. The riders had one more task to endure before the race was finished and that was to complete the 666-metre circuit of the track to try and win the stage and a bonus prize of 100 Francs. The crowd rose and cheered their heroes. Caps and straw boaters were thrown into the air as the crowd shouted 'Vive Le Tour' and 'Vive L'Auto'.

Jean Alavoine leads the peloton into the Parc des Princes stadium.

The exhausted riders set off on their last challenge with gusto. The cheers from the 30,000 crowd rang around the stadium, raising the adrenalin levels of the five riders, each eager to triumph in front their Parisian fans. They sped down the first straight, building up enough speed to launch themselves around the steep banks of the racing circuit. The words 'ALYCON, DUBONNET and HUTCHINSON' flashed in front of their eyes, as the advertising hoardings appeared on the main stands. The crowds were so close, the riders could almost hear them breathing as they completed half a lap. This was going to be close, extremely close. As the riders came into the last bend, they were all still together, the crowd roared and cheered their favourites on. The finishing line approached and suddenly two riders found some energy from their reserves which must have been depleted after 5,560km of racing. Who were they? It was Jean Alavoine, 'Gars Jean' and Luigi Lucotti 'The Italian Job'. Surely Lucotti couldn't deny the French their victory again? This time it was not to be and Gars Jean secured the victory for France by half a length. He looked to the sky and hoped his brother Henri was looking down on him. This win was for France and for Henri.

The other three, the Parisian Barthélémy (Glass Eye), 'The Locomotive' Léon Scieur and 'The Smoker' Jacques Coomans all pulled in together, a further length behind. The Parisian crowd went wild. Eugéne Christophe may have lost the Tour, due to his misfortune, but at least they had a French winner in Paris, and a local man from Versailles as well.

The moment the Tour was won. Firmin Lambot signs in at the Parc des Princes and he becomes the first winner of the Tour de France and the yellow jersey.

The crowd were still celebrating, when a cheer went up from the other side of the stadium. Jules Nempon 'Julot' had appeared and was doing a solo lap of the Parc de Princes with people rising to their feet and applauding the 'Licence B' rider as he passed by the stands. This had truly been a magnificent effort and surely a professional contract would be coming his way soon.

No sooner had the Young Upstart completed his lap, then the cheers started again. It was the yellow jersey! It was the first time the Parisian public had seen Henri Desgrange's new creation and they took it to their hearts. Ok, it wasn't being worn by a Frenchman, but Firmin Lambot was a worthy winner of the first ever 'maillot jaune', given his two top-ten finishes in the last two pre-war Tours. He was followed by his faithful companion Jacques Coomans (The Smoker), who let his fellow countryman, receive the plaudits he deserved and he duly finished a minute behind the yellow jersey.

The crowd settled down. They were now waiting for their hero. However, the next to show his face was the youngster 'Le Gosse (The Kid)' Alfred Steux, who had shown that, despite his boyish looks, he had what it takes to compete with the best and the crowd showed their appreciation for the young Belgian. Alfred had not even reached the finish line, when the whole of the Parc des Princes erupted again. He was here. Eugéne Christophe had made it along with Paul Duboc (The Apple). They entered the stadium. Eugéne looked sheepishly as he started his lap. He couldn't look up at the crowd. He felt he had failed them. He cycled round the track, with the tears rolling down his face. He crossed the line, just behind Duboc, in last place. The Old Gaul, the brave warrior had finished in last place. He just wanted to sign the control sheet and disappear. Never before had he sobbed, and especially not in front of a crowd of 30,000 people. Alphonse Baugé, the marshal, came to his rescue and carried him under the handrail and led him up to the area where the other riders had gathered. Nearby, he could see Henri Desgrange, who whispered under his breath.

"Listen to the crowd Eugéne. They are cheering for you as if you were a God. You are 'Le Vaincu du Destin'."

The Old Gaul listened. It was true. All he could hear were cries of

"Bravo Christophe, Hourra Cri-Cri."

The crowd broke over the barriers and surged towards him. They all wanted to shake his hand and comfort him after his misfortune. Suddenly Gars Jean approached him. He had already washed and changed into his daytime clothes. Alphonse Baugé, poked fun at him.

"He arrived a while ago, Cri-Cri, and he has had the time to dress himself up like a dog's dinner."

"Stop, marshal, be serious for a second. I've come to give to Cri-Cri, the sum we have collected between the other riders. Here my brave Eugéne, take this. You deserve it. Even if what you really deserve is to wear that yellow jersey on your shoulders!"

Firmin Lambot approached and looked at him kindly.

"Would I have preferred to have come to you without the misfortune you have suffered? I don't really know, but what I do know is that I would have preferred to have fought you on equal terms."

Cri-Cri didn't know what to say. He put his arm on the shoulder of Lambot's 'maillot jaune' and turned and departed the Parc.

'The Green-Toothed Witch had defeated the yellow canary'

Jean Alavoine, Firmin Lambot, Honore Barthélémy.

Luigi Lucotti, Eugéne Christophe, Henri Pélissier.

Francis Pélissier , Jean Rossius

Stage 15: Dunkirk – Paris (340km)

1. Jean Alavoine	in 15h 00m 54s
2. Luigi Lucotti	at half a length
3. Honoré Barthélémy	at a length
4. Léon Scieur	at a length
5. Jacques Coomans	at a length
6. Jules. Nempon	in 15h 05m 56s
7. Firmin Lambot	in 15h 11m 03s
8. Joseph Vandaele	in 15h 12m 02s
9. Alfred Steux	in 15h 35m 09s
10. Paul Duboc	in 15h 36m 41s
11. Eugéne Christophe	at a length.

General Classement (G.C.)

1. F. Lambot	(The Saddler)	231h 07m 15s
2. J. Alavoine	(Gars Jean)	232h 50m 09s
3. E. Christophe	(The Old Gaul)	233h 33m 46s
4. L. Scieur	(Locomotive)	233h 59m 30s
5. H. Barthélémy	(Glass Eye)	235h 21m 37s
6. J. Coomans	(The Smoker)	246h 28m 49s
7. L. Lucotti	(The Italian Job)	247h 08m 27s
8. P. Duboc *	(The Apple)	248h 33m 00s
9. A. Steux	(The Kid)	249h 30m 17s
10. J. Vandaele	(Waterloo)	251h 36m 16s
11. J. Nempon	(The Upstart)	252h 51m 27s

* includes 30-minute penalty on Stage 8, Subsequently disqualified for borrowing a car to go and fix a pedal during Stage 15.

Chapter 20 – 'FIN'

That evening, Eugéne Christophe was invited to a celebration to be held in his honour at the L'Ètoile Sportif de Malakoff, the French suburb and place of his birth, five kilometres from the Parc des Princes. He limped into the large function room, using a cane to support himself, due to his wounded knee. The crowd chanted his name 'Cri-Cri, Cri-Cri'. On the stage the President of the Club presented him with a commemorative sheaf and urged him to say a few words. Public speaking was not Eugéne's strong point but he spoke from the heart when he said:

"Yes, my friends, I should have won the Tour de France. I had caught back some time on Lambot after his breakaway, I was riding easily and I was feeling confident just before my accident. What could I do? It was bad luck and that's the truth. It has been written that I will never win the Tour de France. I might as well quit this profession of cycling!"

"No, No," cried the shocked crowd.

"Yes, Yes. I have decided to take up an offer I have had from the owner of the little forge in Raismes, where I repaired my forks. He has made me a good offer to become foreman."

"We'll talk about this tomorrow, Eugéne," whispered Alphonse Baugé, "Haven't you heard? A subscription has been started by L'Auto to collect money on your behalf. They have donated 1,000 francs and it has already reached 1,705.95 FF on its first day."

This brought some cheer to Eugéne. After all, the tactics he'd deployed were in order to retain the yellow jersey, his prime objective. He had not been interested in stage wins and the monetary prizes that came with it. After his accident, and his resulting third position in G.C., his total winnings had been a mere 2,200 FF. Firmin Lambot's winnings had amounted to 6,775 FFs and Jean Alavoine's 5,600 FFs. Even Jules Nempon, the Licence B rider had amassed more than the Old Gaul. Although he had only won 375 FF of the main prizes on offer, Julot had scooped 2,600

FF of the Licence B prizes, giving him a total of 2,975 FFs. At least this subscription would be some recompense!

In the end the subscription raised 13,310.82 FFs and Eugéne ended up receiving nearly double the amount Firmin Lambot received for winning. I wonder if he thought he should return the spontaneous collection made for him by the other riders at the Parc des Princes?

Eugéne was right in one thing; he would never be destined to win the Tour de France. He had to abandon in 1920 and 1921 and worse still he suffered a third broken fork in 1922, coming down the Galibier in the Alps. He was third in the G.C. and guess what? Yes, Firmin Lambot was the winner AGAIN ! His one consolation in 1922, was that he got to wear the yellow jersey again for three stages. He finished 18th in his final Tour in 1925 and at the age of 40 he retired. Despite not winning the race, 'Le Vieux Gaulois' had earned his place as a legend in Tour history. In 1951, he re-enacted that fateful day at Saint-Marie-de-Campan, when a broken fork cost him the race coming off the Tourmalet. A plaque was placed on the forge where he undertook the repair, and he celebrated the occasion with the seven-year-old child Corni, who had pumped the bellows for him, resulting in a ten-minute penalty. In 1965, he was honoured when the great French rider Jacques Anquetil, gave him his Tour de France winners medal. Then, on the 18th July 2014, a bronze statue was unveiled in his honour in Sainte-Marie-de Campan, and the square was renamed the 'Place Eugéne Christophe'. Eugéne had reached the grand old age of 85, when he passed away in the Hôpital Broussais, one kilometre from the place of his birth, Malakoff in Paris.

As for the winner, Firmin Lambot's achievement was nothing short of a miracle. He had been a prisoner of war for four years during the Great War and he'd not sat on a bike or trained, during all of that time. He'd taken part in the Paris-Brussels race, finishing 13th, two weeks before the Tour on the 15th June 1919, but basically that had been it. He'd got fit whilst riding the Tour and his win proved he would be destined for great things. He finished third in the Tour in 1920 and ninth in 1921 before his historic second victory in the Parc des Princes in 1922, where he won the Tour without winning a stage. On this day, he became the oldest winner of the Tour at the age of 36, a record that still stands today. This proved to be the peak of his career, and eventually he retired to become a saddler once again. He died on 19th January 1964, in Bougerhout, a suburb of Antwerp, aged 77.

The eloquent Jean Alavoine, 'Gars Jean', was also destined not to win a Tour de France, finishing second again to Firmin Lambot in the Tour of 1922. However, his stage victories have stood the test of time and he still sits 8th in the all-time stage victory list with 17 stage wins. One can only wonder what would have been the result had 'Gars Jean' not lost over 40 minutes to Firmin Lambot on the first stage, when he fell asleep briefly under a hedge, whilst having punctured. Born in the cycling town of Roubaix, he died in 1943 whilst taking part in a veteran cycle race in Argenteuil, Paris, aged just 55.

Firmin Lambot would have been happy to see the 4th place finish of his protégé, Léon Scieur. He'd encouraged his compatriot, from his hometown in Florennes, to become a professional cyclist and Léon had finished only 25 minutes behind the great Eugéne Christophe. Léon would be part of Belgium's domination of the Tour de France at the turn of the 1920's, coming fourth in 1920 and winning it in 1921, with a stunning performance. After Louis Mottiat's victory on the first stage from Paris to Le Havre, Léon took the yellow jersey on Stage 2 and rode in it all the way to Paris. It was in this Tour, that his ability to pedal fast in a low gear, earned him the nickname of the 'Locomotive'. Léon never ventured far from his home town of Florennes and this was where the Locomotive pulled into his final station in October 1969, aged 81.

As for old Glass Eye, the red headed Honoré Barthélémy was well pleased with his 5th place finish and four stage wins. Mind you, this was surprisingly the most stages he would ever win. In 1920 he finished 8th, but with no stage victories to his name. The following year 1921, he achieved his best ever finish in the Tour with a commendable third place, but with only one stage victory. This was the peak for the red squirrel who kept on competing in the Tour until 1927, but was not able to finish in any of them. He remained in his Parisian home until May 1964, when he passed away aged 72.

Throughout the rest of his cycling career, Jacques Coomans (The Smoker) never finished another Tour de France. After his 6th place showing in 1919, he never got any further than Stage 6 in any of his future outings up to 1925. Despite his penchant for smoking, and his cravings for cigarettes and large cigars, Jacques lived to the ripe old age of 91, passing away in his hometown of Liège, just two months short of his 92nd birthday.

The young 25-year-old Luigi Lucotti (The Italian Job) had a surprisingly short Tour de France career. His only other Tour finish was in 1921, when he finished one place behind his 1919 placing of 7th, winning Stage 8 Perpignan-Toulon. He had one more go in 1925, but only got as far as the finish of Stage 3 in Brest, and abandoned. He subsequently retired from professional cycling and returned to his birthplace in Voghera, Italy where he died peacefully, aged 83.

It was a similar tale for the Belgian, Joseph Vandaele, (Facing his Waterloo) who followed up his respectable 8th place finish in 1919, with a 10th place finish in 1920, but again that was it. In his two attempts in 1921 and 1923, he completed two and seven stages respectively. He passed away in the French city of Amiens, at the relatively young age of 48, (maybe he met Yvonne with her sticky buns) just after the Second World War.

As for his compatriot, Alfred Steux. He was also destined never to complete another Tour de France. He had three more attempts, abandoning on Stage 3 in 1920 and 1921 and then, in what seemed an afterthought, he abandoned after the first stage in 1925. Le Gosse (The Kid) died at the early age of 42 in his adopted home in Paris.

Paul Duboc (The Apple), had signed in at the Parc des Princes in tenth place. However , it was subsequently discovered that 'Le Pomme' had borrowed a car to go and fix his pedal on the morning of the last stage and he was disqualified. Imagine cycling the complete 5,560km of the Tour around France, only to be eliminated at the final hurdle. You may have some sympathy for him or you may think the rules are the rules, and Paul is a 'bad apple'. He may have felt he deserved some recompense after the attempt to poison him in 1911, when he missed out on what should have been his Tour win, and he ended up in second place. Mind you had he borrowed any cars? Who knows? Paul died in Paris, in 1941, at the relatively young age of 57. Maybe the poisoning hadn't helped his longevity!

Of course, Duboc's disqualification was good news for Jules Nempon, the sole Licence 'B' rider, who moved up to tenth place in the standings. He was still in the coveted position of being awarded the prestigious title of 'Lanterne Rouge'. In the Tour de France the rider who finishes last in Paris, rather than dropping out along the way, is accorded the distinction of 'lanterne rouge'. Because of the popularity it affords, riders may compete for last position, rather than settling for a place near the back. Often the rider who comes last is remembered, while those a few places ahead are forgotten. In the 1979 Tour de France, Gerhard Schönbacher and Philippe Tesnière were in the last two spots in the general classification, less than one minute apart. Tesnière had already finished last in the 1978 Tour, so he was aware of the publicity associated with being the lanterne rouge. In the 21st stage, a time trial, Tesnière rode slowly. Unfortunately, he rode so slowly he missed the time cut and was eliminated, and Schönbacher became the new lanterne rouge. Surprisingly, after his good showing in 1919, the following two years were a disaster and Julot did not even get past the first stage. In 1922, he did get to the finish in Paris , finishing 20th and in 1927, he completed all 24 stages, finishing 35th. After another DNF (Did Not Finish) in 1928 Julot hung up his cycle clips and returned to the region of Pas de Calais, and passed away in June 1974, at the age of 84.

And so, just ten riders were deemed to have finished the 1919 Tour de France. The lowest ever in its history. There were times when it looked as though there might not be enough riders left to make it to Paris. As early as Stage 4, after the abandonment of the Pélissier brothers, 50 riders had already left the race and there were only 17 left heading into the mountains. 1919 was also the slowest Tour in the history of the race and Firmin Lambot's average speed of 24.06 km/hour (as a comparison Egan Bernal achieved 40.58 km/hr in 2019) reflected the state of the post war roads, the terrible weather conditions and the general lack of time for training. All in all, though it had been a success and the Tour de France was back up and running.

*

And all in all, my Tour de France had been a success. It had taken me to parts of the country I'd not visited previously and my memories of camping on clifftops overlooking the sea, or on the shores of an iridescent blue lake, or awaking amongst the vineyards of a Bordeaux Chateau are memories and images that will remain with me. There were times when I wondered what the hell I'd undertaken, after the break-in to my camper-van in Nice, the breakdown in Belgium and the broken chain in Alsace. They all came at a cost, both financial and personal. Still, it was a dream realised and somehow the attacks of the 'Green-Toothed Witch' seemed to come at a time that coincided with the attacks on the 'Yellow Canary' in the 1919 Tour. The trip had also given me the chance to go on a personal journey and to follow my young grandfather's footsteps on all three major fronts of the First World War.

I'd learnt a lot about these men of steel. I'd climbed every peak with them, travelled along every boring tree-lined road, shared their frustrations, agonies and injuries and felt their sense of achievement at having completed each stage. As I travelled it made me reflect on the current Tour de France, which is no longer a true journey around France, but rather a series of 21 cycling challenges staged largely in France, but quite often spilling over into other countries. I understood the logic of taking the sport of cycling to other nations, and I for one, loved the opportunity to witness 'Le Grande Boucle' first hand when my friends and I cycled and watched the London to Canterbury stage in 2007. I also understood the necessity of varying the route; to give more towns the opportunity to become a 'ville d'ètape'; to make the stages as challenging at the right moments to ensure a close race all the way to the Champs Èlysées in Paris, and to introduce different spectacles such as the individual and team trials. However, having completed my trip, part of me yearned for a return to these golden days of cycling. Of a man and a bike and an uninterrupted journey around France. In Henri's own words to the sportsman of Belfort:

"The Tour de France, as its name indicates, needs to follow the periphery of our country and not be raced in zigzags."

The 'Grande Boucle' had remained just that, a complete journey around France, either clockwise or anti-clockwise, until 1951 (38th Tour) when it became 'un-boucled' and small gaps in the route started to appear and transfers had to be made between ville d'ètapes. These gaps got bigger in the early 1960's as the Tour started to move into other countries and by 1982 the Tour had become a series of eight separate cycling events.

1. North-east France
2. Belgium, Lille
3. Brittany
4. Bordeaux
5. Pyrénées
6. Marseille (Time Trial)
7. Alps
8. Finish in Paris

I know that Henri Desgrange was draconian with the early morning starts, and over 1,500km of the Tour was cycled during the night, but I'm sure a route could be found that would cover maybe 3,800km and finish with a short race into Paris. Maybe this book will inspire some young rider to attempt to tackle the 1919 Tour de France or even to attempt a stage, setting off at the same time as the 'aces' of Tour did all those years ago. For an idea as to how tough it can be, watch 'Can We Ride And Survive A Stage Of The 1903 Tour de France?' on YouTube. It features Mark Beaumont and Hank Lowsley-Williams tackling the first stage between Paris and Lyon (467km) on fixed wheel bikes. Mark is an endurance cyclist who has cycled around the world and you can discover how hard he found this stage versus modern day cycling.

That night I sat in the bar of my Parisian campsite on the banks of the Seine and chatted with a German couple who had recently toured the UK. One beer led to another, and we told each other the stories of our adventures. They asked me where my favourite parts of France were and it was a difficult question to answer. Every day, the journey had brought new sights, new experiences, new foods and new wines. It brought me into contact with the hometowns of many famous French artists and writers. I saw the development of the French rail and road network and marvelled at some of the construction both old and new. The route, of course, crossed the path of many historic incidents that told the story of the Tour de France, over the last one hundred years.

In France, there is a school book called 'Le Tour de la France par deux enfants' which was written by Augustine Fouillée (under the pseudonym of G. Bruno) in 1877. The book recounts the tale of two young brothers, André and Julien Volden who after the annexation to Prussia of their home town, Phalsbourg in Lorraine

(1871) and the death of their father, go in search of their family members. They travel throughout the provinces of France and the diversity of the people they meet, ensure they learnt more and more about their country. There are passages on the taste of the local foods, the strange patois spoken, the varied geography, trees, animals, birds and fish. It detailed the industries that had grown up in various regions and outlined the history and science behind them. It was designed to give the youth of France a patriotic sense of the wealth of diversity in their homeland. It became known as the' little red book of the Third Republic' and would have been read by a young Henri Desgrange (born in 1865) as a twelve-year-old schoolboy. As I flicked through the pages, I could see the influence it would have had on the young Henri and the eventual creation of his Tour de France.

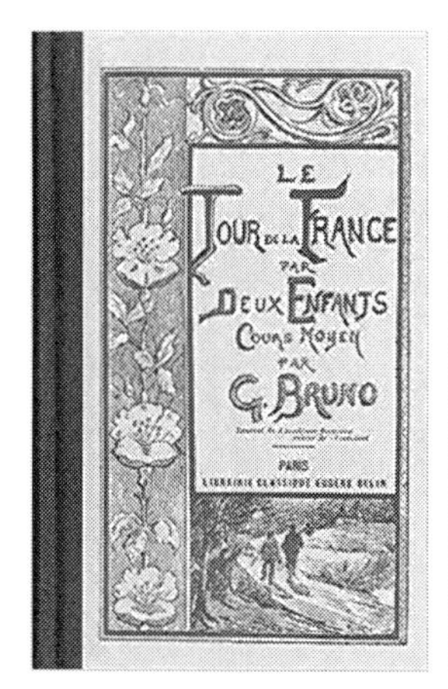

The book has inspired a modern-day rewrite, a film and two TV series. There is also a recent travelogue where two friends realise a lifelong ambition to follow the exact route of the young Volden brothers. They start off from Phalsbourg in Lorraine and drive to Clermont Ferrand in a Peugeot 204. They then sail along part of the Mediterranean, cycle through the Pyrénées, catch a coach to Normandy and Brittany and finish in Paris by train (TGV).

NOW, THERE'S A GOOD IDEA FOR A BOOK!

Appendix 1 : 100 Years of the Yellow Jersey (as at 2019)

1) The first rider to wear the yellow jersey was Eugéne Christophe (FRA) on Stage 10 (Grenoble – Geneva) on Saturday 19th July 1919

2) The first winner of the yellow jersey was Firmin Lambot (BEL) in the Parc des Princes on Sunday 27th July 1919.

3) There have been **283** different wearers on the yellow jersey since the first jersey was awarded in 1919. (as at 2019)

4) There were 24 virtual winners of the Yellow Jersey prior to Eugéne Christophe wearing it on Stage 10 in 1919.

5) The youngest Tour de France winners are:

i.	Henri Cornet	(FRA)	19yrs + 352d (1904)
ii.	François Faber	(LUX)	22yrs + 187d (1909)
iii.	Octave Lapize	(FRA)	22yrs + 280d (1910)

6) The youngest stage winner of the yellow jersey is Felice Gimondi (ITA) in 1965 at the age of 22 yrs +289 days, followed by Philippe Thys at 22 yrs +292 days.

7) Firmin Lambot is the oldest ever winner of the yellow jersey in 1922 aged 36 and 130 days.

8) There are three riders who have worn the yellow jersey throughout the Tour de France.

i.	Octavia Bottechia	(ITA)	1924
ii.	Nicholas Frantz	(LUX)	1928
iii.	Romain Maes	(BEL)	1935

9) Most days in the yellow jersey

i.	Eddy Merckx	(BEL)	96
ii.	Bernard Hinault	(FRA)	79
iii.	Miguel Indurain	(SPA)	60
iv.	Chris Froome	(GBR)	59
v.	Jacques Anquetil	(FRA)	52

10) In 1947, after the death of Henri Desgrange, Jacques Goddet took over as Editor in chief of L'Auto. In honour of the great man he decreed that his initials 'HD' should be stitched into the yellow jersey.

11) Philippe Thys said he was the first to wear yellow in the Tour de France of 1913. This has never been corroborated.

12) On the 8th Stage of the Tour de France 1929, there were three wearers of the yellow jersey, Nicolas Frantz, Victor Fontan and André Leducq as they were all joint equal in the GC standings.

13) Eight riders have won the Tour de France .without winning a stage:

i.	Firmin Lambot	(BEL)	1922
ii.	Roger Walkowiak	(FRA)	1956
iii.	Gastone Nencini	(ITA)	1960
iv.	Lucien Aimar	(FRA)	1966
v.	Greg LeMond	(USA)	1990
vi.	Óscar Pereiro	(ESP)	2006
vii.	Chris Froome	(GBR)	2017
viii.	Egan Bernal	(COL)	2019

14) Sixteen riders have quit whilst wearing the yellow jersey.

i. 1927 Francis Pélissier (Sickness)
ii. 1929 Victor Fontan (Broken bicycle)
iii. 1937 Sylvère Maes (Collective withdrawal of the Belgian team due to threat of French spectators)

iv. 1950 Fiorenzo Magni (Collective withdrawal of the two Italian teams due to threat of French spectators)
v. 1951 Wim Van Est (After a fall in a ravine in Aubisque)
vi. 1965 Bernard Van De Kerkhove (Withdrawal in the climb of Aubisque (sunstroke)
vii. 1971 Luis Ocaña (Fall during a storm in Col de Mente)
viii. 1978 Michel Pollentier (Expelled for fraud attempt in doping test)
ix. 1980 Bernard Hinault (Knee pain)
x. 1983 Pascal Simon (Scapula fracture)
xi. 1991 Rolf Sørensen (Clavicle fracture after fall in the last kilometre)
xii. 1996 Stéphane Heulot (Knee tendinitis)
xiii. 1998 Chris Boardman (Head and neck injury after a severe crash)
xiv. 2007 Michael Rasmussen (Fired by his team due to lying about his whereabouts)
xv. 2015 Fabian Cancellara (Broken vertebrae in Stage 3 crash)
xvi. 2015 Tony Martin (Broken collarbone in Stage 6 crash)

15) On 19 July 1988 there were two stages. Other than the split stages that the Tour de France saw earlier, these two stages were counted as individual stages, so Pedro Delgado received two yellow jerseys on that day.

16) Fabian Cancellara, with twenty-nine days in yellow, is the rider with the most yellow jerseys, not to have won the Tour.

Connect with Ian
email: ianchesteri@btinternet.com
twitter: @Ian20583404
Facebook: Ian Chester
Instagram: chesfox77
Linked-In: Ian Chester

Appendix 2: The 1919 Riders

A full list of the 67 riders who started Stage 1, at the Parc des Princes, Paris on Sunday 29th June 1919.

No.	Race	Name	Nation	Runner
1	1	René Gerwig	France	
2	3	Robert Asse	France	
3	4	François Chevalier	France	
4	6	GastonVan Waesberghe	Belgium	
5	7	Constant Ménager	France	
6	15	Philippe Thys	Belgium	Basset Hound
7	19	Luigi Lucotti	Italy	The Italian Job
8	25	Marcel Buysse	Belgium	
9	26	Lucien Buysse	Belgium	
10	37	Henri Pélissier	France	The Greyhound
11	38	Alexis Michiels	Belgium	
12	39	Hector Tiberghien	Belgium	
13	40	Émile Masson	Belgium	The Unknown
14	41	Jean Rossius	Belgium	Eternal Second
15	42	Jean Alavoine	France	Gars Jean
16	43	Louis Heusghem	Belgium	
17	44	Paul Duboc	France	The Apple
18	45	Firmin Lambot	Belgium	The Saddler
19	46	Eugène Christophe	France	The Old Gaul
20	47	René Vandenhove	France	
21	48	Louis Mottiat	Belgium	The Man of Iron
22	49	Honoré Barthélémy	France	Glass Eye
23	50	Odile Defraye	Belgium	The Unwanted
24	51	Francis Pélissier	France	Young Magician
25	52	Alfons Spiessens	Belgium	
26	53	Charles Juseret	Belgium	
27	54	Jules Masselis	Belgium	
28	55	Joseph Van Daele	Belgium	Facing Waterloo
29	56	Alfred Steux	Belgium	The Kid
30	57	Léon Scieur	Belgium	The Locomotive
31	58	Louis Engel	France	
32	59	Félix Goethals	France	The Sock Seller
33	60	Robert Jacquinot	France	
34	61	René Chassot	France	Cheeky Monkey
35	62	Hector Heusghem	Belgium	
36	63	Jacques Coomans	Belgium	The Smoker
37	65	Albert Dejonghe	Belgium	
38	66	Urbain Anseeuw	Belgium	

39	67	Eugène Dhers	France	
40	68	Basile Matthys	Belgium	
41	69	André Huret	France	
42	70	Charles Hans	France	
43	72	Joseph Verdickt	Belgium	
44	101	Pietro Fasoli	Italy	
45	102	Maurice Borel	France	
46	103	Henri Leclerc	France	
47	104	Edgard Roy	France	
48	105	André Renard	France	
49	106	Etienne Nain	France	Dwarf
50	107	Emile Denys	France	
51	108	Jean Deyries	France	
52	113	Alfred Brailly	France	
53	114	Camille Van Marcke	Belgium	
54	115	José Orduna	Spain	Sole Spaniard
55	119	Maurice Bissiere	France	
56	120	Lucien Decour	France	
57	123	Léon Kopp	France	
58	125	Emile Ledran	France	
59	131	Napoleon Paoli	France	
60	133	Albert Heux	France	
61	137	Ernest Gery	France	
62	138	Paul Zlenck	France	
63	143	Paul Thondoux	France	Soft Tuna
64	149	Henry Allard	Belgium	
65	151	Jules Nempon	France	The Upstart
66	152	Henri Moreillon	France	The Dean
67	155	Alois Verstraeten	Belgium	
	12	Georges Devilly	France	**
	121	Marcel Misserey	France	**

** Note 1: Both riders, Georges Devilly (12) and Marcel Misserey (121) arrived too late to sign in at the start at the Parc des Princes. Consequently, the official number of riders who were declared to have started the race is 67.

Note : There were two abstentions

Ernest, Lemaire, die Solre-le-Château (north), a gunner in Vannes, and Joseph Muller also a soldier in Strasbourg were unable to start, their authorisation having been refused.

APPENDIX 3:

1919 Tour de France – Stage Results

Stage	1919	Route	Distance		Winner	Race leader
1	29-Jun	Paris to Le Havre	388 km	Plain stage	Jean Rossius (BEL)	Henri Pélissier (FRA)
2	01-Jul	Le Havre to Cherbourg	364 km	Plain stage	Henri Pélissier (FRA)	Henri Pélissier (FRA)
3	03-Jul	Cherbourg to Brest	405 km	Plain stage	Francis Pélissier (FRA)	Henri Pélissier (FRA)
4	05-Jul	Brest to Les Sables-d'Olonne	412 km	Plain stage	Jean Alavoine (FRA)	Eugène Christophe (FRA)
5	07-Jul	Les Sables-d'Olonne to Bayonne	482 km	Plain stage	Jean Alavoine (FRA)	Eugène Christophe (FRA)
6	09-Jul	Bayonne to Luchon	326 km	Stage with mountain	Honore Barthelemy (FRA)	Eugène Christophe (FRA)
7	11-Jul	Luchon to Perpignan	323 km	Stage with mountain	Jean Alavoine (FRA)	Eugène Christophe (FRA)
8	13-Jul	Perpignan to Marseille	370 km	Plain stage	Jean Alavoine (FRA)	Eugène Christophe (FRA)
9	15-Jul	Marseille to Nice	338 km	Stage with mountain	Honoré Barthélemy (FRA)	Eugène Christophe (FRA)
10	17-Jul	Nice to Grenoble	333 km	Stage with mountain	Honoré Barthélemy (FRA)	Eugène Christophe (FRA)
11	19-Jul	Grenoble to Geneva	325 km	Stage with mountain	Honoré Barthélemy (FRA)	Eugène Christophe (FRA)
12	21-Jul	Geneva to Strasbourg	371 km	Stage with mountain	Luigi Lucotti (ITA)	Eugène Christophe (FRA)
13	23-Jul	Strasbourg to Metz	315 km	Plain stage	Luigi Lucotti (ITA)	Eugène Christophe (FRA)
14	25-Jul	Metz to Dunkerque	468 km	Plain stage	Firmin Lambot (BEL)	Firmin Lambot (BEL)
15	27-Jul	Dunkerque to Paris	340 km	Plain stage	Jean Alavoine (FRA)	Firmin Lambot (BEL)
		Total	5,560 km			

APPENDIX 4: Race comparison 1919 v 2019

Tour de France 1919 v 2019	1919	2019	%
Total Km's	5,560	3,460	62%
Total miles	3,445	2,144	62%
Total No. of stages	15	21	
No. of rest days	14	2	14%
Average length of stage (km)	371	165	44%
Average kms per day	192	150	78%
Time taken (yellow Jersey)	231h 07m	82h 57m	36%
Average speed (km/hr)	24.056	40.580	59%
Longest stage (kms)	482	280	58%
Longest stage (miles)	299	173	58%
No. of individual stage winners	7	15	
Stages won by winner	1	0	
No. of wearers of yellow jersey *	3	4	
No. of riders at the start	67	176	
No. of riders at the finish	10	155	
% Finish	15%	88%	

* includes Henri Pelissier

If you have in anyway enjoyed this book, and feel so inclined, please leave a review on the Amazon or Goodreads website. As a self-published author, online reviews are like gold dust and open the door to the larger audiences accessible by the major publishers.

Thanks in advance.

Ian Chester, Warwickshire, England.

Bibliography: Tour De France

Le Tour: Geoffrey Wheatcroft, Simon & Schuster 2003.

Blazing Saddles : Matt Rendell, Quercus, 2007.

It's all about the bike: Robert Penn, Particular Books, 2010.

Eugéne Christophe, le damne de la route : Jean-Paul Rey, Editions Cairn, 2013.

Mapping Le Tour, Ellis Bacon, Harper Collins, 2013.

Maillots Jaunes, Pascal Sergent, Editions Jacob-Duvernet, 2013.

Tour De France : F & S. Laget, P. Cazaban, G. Montgermont, Quercus, 2013.

The Shattered Peloton : Graham Healy, Breakaway Books, 2014.

1919 Le Tour renait de l'enfer : Jean-Paul Bourgier, Le Pas d'oiseau, 2014.

Cartes du Tour : Paul Fournel, Rapha Racing Ltd, 2018.

100 ans de maillot jaune : Serge Laget, Hugo Sport, 2018.

Tour de France – Legendary climbs : Richard Abraham, arlton Books Ltd, 2018.

Riding in the zone rouge: Tom Issitt, W&N, 2019.

Bibliography: World War 1

The Oxford & Bucks Light Infantry: Philip Booth, Lee Cooper Ltd, 1971.

Delville Wood: Nigel Cave, Leo cooper Ltd., 1999.

Flers & Gueudecourt, Trevor Pidgeon, Pen & Sword, 2002.

A Storm in Flanders: Winston Groom, Cassell, 2002.

The Battle of Bellewaarde Farm: Carole McEntee-Taylor, Pen & Sword, 2014.

First World War Diary: 14 Division, 42nd Infantry Brigade, Oxfordshire and Buckinghamshire Light Infantry 5th Battalion, Naval & Military Press Ltd, 2015.

Over the Top: Martin Marix Evans, Arcturus Publishing Ltd, 2018.

Articles :

A Day of Eating for a Tour de France Cyclist By Jiří Kaloč, July 7, 2016 – welovecycling.com

Sex and the Somme: By Clare Makepeace, Mail Online Updated: 01:11, 29 October 2011, Posted on centenarynews.com on 20 June 2014

Inside the brothels that served the Western Front: .John Lichfield Independent News - Sunday 3 August 2014

Cumming, Elsie May & Gillings, Jennifer Mary & Richards, Julieanne 2008, In all those lines : the diary of Sister Elsie Tranter 1916-1919, J.M. Gillings & J. Richards, Newstead, Tas

How do cyclists pee whilst racing the Tour de France?' Cycling Weekly Michelle Arthurs-Brennan July 18, 2019

Photo acknowledgements:

I would like to extend my thanks to the Bibliotheque Francophone Numerique (www,gallica.bfn.fr) for the access to the editions on L'Auto for 1919 and for the photos below. (Public domain).

Page

Eugéne Christophe: Bordeaux-Paris, 22nd May 1921 **Front cover**
Référence bibliographique : Rol, 66233 , public domain
Collection numérique : Photographies de l'Agence Rol
Identifier : ark:/12148/btv1b53067663k
Source :Bibliothèque nationale de France, département Estampes et photographie, EI-13 (790)

Henri Desgrange **2**
Référence bibliographique : Rol, 38459, public domain
Collection numérique : Photographies de l'Agence Rol
Identifier : ark:/12148/btv1b6929536j
Source :Bibliothèque nationale de France, département Estampes et photographie, EST EI-13 (351)

Ravitaillement – Oloron Sainte Marie Tour de France 1922 **51**
Référence bibliographique : Rol, 76019, public domain
Collection numérique : Photographies de l'Agence Rol
Collection numérique : Fonds régional : Aquitaine
Collection numérique : Bibliothèque Pireneas (Pau)

Jean Alavoine leads Peloton into Parc des Princes, Paris **305**
Référence bibliographique : Meurisse, 74389, public domain
Collection numérique : Photographies de l'Agence Meurisse
Identifier : ark:/12148/btv1b90324286
Source :Bibliothèque nationale de France, département Estampes et photographie, EI-13 (2604)

Firmin Lambot signs the control sheet, Parc des Princes: **306**
Référence bibliographique : Meurisse, 74395, public domain
Collection numérique : Photographies de l'Agence Meurisse
Identifier : ark:/12148/btv1b9032435b
Source : Bibliothèque nationale de France, département Estampes et photographie, EI-13 (2604)

(La Vie au grand air, no. 845, 15 Aout 1919, coll. G.Salmon)

René Chassot arrives in St.Brieuc	93
Jean Alavoine, wins Stage 4 in Sables d'Olonne	113
Luigi Lucotti attacks on the Col d'Aubisque	147
F. Lambot and H. Barthelemy climbing the Tourmalet	150
Jean Alavoine and Paul Duboc lead the peloton at Beziers	177
Les Laureats de Tour de France	308
Eugéne Christophe, Col de Port : (public domain)	161

Printed in Great Britain
by Amazon